French Writers and their Society
1715–1800

French Writers and their Society 1715–1800

Haydn Mason

To A.M.R.

First published 1982 by
THE MACMILLAN PRESS LTD
London and Basingstoke
Companies and representatives
throughout the world

ISBN 0 333 26465 7

Typeset in Great Britain by
Redwood Burn Limited
Trowbridge & Esher
and printed in Hong Kong

Contents

Introduction

The basic assumption underlying this book is very simple: literature does not arise in a vacuum. Like every other human activity, it is 'in situation', however much it may ultimately transcend that condition in its final form. There is of course nothing new about this approach, and if it needs justification afresh these days, the reason lies to some extent in the harm which has been done by abusing it so often in the past. Taine's brilliant but excessive insistence upon 'race', 'milieu' and 'moment' in the formation of the writer has done as much damage to literary criticism as the Marxist orthodoxy that the class struggle will illuminate all. It is hardly surprising that many a critic, horrified by explanations that explain nothing or, worse, deform the literary work completely, has reacted by asserting that the text is supreme and all extrinsic considerations irrelevant. But this approach, while not without validity on particular occasions, cannot serve as a complete answer. It makes for an increasingly esoteric cult, a purism which must remain wholly theoretical and sterile on many of the larger questions we may ask ourselves about literature. To study, say, the collocation of images in *Candide* or *Le Neveu de Rameau* may not require much reference outside the works themselves (though the critic might be unwise in choosing to ignore whether Voltaire or Diderot use similar imagery in, for example, their correspondence of the same period). But to attempt any discussion on the general significance of these works would be foolish if one is not prepared to consult all the information available – which involves one in Voltaire's commercial activities in shipping, Diderot's other comments on the rôle of genius in society, and much else besides. There will still be an enigma at the end of it all, great literature being by its nature ambiguous and susceptible of diverse interpretations; but at least one may delimit the area of that ambiguity, confirm or deny specific details of fact and circumstances, and then arrive at the rich task of critical evaluation with much spare ballast jettisoned. Though his concern was somewhat different from ours, Daniel Mornet summed up the situation with his usual lucidity and commonsense: 'L'histoire complète de la pensée et du goût permet de tracer avec beaucoup plus de précision le cercle à l'intérieur duquel il faut seulement chercher le secret de son génie'.[1] Purely textual literary criticism, when it poses as the whole discipline rather than a part of it, contributes to that ' "balkanization" of knowledge and culture' against which Malcolm Bradbury has registered protest. As he rightly argues, literature 'coheres, structures and illuminates' many of society's most profound meanings.[2] Literature and sociology have much to gain from one another, and this interdisciplinary study is but the new form, in a more rigorous mode, of an old subject.

What then are the questions we must ask in such a study of literature and society? First of all, we must delineate the writer's social context. We must define his background, education, training, occupation; we must find out how he was placed financially and how dependent he was on the social establishment of his day. Such questions broaden out into fundamental considerations of the class structure, the educational institutions, the economics of patronage (which implicitly, and often in the eighteenth century explicitly, involves censorship). How are books produced and distributed and what do they cost? Who pays? What is the status of the writing profession? How does all this affect the social affiliation and ideology of the writer?

A second series of questions, closely related to the first, concerns the writer's audience. As Sartre put it in his famous essay *Qu'est-ce que la littérature?*: 'Pour qui écrit-on?' The extent and nature of the reading public are closely bound up with education and literacy, particularly in an earlier period like the eighteenth century. Who constitutes the cultured class? Is it a unity or fragmented into subgroups? What are the means available by which authors reach their readers, either directly or by general publicity of their works and ideas? Here we need to consider the various rôles of eighteenth-century media: not only books but theatre, cafés, salons, newspapers and periodicals. The question of censorship is of course most pertinent here, the relationship between works that were officially (or unofficially) approved and those that circulated being a highly complex one. The signifi-

cance of cafés and salons is harder still to establish, their contribution being essentially an oral and ephemeral one; but it must
not be ignored.

All this needs to be related to the general manifestations of the
time: the growth of scientific and technological change, the struggles between the monarchy and the *Parlements*, the foundering of
the State finances, the inequities of taxation, the overwhelmingly
rural nature of France in the eighteenth century, and so on.

Finally, and not least, we must consider the social content,
purpose and influence of these literary documents. How do works
of literature order and present the social scene, and to what
effect? Here it needs to be said with the greatest firmness that the
creative rôle of literature must never be forgotten. To study
literature as no more than a response to society is already to
throw in one's lot with sociology at the expense of criticism. The
present writer, however imperfectly, will hope to convey something of his conviction that literature, as one of man's richest pursuits, can never be reducible to other phenomena or totally
explained by reference to them. The task of studying literature in
a social context would for him be meaningless if that literature
were lacking in its own unique qualities. The nature of this study
carries with it a certain predisposition to examine society first
and literature second; it is hoped that the result has not been to
demote the latter. In line with these views, the literature that
mainly figures here is serious and complex in thought and form.
This emphasis is however not exclusive. A general study that
omitted all reference to more popular literature in this period
would be misleading, and so it is included, albeit briefly. The traditional mass literature and the new mass journalism are themselves fascinating topics of enquiry, and they would have
occupied a more important position if this book were concerned
with cultural sociology rather than literature in its social setting.

The foregoing questions would be formidable enough if we
were dealing with a static model. In fact, France between 1715
and 1800 was in a process of ceaseless and ever greater change
and turmoil; and the last decade is one of revolution and in-
numerable obscure confusions to which a whole library of books
has been exclusively devoted. Not only must the basic points be
raised, they must be raised repeatedly at each important landmark. The task ideally requires the wisdom of Solomon and the
patience of Sisyphus.

In view of all this, certain bold options have been taken, which may not be to the liking of every reader. It would have been feasible to spin a web of generalities, giving due proportion to every single movement and writer within the space available. The danger of this approach would be to take a helicopter view which never came down to ground level, a danger which has too often afflicted the study of literature and society in the past. It was thought that, if the essential 'feel' of the period was to be conveyed, this would be best achieved by looking at a number of writers and works across the 85 years between Louis XIV and Napoleon, from which mosaic a more immediate sense of the writer in society would, it was hoped, arise. In this way, too, the creative autonomy of the literary work stands a better chance of being preserved. That in itself is, naturally, not enough to provide a synoptic framework of the period, so with such a framework this study will begin. Thereafter the 'case histories' will, one trusts, illuminate in enough diverse ways to contribute something like a total impression of eighteenth-century French literature in this context. Inevitably, the selections would have been different ones in others' hands; it is to be hoped that readers will at least find them representative.

This book would not have been possible but for the enlightened arrangements of the University of East Anglia, which generously granted me a period of leave to write it; to its wise and helpful policies I owe and acknowledge much gratitude, whatever their practical result on this occasion. Its library, furthermore, generously assisted me in my every request, often far beyond the call of duty. I wish to thank Mrs Mary Davidson for her accurate, rapid and efficient typing of the manuscript. My wife Gretchen gave precious advice and support, especially in the initial stages. Finally, Adrienne Redshaw encouraged me to take the work up again after it had long been put aside and helped me to carry it through to completion; without her it would not have seen the light of day, and to her it is dedicated.

NOTES

1. 'Méthode d'un cours sur l'histoire de la pensée et du goût en France au XVIIe siècle', *Romanic Review* 39 (1948), p. 205. See also L. Gossman's useful comments in his *French Society and Culture* (Englewood Cliffs, New Jersey: Prentice-Hall, 1972), pp. 112–20.
2. *The Social Context of Modern English Literature* (Oxford: Blackwell, 1971), pp. xii–xiii.

Part I
General Matters

1 Politics and Society

> Le monarque qui a si longtemps régné n'est plus.
> Il a bien fait parler des gens pendant sa vie; tout
> le monde s'est tu à sa mort. Ferme et courageux
> dans ce dernier moment, il a paru ne céder qu'au
> destin. Ainsi mourut le grand Cha-Abas, après
> avoir rempli toute la terre de son nom.
>
> (*Lettres persanes*, XCII)

In these simple, measured terms Montesquieu records the death of Louis XIV. An age was at an end. The old king having lived so long as to survive both son and grandson, the succession passed to a five-year-old boy. After the wearisome years of royal oppressiveness, suddenly the centre of authority was removed, and no one quite knew what form it would now take. True, a regency was certain, and also certain was that the duc Philippe d'Orléans would be regent, since he was the late King's nephew and therefore nearest to the throne. But how he would act and with whom he would make common cause were total enigmas. It is not surprising that Montesquieu continues dryly: 'Ne crois pas que ce grand événement n'ait fait faire ici que des réflexions morales. Chacun a pensé à ses affaires et à prendre ses avantages dans ce changement.' Everything was possible at first under the Regency, even an alliance with the Jansenists or an amnesty for the Protestants.[1] It is symptomatic of the transition that a considerable debate arose over what precisely were Louis XIV's last words to his infant successor. Some accounts reflected only traditional piety, but most managed to incorporate a sense of changed values felt under the new king.[2] At home all was in flux. Abroad too France's defeat in the War of the Spanish Succession and the signing of the peace agreements over the years 1713–15 had disturbed the balance of power; no nation was now strong enough to dominate Europe, the new-found equilibrium helping to give 25 years of peace until the War of the Austrian Succession. While all epochal dates must be distortions of the basic continuity in human affairs, 1715 will serve as better than most to delimit the period of increased questioning of the social, political and religious system that we now associate with the Enlightenment.[3]

One further point, accidental but important, confirms the usefulness of this watershed. Most of the great writers of Louis XIV's reign were dead. Very few who were active under the Roi Soleil continued to be so under his successor. One thinks of such authors as Fontenelle, Massillon, Crébillon *père*, Le Sage; but except for the latter two, their important work tends to be associated with one reign or the other. Younger writers like Marivaux, Montesquieu and Voltaire had not begun to make a mark in 1715. It was as if the great king had, Samson-like, pulled down the cultural edifice around him before he died, so that literature after 1715 would begin anew. The date does not of itself mark the beginnings of critical thought in France, as Paul Hazard made abundantly clear in his *Crise de la conscience européenne* as long ago as 1935.[4] But though the necessary intellectual climate for such works existed from about 1680, it was not until 1715 that the political circumstances in France lent them the opportunity of appearing more openly. The Regency, despite not being as lenient in its censorship as is sometimes claimed, removed much of the repression on writers; thoughts formerly unprintable could now be written with impunity, as the *Lettres persanes* would demonstrate.[5] Buvat's *Journal de la Régence* reflects this freedom: 'C'est un plaisir de voir la liberté qui règne à présent dans l'imprimerie; on ne voit que brochures sur brochures sur toutes les matières du temps sans aucune permission'.[6] The only books condemned until 1733 as being subversive were not free-thinking, but Jansenist; and up to 1744 the latter category still remained in the majority.[7]

As events were to prove, however, the Regency was a false dawn. Nothing essentially had changed or been reformed, indeed in some respects it marked a step backwards; for the aristocracy, granted by the duc d'Orléans a freedom that it had not known under Louis XIV, was to cling to its prerogatives in an increasingly reactionary way as the century went on. The Ancien

Régime merely passed another landmark in 1715; its demise was still 74 years away.

* * *

How best to sum up this form of government and society? Pierre Goubert's excellent study begins on a discouraging note:

> Il est difficile de présenter simplement un régime qui n'a pas eu d'acte de naissance, même pas de constitution écrite, et qui a toujours cultivé la confusion. Il est même impossible, et peut-être malhonnête, d'apporter une lumineuse clarté là où elle n'a jamais régné, là où il lui fut refusé de pénétrer: en un sens, la méthode de Descartes, cet exilé volontaire, est l'antithèse probable de l'Ancien Régime.[8]

The reason for this chaotic structure lies in its casually empirical past: 'Il est un magma de choses habituellement séculaires, parfois millénaires, dont il n'a jamais supprimé aucune. Il fut profondément conservateur....'[9] Any attempt at describing the system must therefore allow for this fundamental difficulty that the object eludes simple definition. Certain of its essential features can however be charted. As Goubert makes clear, it grew out of habits that became customs, conventions, laws. It was hierarchical, corporate, based on privilege, which was itself extended to groups, not individuals (except the King); and these groups, whether they were social orders (like the clergy and nobility) or particular bodies (like guilds or *Parlements*) or specific territories (like certain towns or provinces), naturally clung to their special rights. By contrast, individual rights such as freedom of speech, press, or worship were denied. There was no rule of law applicable to all, but a multitude of different practices according to time, place and social class. Imprisonment was arbitrary, without trial, and of indefinite length. This was a religious society, centred on the primacy of the Catholic Church, which baptised, married and buried all but the outcasts, and which directed almost all the education there was. The monarchy was absolute, the King ruling by Divine Right, hence supreme and above the laws. The King's person was sacred. On the morrow of Louis XV's coronation in 1722 more than 2000 victims of scrofula, on their knees before him at Reims, enacted the ancient ritual of touching for the King's evil, as he passed them one by one, saying to each: 'Dieu te guérisse, le roi te touche'.[10] The

practice continued into Louis XVI's reign and probably right up
to 1789.[11] Such personal authority would not be shaken by
normal events, and indeed it was not until some time after the
storming of the Bastille that the King became a mere mortal like
all others.

But the Ancien Régime was also compartmented in diverse
ways. At Court there were numerous shifting factions, owing allegiance to a Queen or King's mistress or a powerful minister.
There was thus no consistent policy, and a sudden promising
move towards reform could die as suddenly, if the King lost interest or another group found favour. Justice was administered
by 31 *cours souveraines*, with the fifteen *Parlements* at their head;
over 300 different sets of customary laws prevailed. Communica-
tions were fragmented too. In 1715 nearly 5700 privately owned
tolls on French roads and rivers existed. Around 1750, 'it was
alleged that a boatman taking a load of staves from Lorraine to
Languedoc had to stop twenty-two times to pay thirty-eight different tolls and duties'.[12] The speed of transport, by road or
waterway, had not changed between medieval times and mid-
century and, despite the new roads and canals, did not improve
greatly thereafter before 1800. It was, finally, a rural society, in
which perhaps as few as two per cent were not in some way linked
to the soil. Ancien Régime society was traditional, conservative,
localised, and never far from anarchy.

Any attempt to impose some kind of periodisation upon such
untractable material is fraught with danger. One should bear in
mind Francastel's wise dictum: 'Il n'y a pas eu, au XVIIIᵉ siècle,
une succession d'époques tranchées, marquées chacune par un
idéal absolu'.[13] Yet the attempt must be made, for there is a
broad pattern of development through the century, and this is of
the utmost relevance for the link between literature and society;
an early work like Montesquieu's *Lettres persanes* is quite different
in attitude from *philosophe* writings of the 1760s and 1770s. The
period 1715–1800 can perhaps be broken down into four phases,
during each of which, despite the unbroken sequence of human
pursuits, a new mood made itself felt: 1715–40; 1740–70; 1770–
89; 1789–1800.

The quarter-century up to 1740 presents certain unitary
characteristics, albeit that it is sharply divided at 1723 by the
death of the duc d'Orléans. Although there is a sharp reaction
against the dissoluteness of the Regency in the years that fol-

lowed, governmental policies and literary productions alike
reflect the belief that criticism has not crossed the borderline into
subversiveness or revolt. Antoine Adam's remark generally holds
true: 'C'est l'un des traits de cette première moitié du siècle que
les penseurs les plus audacieux, les plus libérés de tout esprit
d'orthodoxie, ne veulent en aucune manière troubler les croyances de la nation'[14] – if one assumes that for him 'troubler' has
the sense of 'bouleverser', not the more superficial meaning of its
English equivalent. As we have seen, most of the repressive activity against new books was anti-Jansenist; indeed, the Jansenist
problem occasioned the only divisive quarrel during these years.
But the seeds of future disorder were already sown, for by 1717
the Regent's honeymoon with the *Parlement* of Paris had ended.
At first the quarrel was over financial matters, the Regent acced-
ing to the *parlementaires'* demands; but the following year saw the
beginning of a firmer reaction from the government, leading to
the first of many orders of exile for the magistrates in 1720. The
new assertiveness of the Paris *Parlement* was to find its most fruitful cause in the Jansenist controversy.

Jansenism had of course been a longstanding source of trouble
in France, but with the demolition of the Port-Royal nunnery in
1710 such resistance might have seemed at an end. In 1713 the
Pope condemned the Jansenist propositions uttered by Pasquier
Quesnel 40 years before. This condemnation, in the Papal Bull
Unigenitus, proved to be the starting-point for the new campaign.
It revealed a split between the Ultramontane party, mainly
Jesuit or sympathetic to that Order, who acknowledged the
Pope's absolute authority in matters of faith, and the Gallicans,
who sought a measure of independence from Rome and numbered amongst their members the majority of *parlementaires*. This
quarrel was not to be resolved until the 1750s, and although the
Church in the end scored a technical victory over Jansenism, the
dispute weakened the Jesuits to the point where an incidental in-
discretion led to the suppression of their Order in 1762. It put the
Parlements firmly back in a strong tactical position which they
were not to abandon till the Revolution; and it gravely affected
the prestige of the Church. Barbier records in his *Journal* for July
1752, *à propos* of the quarrel: 'On commence à tourner en dérision
les choses spirituelles et les plus sérieuses de la religion; mais elles
le méritent bien un peu'. Undoubtedly, the lasting effects of the
Jansenist controversy did much harm to the social fabric in

general.[15]

But these effects had not made themselves fully felt before 1740. The troubles with the *Parlements* reached a climax in 1732, when a pamphlet commonly known as the *Judicium Francorum* appeared, arguing that the *Parlement* of Paris dated from the birth of France and represented the nation. But this document, though of ominous import for the future, in fact preceded a lull in the struggle which was to last for twenty years. The collapse of Law's financial system was demoralising, as Montesquieu's *Lettres persanes* were to bear out, and it came with catastrophic suddenness. His trading company, which for a while had cornered all French trade overseas, collapsed in a matter of weeks, dragging down the French currency with it. On 4 June 1720, the 100-*livre* note was worth 110 *livres*; by 17 September it had declined to 30 *livres*. During the same period the 1000-*livre* note fell to a quarter of its nominal value.[16] Yet despite the ruin of many personal fortunes the economy recovered, and from 1726 the currency was definitively stabilised until the Revolution. But the overall damage done was of longer effect. Law had tried to establish a State Bank based on credit and paper currency, and his failure meant the end of any such institution until Napoleon founded the Banque de France in 1800.

The period 1715–40 is full of disturbing portents. But there was a steady economic improvement during the period, and under Fleury as prime minister (1726–43) France enjoyed a period of domestic calm. Abroad, only the War of the Polish Succession (1733–35) disturbed the peace, and this was brief and relatively painless. But 1740 heralded a change that nevertheless took a decade to manifest itself fully. As Norman Hampson says: 'The wars of 1740–63 form a watershed within the eighteenth century'.[17] The War of the Austrian Succession (1740–48) plunged the State finances once again into an imbalance from which they were not to recover under the Ancien Régime. Politically, it failed to resolve the struggle for colonial supremacy between England and France, and another bloodier conflict, the Seven Years War (1756–63) proved necessary for this. The outcome of the latter was total defeat for France, which lost its colonial empire in North America and India.

Meantime at home, latent internal conflicts had attained maturity. Machault, appointed *contrôleur général des finances* in 1745, sought a way out of the financial impasse by reforming the tax system. His main proposal, set forth in a royal edict of 1749, was to establish a new permanent tax, the *vingtième*, levied on all without distinction. This dared to offend the ancient tax privileges of clergy, nobility and other particular groups, for no such direct tax had ever been imposed indiscriminately, except as a short-term emergency in wartime. The *pays d'états*, provinces on the periphery like Languedoc and Brittany, protested fiercely at this initiative, for it would have seriously undermined their favourable position in matters of taxation; but the most obdurate opposition of all came from the clergy, with considerable help from the devout party at Court. In consequence, despite much support for his proposals from writers like Voltaire, Machault had to acknowledge defeat. The privileged parties, resolutely united against an indecisive government, had won their case; but it was a bad loss for the Ancien Régime. An important attempt to introduce some order and justice into an anomalous tax system had failed.

Yet the public financial deficit was serious. In November 1759, Barbier records that people were being urged to take their *vaisselle d'argent* to the Mint for melting down – 'ordinairement la dernière ressource dans les calamités de l'Etat'. Pre-Revolutionary France was never to be solvent again after 1741. But economic prosperity prevailed, and by regularly writing off a part of its debts, the State managed to avoid total bankruptcy. Besides, the political situation at home markedly improved under the judicious control of Choiseul (1758–70), nominally no more than Secretary for Foreign Affairs but in practice much more like a prime minister. The new political leader helped France to recover from the Seven Years War by reforming and rebuilding the army and navy. Corsica and Lorraine were annexed to the kingdom, and trading links with the colonies improved. Choiseul looked benevolently upon Voltaire's crusade against intolerance, and supported moves towards liberalising trade and promoting agricultural development. But his achievements were bought at the price of capitulation to the *Parlements*, a notable sign of the times. During his reign the Jesuit Order was abolished (1764), while the *Parlement* of Toulouse delivered notorious judgements on Calas and Sirven in 1762 and 1764 respectively and that of Paris on La Barre in 1766.

Around midcentury, writers grew bolder. In the period 1745–51, Diderot's and Rousseau's first philosophical works and Voltaire's first *contes* appeared, as well as La Mettrie's materialistic *L'Homme machine* and Condillac's sensationalist psychology in the *Traité des systèmes*; the *Encyclopédie* began to unfold. The year 1748 is often cited by historians as a turning-point because it saw the publication of Montesquieu's *De l'esprit des lois*. Until then writers had been reticent on political matters; after Montesquieu's great work this was no longer so. Barbier speaks of the great number of arrests being made in 1749, the imprisoned including men of letters like Diderot. Established religion had come under question much earlier than the political régime, but in the latter too attacks now grew more audacious, while in philosophical writings materialism and atheism began to share prominence with the deist expressions of faith voiced earlier. Despite governmental opposition, the number and influence of critical works increased. The *philosophes*, like the *Parlements*, had become a force to be reckoned with.

The final Act of the Ancien Régime may be said to commence with Choiseul's fall in 1770 and the ensuing consequences. Choiseul tried to support Spain in a dispute with Britain, but the state of the Exchequer ruled out armed intervention and the King dismissed him. The new power behind the throne was Maupeou, the *Chancelier*; and Maupeou was a firm supporter of the King against the *Parlements*. These latter bodies, especially the one in Paris, had renewed their agitation since the early 1750s. For over a decade, Choiseul's sympathetic attitude had prevented their total opposition, but towards the end of his ministry they found an excellent case for exploitation in the government's chronic need of money, the Paris *Parlement's* support being required for the issuance of financial edicts to remedy the situation. By contrast with Choiseul's flexible approach, Maupeou and Terray (Maupeou's nominee as *contrôleur général*) pursued a more authoritarian policy. In 1771, Maupeou used the Paris *Parlement's* opposition to exile its members, not as formerly to a comfortable abode nearby but to distant and often unattractive places. Unlike previous occasions, the *Parlement's* functions were largely assumed by a royal council, the *Conseil des Parties*, and new courts set up in the provinces, so that its range of activities was severely reduced; venality of offices was abolished. Provincial *Parlements* were also reformed in due course. Despite bitter opposition, refusals to serve, demands for the summoning of the *Etats généraux*, support for the *parlementaires* from the nobility as a whole and even (with the important exception of Voltaire) from the *philosophes*, Maupeou persisted. What had seemed to many at first an act of barbaric despotism became less unpopular as the new system began to function, with particularly beneficial effects upon the tax system. But no final victory had been won; and when Louis XV died in 1774, the *Parlements* exploited the new situation so effectively that before the year was out the new king had reinstated the Paris *Parlement* and dismissed Maupeou. This decision has been seen as the fundamental political choice of Louis XVI's reign;[18] thereafter no hope remained for serious reform of ancient privilege.

Over the next fifteen years the situation became ever more discouraging. Louis XVI, flirting with various combinations of appeals to public opinion, bouts of despotism and concessions to privilege, failed to arrest the growing crisis. The aristocratic reaction against reform was paralleled by an increasing radicalism amongst writers, who openly denounced the archaic state of political institutions. By 1789 an important group, including La Fayette, Mirabeau, Sieyès, Condorcet, Talleyrand and Chastellux, were demonstrating their warm support for the American revolutionaries and seeking to emulate them in establishing a united nation free of the inequities of privilege. Even so there was no mass movement for change until 1788; but events were now to prove inexorable. To all the existing difficulties was added a new problem; the period of economic advance which had gone on, with only brief interruptions, since the 1730s reached a plateau in the late 70s, and then a recession set in. This situation, in a predominantly agricultural economy, was much exacerbated by the bad harvest of 1788, followed by another poor one the next year. Rising expectations were affronted.

More immediately, the unprivileged, particularly the peasant, suffered from the drop in agricultural produce and the increased financial demands. The State Treasury, already precarious, had incurred the additional burden of supporting the American colonists in their War of Independence. Once again the government found itself vulnerable to the *Parlements*, this time fatally. An *Assemblée des Notables* was convened in 1787, but this was not enough for the *Parlements*, who successfully insisted on summoning the *États Généraux*. It was another crucial decision, signifying the end of absolute monarchy. But before the *États* met in May 1789, the *Parlements* had already discovered that they had won only a

Pyrrhic victory, for the *Tiers État* secured a promise that their own numbers would be equal to the clergy and nobility combined. By January 1789, Mallet du Pan could write: 'Le débat public a changé de face. Il ne s'agit plus que très secondairement du roi, du despotisme, de la constitution; c'est une guerre entre le tiers état et les deux autres ordres.'[19] In agreeing with Hampson that the main political conflict of eighteenth-century France is the struggle of the aristocracy against the declining power of royal absolutism,[20] one must also note that that conflict is already at an end in 1789. By their unique concern for their own interests, the *Parlements* lost the popularity which they had attained in posing as guardians of the nation and found themselves classed with the governmental establishment as objects of equal hostility; they were put on indefinite vacation before the end of the year and abolished in 1790.

The Revolution was therefore the product of a wide range of causes to which particular circumstances applied the necessary explosive factor. The last decade of the century was to see the ferment play itself out through the abolition of feudal rights on the famous *nuit du 4 août 1789*, the establishment of a constitution in 1791, war abroad from 1792 and deepening conflict at home, leading to general revolt and virtual civil strife, desperate remedies by Robespierre, the counter-revolutionary reaction after his death (1794), the *Directoire* interregnum and the growing prestige of Napoleon. On 9 November 1799 (the *18 brumaire*) the latter's *coup d'état* ended France's first attempt at republican government. When, on 15 December, he announced a new constitution with the words: 'Citizens, the Revolution is established upon its original principles. It is over,'[21] one may say that the history of eighteenth-century France was at last at an end. Despite the return to authoritarian rule, however, many permanent changes had occurred. Henceforth the notion was accepted that all were equal before the law,[22] which was the same for all France. Taxation became equitable, arbitrary government and legalised class privilege were swept away. The Catholic Church lost its position of supremacy as the State religion. The way was paved for a national educational system. With the abolition of feudal dues, peasants could become landowners in the full sense of the term. Many of the most important changes inaugurating the birth of modern France still lay ahead, especially improved transport and industrialisation. But the Revolution made France a unified nation in political, juridical and administrative terms, and the sense of the *patrie* was henceforth ineradicable.

Having seen what became of this society, let us now take a brief glance at its structure. We have noted that it was hierarchical and seen some of the struggles that occurred between conflicting groups. How did this hierarchy operate in the eighteenth century? More precisely, what was the relationship of lords to commoners? It is important to stress that, when we describe the Church as the first Estate, the nobility as the second and the rest of the population as the third, we should not confuse these categories with social classes of today. On the one side, wealth was a great leveller between the different Estates, for wealth could buy privilege, including nobility; on the other, it matters a great deal to know which part of the aristocracy or commonalty is being considered. As with all else about the Ancien Régime, complexity is the first defining principle.

Even to establish who were the nobility is not simple; it ranged across the whole economic spectrum, from lavish wealth to virtual destitution. The only safe criterion is a circular one – those who were recognised as such by the monarchy. For if one defines nobles by their privileges exceptions quickly appear. It is commonly stated that the aristocracy did not pay direct taxes. But in fact they paid both the *capitation* (instituted in 1695) and the *vingtième*, albeit at a special rate; and if one limits this rule to the feudal *taille*, it does not hold true for the Midi, where this tax was levied on the land rather than the person, so that lords and commoners paid alike. Besides, as we have noticed, tax privileges extended to other groups too, like particular towns and provinces. Nonetheless, the nobility existed as a clearly defined order under the Ancien Régime, was transmitted from father to son[23] and enjoyed special prerogatives. In the main, it avoided most of the direct taxation, the *corvée* (compulsory unpaid labour on the roads) and militia service. Beyond that, it exercised privileges over the dependent peasants, who had to deliver up a considerable share of their own produce, suffer the depredations of hunting over their land and the like; besides, the peasants could often not escape falling into debt with their masters, so that to the former's many problems were added the miseries of usury.

The nobility is essentially defined, as Goubert says, by its opposite, 'la roture'.[24] Only nobles were not born with some basic stigma; they represented the prime status symbol. In the circumstances, it is not to be wondered at that the goal of ambitious bourgeois was to purchase the right to 'vivre noblement'. No reading of eighteenth-century French literature can ignore the fundamentally aristocratic tone to society and culture that existed right up to the Revolution. The bourgeois was, as Ernest Labrousse put it in a memorable phrase, a 'refoulé social'; Mauzi adds rightly that he was also a 'refoulé moral'.[25] Aristocrats like the comte de Horn and the capitaine de Mille could be executed, but the rarity of such exceptions proves the rule. The Regent agreed to their sentence only because of the growing public disorder following John Law's transactions, and after resisting great personal pressure on their behalf. By contrast, the comte de Charolais, a prince of the Royal Family who, according to Barbier's *Journal* (May 1723), shot down a bourgeois one night in a sort of apparent *acte gratuit*, obtained an immediate pardon from the Regent. Nobles were tried in special courts by their peers and generally got off with lighter punishments. All these advantages were theoretically justified by the duties incumbent upon them, above all the obligation to serve the king against his enemies; but these services were largely outmoded in a State that was no longer rent by wars at home, less heavily involved in wars abroad and in the process of acquiring an increasingly professional army. The situation of the aristocracy seemed attractive, at least as seen from outside. But rights without duties are often demoralising, and one may argue that the aristocratic resentment which pervades the period stemmed above all from the knowledge that the nobility had lost one rôle and not found another.

A political change had also occurred within the noble ranks during the first half of the century. The *noblesse d'épée*, increasingly outmoded, conceded leadership to the *noblesse de robe* who were engaged in administration and the judiciary. Though differences of lifestyle existed between them, in social prestige they were equal (apart from a very few of the greatest nobles in the land). As the age progressed, the main opposition to the monarchy came, as we have seen, from one branch of the *robe*, the *Parlements*, who wielded much power yet lacked the political rôle as representatives of the nation which they sought. The mentality of the nobles as a group was defensive alike towards the king and those below them. As time went on, more and more avenues of ennoblement available to the seventeenth-century bourgeois like Colbert were closed. The highest posts in the army, administration and civil service became restricted to nobility. The only commoner to serve as minister under Louis XVI (out of 36 in all) was Necker (and his daughter, Madame de Staël, became an aristocrat by marriage). The key positions in the Church were similarly a noble fief; all the 143 bishops in 1789 were aristocratic. The further the Ancien Régime progressed during the century, the less opportunity of social advancement there was for the bourgeoisie. This added a potent source of discord to the gathering storm.

Meantime, the bourgeois were growing in economic and cultural importance. Who were the bourgeois in eighteenth-century France? One can broadly divide them into two categories, the business group and the professional class. At the top of the former hierarchy sat the *négociant*, the large-scale merchant, usually in the wholesale trade. Many were men of enormous resources, like the Roux brothers in Marseilles who were worth 30 million *livres*, or François Durand of Montpellier who possessed a considerable trading empire.[26] Typically, the *négociant* also provided banking services; G. V. Taylor argues that 'in merchant capitalism banking was inseparable from trade. All merchants of any importance accepted deposits and bought and sold drafts.... The flow of money and credit was broadly diffused in the commercial and industrial sector.'[27] Indeed, very few bankers were entirely divorced from commerce in the eighteenth century, the exceptions being generally domiciled in Paris. Any hopes of establishing a sound banking system had been destroyed with the crash of John Law, and it was not until 1800 and the creation of the Banque de France that a state system of financial credit began to be possible. In this respect France lagged far behind city-states like Genoa and Venice which had enjoyed central banks since the sixteenth century, or Holland with its *Wisselbank* at Amsterdam since 1609, or the Bank of England (1694). Below the *négociants* in dignity came the *marchands*, more commonly engaged in retail trade and distributed widely through the small market towns of France. Finance naturally led to involvement in the burgeoning industrial world; but industry was not by any means exclusively a bourgeois concern, the merchant capitalists often coming from the ranks of the nobility. In any case, there was little large-scale industry in France at this period, and its development was well behind that of England.

Commerce, however, was a social leveller, working against

established privileges; but as such its prestige was precarious. The aim of most merchants was simply to buy their way into the nobility, either for themselves or their children: 'La noblesse est la décoration finale de familles négociantes qui ont réussi'.[28] Commerce, despite official attempts to the contrary, despite the blows struck on its behalf by such as Voltaire in the *Lettres philosophiques* (1734) and Sedaine in *Le Philosophe sans le savoir* (1765), continued to carry a social stigma throughout the Ancien Régime.[29]

The commercial bourgeoisie were not generally involved in the *philosophe* movement; the latter depended heavily upon the professional middle class, as we shall see in the make-up of the Encyclopaedists.[30] The two bourgeois groups can be differentiated with a fair measure of clarity. The worlds of commerce and finance do not appear to impinge upon the Academies that formed the chief centres of culture in the provinces[31] and their members did not contribute to the *Encyclopédie*. As Darnton has pointed out, there is no sign here to support Marxist ideology in discerning the rise of a new economic class with modernist ideas.[32] The intellectual bourgeoisie tended to come from traditional backgrounds like medicine, administration, the landed gentry. Furthermore, of all the middle-class groups (with the possible exception of the wealthiest *négociants*) they enjoyed the closest relations with the nobility; and many leading writers were of course titled noblemen. The social situation of the writer, however, requires a more extensive treatment; we shall return to it in the next chapter.

At the lower end of the bourgeoisie there is an overlap between businessman and artisan. The *Encyclopédie* devoted much time to recording and illustrating the diverse trades being carried on in France, and in so doing it broke new ground, as we shall later see. At the same period, the voice of the artisan is making itself heard through Rousseau's pen, so that a group hitherto submerged begins around mid-century to appear in literature. Here is a world dominated by the medieval guild system, composed of closed societies whose original function, to enforce proper standards of workmanship within their respective crafts, had generally deteriorated into a rearguard battle against the new forces at work in industry. Most of the guilds embraced three grades: master, journeyman, apprentice; but while promotion to journeyman after serving one's apprenticeship was usually straightforward, access to the rank of master was entirely another matter. Entrance examinations of prohibitive length or cost excluded many; nepotism was rife. In this way competition and unemployment were avoided and prices kept high. When journeymen tried to organise themselves into *compagnonnages* and take strike action, they were prevented by government edicts of 1749 and 1760 against collective bargaining.[33] But the position of the guilds was also being undermined by the Crown, which was selling guild memberships to anyone who could afford them. In this way they struck at the guilds' monopoly and source of revenue. Weakened by official demands, outflanked by new competition, the guilds gradually declined in power and wealth. Turgot as *contrôleur général des finances* abolished most of them in 1776, but he was powerless against the office-holders, as expropriation would have meant reimbursement, an impractical proposition in view of the precarious State finances. Further trouble struck these corporations when France and England signed a reciprocal treaty in 1786 cutting duties on certain important products of the other nations, thereby introducing a new source of competition. When they were suppressed in 1791 the guilds were already moribund, a striking symbol of an Ancien Régime institution that had long since lost its reason for existence.[34]

But the ordinary craftsman as an individual in his own right is still largely missing as the object of literary study. Even more so is it true of the peasants who formed the overwhelming bulk of the population. When they appear, it is generally as a sentimentalised background to some picture of country life. This happens even on the rare occasion when a writer hails from the peasantry; Restif de La Bretonne grew up on his father's farm in Burgundy but the picture of the countryside which he paints in his writings is a 'literary pastoral, not a reproduction of actual reality', as Richard Fargher has ably demonstrated.[35] The reality emerges in the abbé Meslier's *Mémoire*, which denounces the idle rich, gnawing away like vermin at 'les pauvres peuples'; while the rich man in his castle dwells in prosperity, pleasure, joy, the poor man at his gate hard by suffers 'les peines et les supplices de l'enfer'.[36] Meslier's bitterness is understandable when one learns that in his own village of Etrépigny bad harvests and child mortality went together; during the year 1724, for instance, no fewer than twelve children died, in a community numbering under 150 inhabitants.[37] But even Meslier does not tell us these explicit details;

first-hand testimony on the miseries of the poor is fragmentary. Those who suffered were rarely literate enough to write about it; and the literate tended on the whole to avert their eyes from too directly gazing at a problem for which there was no adequate remedy.[38]

The peasant lived in an economy where the price of bread was the determining factor. Bad harvests led to soaring prices, hunger, increased mortality, widespread riots. Although the vast majority of peasants were legally free persons, economically the feudal dues and taxes which they were called upon to pay left them no margin for emergencies. True, a small group of rich proprietors was comfortably off, but in the nature of things they could not be more than a small minority of the population. Between feudal dues and direct taxation, the burden was crushing. Turgot, when *intendant* in the Limousin in 1766, estimated that the peasant proprietors in two districts which he studied were paying 50 to 60 per cent of the gross value of their produce (before the deduction that had to be made for seed) in direct taxes. This, he reckoned, was common in the provinces subject to *métayage* (sharecropping).[39]

Not surprisingly, then, the average expectation of life was around 22 years until well into the eighteenth century.[40] It was therefore all the harder, after the relative prosperity which had developed since 1730, to bear the new recession that intervened from about 1778 and built up to the markedly bad harvests of 1788 and 1789. It was not a complete reversion to the bad old times; neither winter provoked a famine to equal the catastrophes of the past. But objective facts meant little for people who saw only a return to the distress and insecurity they had begun to forget, and the subjective impression was that calamity had struck once more. In the circumstances, demands by King and feudal lord appeared intolerable, and here too the spark was applied to the gunpowder. It had become clear that no escape from misery was possible for the peasant under the existing system; it needed only the appropriate climatic conditions to unleash the whole train of sufferings to which he had been traditionally heir.

What cultural solace was available to the poor? Only, it would seem, the romantic and magical tales of the cheap literature which was turned out in large quantities for them.[41] These books were presumably read aloud in groups, since widespread illiteracy prevailed. A survey of illiteracy was undertaken by Maggiolo a hundred years ago, and though the evidence has required reassessment in the light of recent research, it still offers much that is basically sound. Defining literacy as the capacity to sign one's name in the marriage register, Maggiolo discovered that in the years 1786–90 52.5 per cent of the men and 73 per cent of the women did not sign. Some progress had been made since a hundred years before, when the corresponding figures had been 71 per cent and 86 per cent. Even so, illiteracy was clearly widespread; and besides, the advances had occurred almost entirely in the most enlightened areas.[42] The West, Centre and Midi (except for Protestant areas) were much worse off than those areas north of a line from Saint-Malo in Brittany to Geneva, and the evidence from another study suggests a positive correlation between the degree of religious instruction and the literate level. Where, as in Lorraine and Normandy, the distribution of pious literature was particularly strong, the literacy figures are high; the converse also holds true in especially ignorant areas like the Massif Central and the whole of the South outside Toulouse and Languedoc.[43] The general conclusion seems proven: education is the province of the Church in eighteenth-century France. The rare exceptions such as State-run institutions like the *Ecole des ponts et chaussées* and the *Jardin du Roi* prove the rule.

Primary education in the *petites écoles* came under the authority of the bishop in each diocese and was organised by the local clergy (often from one of the twenty teaching congregations in France), with the supplementary aid of lay teachers; amongst the religious communities the Christian Brothers were predominant and the most competent, particularly in educating boys. Though unevenly distributed elementary instruction was widespread, since the Catholic Church saw its duty as providing in this respect for all regardless of means. But it was generally restricted to the three R's, plus religious instruction and sometimes vocational training, and it gave the average pupil little chance of progressing to the secondary level. Nor is the rate of attendance in the different provinces entirely clear.

In 1789, secondary schooling was being provided in 271 *collèges* for some 48,000 pupils, that is, roughly two per cent of the male population between eight and eighteen years of age drawn, inevitably, from the upper classes.[44] Though the curriculum was still based firmly upon the study of Latin, grammar and rhetoric in accordance with the old humanist ideal, a gradual evolution can be discerned during the century whereby history and, more so, French, assume greater importance in the programme. Even the teaching of science, particularly of mathematics and physics, shows a marked improvement. But the aim of such education is profoundly conservative and in no way can the secondary schools be said to have consciously prepared the Revolution, though by the 1770s most of the future revolutionary leaders were passing through them.

As for the 24 universities, there is little point in lingering. With rare exceptions like medicine at Montpellier they formed an intellectual backwater. Their curriculum was out of date, based on a mechanical approach to philosophy, logic, law and theology, taught in Latin; yet it continued right up to the Revolution. We shall later see where the ferment of ideas, particularly in science, arose; virtually nothing except opposition to new developments came out of the universities.[45]

If the education of boys left much to be desired, that of girls was much worse. The abbé de Saint-Pierre wrote that he knew of only one *collège* entirely devoted to female education.[46] Otherwise, he added, a few convents cater for girls, who emerge in total ignorance of the most essential things. A similar point is made a half-century later in d'Holbach's *Des femmes* (1773), which claims that the sole education a girl is likely to get is from the convent, equipping her only with a knowledge of music, dance, posture, the cosmetic arts and of course faith.[47] The disastrous effect of such convent-trained ignorance is exemplified with crystal clarity in Laclos's *Les Liaisons dangereuses*.[48] But despite the many feminist supporters during the Enlightenment, women's position *vis-à-vis* men did not improve before the Revolution or as a consequence of it.[49]

An illiterate person is a potential victim of all those in power: the landowner, the tax-collector, the feudal lord, the law courts, occasionally the *curé*. Yet Goubert, making this observation, goes on to add that the great majority of cultivated people were hostile to mass education (p. 245). The eighteenth century is on the farther side of the Industrial Revolution, mass movements were sporadic, fragmentary and ineffectual before 1789; even the upheavals of the last decade did not advance popular representation. The tone of eighteenth-century society remains aristocratic until the Revolution and is not destroyed by the events of 1789–94.

The Enlightenment period is not even bourgeois in its outlook, let alone democratic. Reformist ideas attack the hierarchical edifice; the growth of public opinion as a factor represents one of the greatest achievements in the move towards a more broadly based consensus; but in 1789 the aristocracy are still in power.

If the Enlightenment made a real impact upon contemporary thinking, it was more in the domain of religion than politics. Democratisation proceeded apace with hesitant step; but the movement towards secularisation found more mature soil in which to work. The Church occupied, until 1789, a position of extraordinary authority and independence in the State. Education was its province, almost exclusively, and it was one of the main sources of medical aid. Every individual who required to be baptised, married or buried needed the services of the Church. Only the Protestants as a group tried to defy these rules within their own communities, and for that they suffered persecution through most of the century, pastors being executed as late as 1762. It was 1787 before a royal edict of tolerance was promulgated, granting Protestants civil rights and civil marriage.[50] Although many of the Catholic clergy were poor and scarcely distinguishable in their way of life from the peasantry they served, the Church itself was immensely wealthy, possessing vast tracts of land[51] and receiving tithes levied in all parishes of the kingdom. Exempt from royal taxes, it agreed a quinquennial *don gratuit* to the Crown, the title indicating that it was a voluntary contribution. Machault's attempt to impose a regular system of taxation ended, as we have seen, in defeat, and so did all subsequent efforts by *philosophes* and others up to 1789.

But important though its social and economic situation was, the Church's full authority was to be seen above all in its control of ideas. On one level the weekly sermon from the parish priest assured a dominance over the faith and morals of his congregation; given their general illiteracy, he was their one and only guide and mentor. On another, the Church played an active rôle in book censorship, rivalling the powers of government and *Parlements* in these fields. But the total effect of the Church was more pervasive even than this, for society functioned according to its basic assumptions: hierarchy, order, resignation to present ills and injustices in hopes of the world to come. The criteria for living were transcendental; what happened in the observable world of here and now was unimportant, except as symbolic of the kingdom of God.

It is the erosion of these values in particular that we witness in eighteenth-century France. The age is not irreligious, still less atheist; but it moves steadily in the direction of supplanting a way of life based on the divine by a secular style centred on reason, knowledge, humanity.[52] Religious tolerance can begin to find a place when men no longer feel that God's name and honour will be scandalised if he is prayed to in the wrong faith. Science can take its rise when the measurable world becomes worthy of interest in its own right. Knowledge acquires value when its contribution to progress becomes discernible. Progress itself takes pride of place when the temporal and finite seem of more interest than the eternal. The idea of civilisation as a good in itself, embracing all these aspects, becomes possible for the first time in the Christian world.

Needless to say, these momentous changes do not begin in 1715. They have an ancestry reaching back to the Renaissance and in some respects even beyond. It is the particular feature of the Enlightenment to grasp these new ideas consciously, to urge their development with a firmness not seen before, and above all to develop the sense of man as centre of the universe. The growth of scientific study is of particular interest here. From the mid-seventeenth century a veritable explosion of interest in science had occurred. In the first instance much of the impetus in France came from royal patronage. The *Académie royale des sciences*, founded in 1666, became 'un élément essentiel du progrès scientifique en France'[53] from about 1700, aided by all the pensions, privileges and subsidies which the Crown could contribute to an enterprise that it looked on with favour; election to the *Académie des sciences* soon became a badge of the highest status. From 1703 its *Histoire* and *Mémoires* began to appear, 'la Bible du nouvel âge scientifique'.[54] Later in the century, Maupertuis organised his famous expedition to Lapland in 1736–37 under the aegis of the *Académie des sciences* in order to measure a degree of the meridian and thereby prove that, as Newton had predicted, gravity caused a flattening of the earth's surface at the poles. Wars too had stimulated scientific discovery; from the sophisticated advances in siege warfare developed, for instance, a new interest in engineering.[55]

In the second half of the seventeenth century the periodical press also began to make an impact, starting with the influential *Journal des savants*, which first appeared in 1665 and, like subsequent journals, reached the international audience of the 'République des lettres', made up of writers and thinkers all over Western and Central Europe (with Russia and the American colonies sharing in the intellectual expansion more and more as the eighteenth century advanced). The *Jardin du Roi*, founded in 1626 and concerned with the education of doctors and chemists, came to play a rôle of ever greater importance. From 1673 it gave free, public courses attended by 400 or 500 people at a time, exciting the jealousy of the University of Paris which languished in this field as in most others.[56] Before 1700 a complete demonstration of the human anatomy was being undertaken with the corpses of hanged criminals. Throughout the eighteenth century the *Jardin* was run by a member of the *Académie des sciences*, a happy case of fruitful interaction between official institutions. The really dramatic rise in popularity at the *Jardin du Roi* occurred however when Buffon took over as *intendant* in 1739, a post he was to hold till his death in 1788. By contrast with the closed world of the universities, where theology and Latin held sway, here were demonstrations open to all, in the vernacular, and stressing practice rather than theory.[57] Success under such conditions was almost automatic.

Royal patronage also extended into technology, an area closely linked with the life-sciences, more particularly when such aspects as mineralogy (taught at the *Jardin du Roi* from 1745) were involved. Mining was taught at the *École des ponts et chaussées* from mid-century, opening the way for the creation of the *École des mines* in 1783.[58] The *École du corps royal du Génie* was established in 1748 and the *École royale militaire* in 1751. The *Collège royal*, which François I had founded in 1529 outside the University, served as another focal point for scientific innovation. Here under Louis XV was to be found the biggest collection of scientific instruments in the land; by 1770 seven of the nineteen professorial chairs were given over to science.[59] One of the most dynamic teachers in the field, the *abbé* Nollet (already closely connected with the *Académie des sciences* and the *Jardin du Roi*) was appointed in 1738 to a new chair at the *Collège royal* in experimental physics (the inauguration of the chair was itself a triumph for the discipline). Nollet, a lively man, specialised in the lively subject of electricity. His experiments were remarkable, with a touch of the grand impresario about them; one of his achievements was to give an electric shock to 180 royal guards, another to 700 monks holding hands 'so that they all jumped into the air simultaneously, to the intense satisfaction of the spectators'.[60] Not surprisingly, crowds poured into his classes, including distinguished royal figures like the Queen and the Dauphin.

Although our concern here is with France alone, some mention must be made of the scientific institutions on the international scene, for science, then as now, ignored frontiers. In England the Royal Society (established in 1660) had assisted a similar expansion; fittingly, Newton was its President from 1703 until his death in 1727. Newton's authority on the Continent in the eighteenth century is one of the most significant elements of the whole Enlightenment.[61] But in France he triumphed only after some resistance; by contrast, in Holland he found ready disciples at the University of Leyden in Boerhaave and s'Gravesande, and Newtonianism had swept the Netherlands by the late 1730s while still beginning to make headway in France.[62] In Frederick II's Prussia, too, Maupertuis was striving from the time of his appointment as President of the Berlin Academy in 1746 to renovate that neglected body and turn it into an institution worthy of its London and Paris counterparts; his success long survived his death in 1759.[63] But Maupertuis's migration to another culture is only one among many by scientists and scholars in the century. Frederick competed with Catherine of Russia for the famous Swiss mathematician Euler, the Swiss naturalist Haller left Berne for Göttingen, the Berlin Academy attracted such as Voltaire and La Mettrie, Goldoni and the abbé Galiani came to Paris – the list could be multiplied at length.

Science was in the fashion – it had been so since at least 1658, claims Jacques Roger:[64] the salons were increasingly discussing it. Works of popular science began to emerge on matters like astronomy, such as the abbé de Gérard's aptly titled *La Philosophie des gens de cour* (1680), one of whose sections was headed 'Que les dames doivent s'appliquer à l'étude de la philosophie'. A similar but much more celebrated work on a kindred topic appeared a few years later, Fontenelle's *Entretiens sur la pluralité des mondes* (1686), cast, like the abbé de Gérard's work, in the form of dialogues intended for easy reading.[65] Helvétius was later in *De l'esprit* (1758) to render Fontenelle the justice due to him as one of the first popularisers of knowledge, 'un des premiers qui

... établit un pont de communication entre la science et l'ignorance'.[66]

Nowhere was the new secular mood more clearly seen than in the growth of sensibility. The attenuation of the doctrine of Original Sin, the influence of Locke's philosophy reducing man to a series of sense impressions (governed, in Locke's case, by the capacity for reflection – but his disciples in France were to throw out the reflective and retain only the sensationalist element), the growth of interest in the individual *per se*, the increased belief that an emotional man was also a virtuous man – all these concepts belong as much to intellectual history. But some of their consequences are primarily enshrined in the notion of *bienfaisance*, the sense of promoting the good of society through care for one's fellow men. This is at the heart of all Enlightenment enterprises, and we shall find it all-pervasive in the literature of the period.

Linked increasingly to this new sensibility as the century moved forward was a feeling for nature. After 1750 the practice of taking a country house became widespread among those who could afford it. Interest in the wilder scenery of the Alps took longer to build up, but Rousseau's *La Nouvelle Héloïse* (1761) made the Swiss mountains fashionable, and subsequently the French mountains were discovered in their turn. Until 1750 agriculture had been largely disdained, but within the next decade a great concern for it develops, with the founding of agricultural societies to channel the new development. Gardening became a popular subject, particularly with the discovery of English gardens. Characteristically, as eighteenth-century men of culture Voltaire and Rousseau were both keenly interested in the subject, and gardens are intimately woven into the fabric of both *Candide* and *La Nouvelle Héloïse*; but whereas Voltaire's taste looks back to the symmetrical patterns of Versailles, Rousseau's ideal garden is essentially pure nature, untouched by man.[67]

Such are the lineaments of this society: hierarchical, élitist, oligarchic, but also becoming secular, empirical, reformist, and cosmopolitan. Through the decaying structures pulsated an energy that was ultimately to be explosive; it was new wine in old bottles. The time has come to look at the power more directly wielded by the pen and to see the precise nature of its symbiotic relationship with the society of which it was part.[68]

NOTES

1. See R. Shackleton: 'Jansenism and the Enlightenment', *Studies on Voltaire and the Eighteenth Century* (hereafter *Studs. Volt.*), 57 (1967), pp. 1387–97; J. H. Shennan, *Philippe, Duke of Orleans: Regent of France 1715–1723* (Thames and Hudson, 1979), pp. 77–9. One of the *chansonniers* of the period wrote of the Regent: 'Il a rétabli les duels,/Remis le jansénisme;/Bientôt nous verrons des autels/Rendus au calvinisme'. The Regent considered recalling the Protestant refugees to France; see Saint-Simon, *Mémoires*, edited by G. Truc (Paris: Nouvelle Revue Française, hereafter NRF, Bibliothèque de la Pléiade), Vol. V (1965), pp. 307–8. I am indebted to Dr G. Gargett for this reference. There is also a brief allusion to the Regent's attitude toward Protestants in Montesquieu's *Lettres persanes*, LX.

2. See N. R. Johnson, 'Louis XIV and the Age of the Enlightenment: the Myth of the Sun King from 1715 to 1789', *Studs. Volt.*, 182 (1978), pp. 87–96.

3. A strong case for still considering 1715 as a dividing line is made by F.L. Ford, *Robe and Sword : The Regrouping of the French Aristocracy after Louis XIV* (Harvard University Press, 1953), Chapter I. See also Franco Venturi's opinion that 'the death of Louis XIV was enough for the idea of toleration and the burgeoning Enlightenment to find their centre in the very heart of the greatest monarchical state, in Paris and in France', *Utopia and Reform in the Enlightenment* (Cambridge University Press, 1971), p. 65. A. C. Keller gives reasons for ignoring 1715 as an important landmark (G. Atkinson and A. C. Keller, *Prelude to the Enlightenment: French Literature, 1690–1740* (Allen and Unwin, 1971), pp. 205–6). His arguments, though valid, seem partial and do not take account of the full range of developments in France.

4. 'The great battle of ideas took place before 1715, and even before 1700', A. Cobban, 'The Enlightenment', in *The New Cambridge Modern History*, Vol. VII, *The Old Régime 1713–63*, edited by J. O. Lindsay (Cambridge University Press, 1957), p. 85. Similarly, Gustave Lanson argued that the political doctrines of the later eighteenth century do not grow out of abstraction, but have an experiential basis in the miseries of the final years of Louis XIV's reign: 'Le Rôle de l'expérience dans la formation de la philosophie du XVIIIᵉ siècle en France', in *Etudes d'histoire littéraire* (Paris: Champion, 1929), pp. 164–209.

5. It should however be added that Montesquieu's work could not expect to receive any official authorisation to print, nor indeed did it seek any.

6. 7 September 1716; cited in R. Laufer, *Lesage ou le métier de romancier* (Paris: Gallimard, 1971), pp. 125–6.

7. A. Adam, *Le Mouvement philosophique dans la première moitié du XVIIIᵉ siècle* (Paris: Société d'Editions d'Enseignement Supérieur, hereafter S.E.D.E.S., 1967), p. 36. After 1737, however, the situation began to deteriorate, especially with the proscription laid upon novels by the government (see below, p. 100).

8. *L'Ancien Régime*, Vol. I, *La Société* (Paris: Colin, 1969), p. 6.

9. *L'Ancien Régime*, p. 23. This is a slight exaggeration; some institutions and

practices, like the Jesuit Order, most guilds, and judicial torture, were suppressed or modified before 1789. But Goubert's study stops at 1750, which makes the broad assertions substantially correct within his limits.

10. C. Kunstler, *La Vie quotidienne sous la Régence* (Paris: Hachette, 1960), p. 165; M. Bloch, *Les Rois thaumaturges* (Paris: Istra, 1924), p. 397.

11. Bloch, *Les Rois thaumaturges*, p. 401.

12. M. S. Anderson, *18th Century Europe 1713-1789* (Oxford University Press, 1966), p. 77.

13. P. Francastel, 'L'esthétique des Lumières', in *Utopie et institutions au XVIIIᵉ siècle*, edited by P. Francastel (Paris/The Hague: Mouton, 1963), p. 352.

14. *Le Mouvement philosophique*, p. 14.

15. For a succinct and lucid account of the affair, see J. Lough, *An Introduction to Eighteenth Century France* (Longmans, 1960), pp. 139–42, 151–3, 155–7, 170–5.

16. Kunstler, *La Vie quotidienne sous la Régence*, p. 129; see also Shennan, *Philippe, Duke of Orleans*, especially pp. 112–16.

17. *The Enlightenment* (Penguin, 1968), p. 174.

18. H. Méthivier, *La Fin de l'Ancien Régime* (Paris: Presses Universitaires de France, hereafter P.U.F., 'Que sais-je?', 1970), p. 26. See also: 'One might almost say it was the recalling of the *Parlement* in 1774 which led Louis XVI to the guillotine', R. B. Jones, *The French Revolution* (University of London Press, 1967), p. 37.

19. *Mémoires et correspondance*, edited by A. Sayous (Paris, 1851), 2 vols., Vol. I, p. 163; cited in J. Lough, *An Introduction to Eighteenth Century France* (Longmans, 1960), p. 229.

20. *A Social History of the French Revolution* (Routledge, 1966), p. 4.

21. M. J. Sydenham, *The French Revolution* (Methuen, 1969), p. 233.

22. But a woman's rights *vis-à-vis* her husband were to remain inferior: see D. Williams, 'The Politics of Feminism in the French Enlightenment', *The Varied Pattern: Studies in the 18th Century*, edited by P. Hughes and D. Williams (Toronto: Hakkert, 1971), pp. 338, 349–51.

23. 'noblesse, c'est liqueur séminale' (Valéry); cited in P. Goubert, *L'Ancien Régime*, Vol. I, p. 152.

24. *L'Ancien Régime*, Vol. I, p. 152. For a detailed description of 'la noblesse' see R. Mousnier, *Les Institutions de la France sous la monarchie absolue, 1598–1789*, Vol. 1 (Paris: P.U.F., 1974), pp. 94–171.

25. R. Mauzi, *L'Idée du bonheur dans la littérature et la pensée françaises au XVIIIᵉ siècle* (Paris: Colin, 1967), p. 271.

26. E. G. Barber, *The Bourgeoisie in 18th Century France* (Princeton University Press, 1955), pp. 28–9.

27. G. V. Taylor, 'Types of Capitalism in Eighteenth-Century France', *English Historical Review*, 79 (1964), p. 487.

28. Goubert, *L'Ancien Régime*, Vol. I, p. 179.

29. The implications of this position are developed at greater length below (see pp. 149–52).

30. See below, p. 120.

31. D. Roche, *Le Siècle des lumières en province : Académies et académiciens provinciaux, 1680–1789* (Paris/The Hague: Mouton, 1978), 2 vols., I, pp. 249–55, II, p. 96.

32. R. Darnton, 'In Search of the Enlightenment', *Journal of Modern History*, 43 (1971), p. 130.
33. Hampson, *A Social History of the French Revolution* pp. 19–20.
34. See D. Ogg, *Europe of the Ancien Régime, 1715–1783* (Collins, 1965), pp. 22–9; J. S. Schapiro, *Condorcet and the Rise of Liberalism* (New York: Octagon, 1963), pp. 10–13; H. Sée, *La France économique et sociale au XVIIIᵉ siècle* (Paris: Colin, 1925), pp. 100–11.
35. In *Life and Letters in France : the Eighteenth Century* (Nelson, 1970), pp. 190–8.
36. *Oeuvres complètes*, edited by R. Desné *et al.* (Paris: Anthropos, 1970–72), 3 vols., II, pp. 26, 64–5.
37. *Oeuvres complètes*, p. 541.
38. The rare exception of a literate agricultural worker, who eloquently recounts his terrible sufferings during the notorious winter of 1709, is to be found in the *Vie de Duval*, an excerpt from which is printed in J.-M. Goulemot and M. Launay, *Le Siècle des lumières* (Paris: Seuil, 1968), pp. 31–6.
39. Cited in C. B. A. Behrens, *The Ancien Régime* (Thames and Hudson, 1967), p. 32.
40. R. Mandrou, *La France aux XVIIᵉ et XVIIIᵉ siècles* (Paris: P.U.F., 1970), p. 96; see R. Favre, *La Mort dans la littérature et la pensée françaises au siècle des lumières* (Lyon: Presses Universitaires, 1978), pp. 43–5.
41. See below, pp. 232–8.
42. Goubert, pp. 244–5, 258–9. The strengths and weaknesses of Maggiolo's study, undertaken in 1877, are concisely summed up in R. Chartier *et al.*, *L'Education en France du XVIᵉ au XVIIIᵉ siècle* (Paris: S.E.D.E.S., 1976), pp. 87–109. New research has been published recently in F. Furet and J. Ozouf, *Lire et écrire : l'alphabétisation des Français de Calvin à Jules Ferry* (Paris: Editions de Minuit, 1977).
43. J. Brancolini and M.-T. Bouyssy, 'La Vie provinciale du livre à la fin de l'Ancien Régime', *Livre et société dans la France du XVIIIᵉ siècle*, Vol. II (Paris/The Hague: Mouton, 1970), pp. 20–3.
44. D. Julia and P. Pressly, 'La Population scolaire en 1789', *Annales*, 30 (1975), pp. 1516–61; Chartier *et al.*, *L'Education*, pp. 186–206.
45. Apart from the authorities cited, the following have also been useful in preparing this section: H. C. Barnard, *Education and the French Revolution* (Cambridge University Press, 1969), pp. 1–15; A. Léon, *Histoire de l'enseignement en France* (Paris: P.U.F., 'Que sais-je?', 1967), pp. 36–46; F. C. Green, *The Ancien Régime: A Manual of French Institutions and Social Classes* (Edinburgh University Press, 1958), pp. 52–8; F. de la Fontainerie, *French Liberalism and Education in the Eighteenth Century* (New York: McGraw-Hill, 1932), pp. 1–25.
46. Cited in Atkinson and Keller, *Prelude to the Enlightenment*, p. 115.
47. D. Williams, 'The Politics of Feminism', p. 344.
48. See below, p. 200.
49. See above, note 22. Some details on female education are provided in Chartier *et al.*, *L'Education*, pp. 231–47.
50. Cf. Fargher, pp. 128–42. The classic study on the subject is E. G. Léonard, *Histoire générale du protestantisme* (Paris: P.U.F., 1961–64), 3 vols.
51. Lough estimates that the Church owned about six per cent of the country's land (*An Introduction*, p. 98).
52. A number of recent studies exemplifying this trend are briefly noticed in R.

Mauzi and S. Menant, *Le XVIIIe Siècle: II, 1750–1778* (Paris: Arthaud, 1977), p. 17.

53. J. Roger, *Les Sciences de la vie dans la pensée française du XVIIIe siècle* (Paris: Colin, 1963), p. 174. See also R. Hahn, *The Anatomy of a Scientific Institution: The Paris Academy of Sciences, 1666–1803* (University of California Press, 1971).

54. Roger, *Les Sciences de la vie*, p. 181.

55. C. Kiernan, 'Science and the Enlightenment in Eighteenth-century France', *Studs. Volt.*, 59 (1968), p. 47.

56. Kiernan, 'Science and the Enlightenment', pp. 58–60; Roger, *Les Sciences de la vie*, p. 175.

57. Kiernan, 'Science and the Enlightenment', pp. 48–9.

58. Kiernan, 'Science and the Enlightenment', p. 52; Hahn, *The Anatomy of a Scientific Institution*, p. 96.

59. Kiernan, 'Science and the Enlightenment', p. 53.

60. Kiernan, 'Science and the Enlightenment', p. 54; see also G. Gusdorf, *Les Principes de la pensée au siècle des lumières* (Paris: Payot, 1971), pp. 176–7. Beyond the sophisticated world, however, the manifestations of electricity could still be highly disturbing. An aristocrat in Saint-Omer erected a sword on his house as a lightning conductor in 1783; the populace saw the action as blasphemous and the imprudent experimenter was saved from trouble only through the eloquence of a young lawyer from Arras – Maximilien de Robespierre (A. Dupront, *Les Lettres, les sciences, la religion et les arts dans la société française de la deuxième moitié du XVIIIe siècle* (Paris: Centre de Documentation Universitaire, n.d. [1962]), p. 32.

61. See Gusdorf's chapters 'Le Modèle newtonien' and 'La Généralisation du paradigme newtonien', in *Les Principes de la pensée*, pp. 151–212, for an excellent discussion of the question.

62. P. Gay, *The Enlightenment*, Vol. II (Weidenfeld and Nicolson, 1970) pp. 135–6.

63. H. Brown, 'Maupertuis *philosophe*: Enlightenment and the Berlin academy', *Studs. Volt.*, 24 (1963), pp. 255–69.

64. *Les Sciences de la vie*, p. 181.

65. Fontenelle, *Entretiens sur la pluralité des mondes*, edited by R. Shackleton (Oxford: Clarendon Press, 1955), pp. 7–9.

66. (Paris, 1758), p. 523; cited in Shackleton (ed.). *Entretiens*, p. 30.

67. See C. Thacker, 'Voltaire and Rousseau: Eighteenth-century Gardeners' *Studs. Volt.*, 90 (1972), pp. 1595–614. The classic study on love of nature in eighteenth-century France remains D. Mornet, *Le Sentiment de la nature en France de Jean-Jacques Rousseau à Bernardin de Saint-Pierre* (Paris: Hachette, 1907).

68. The following works have been of particular help in compiling this chapter: Goubert, *L'Ancien Régime*, Vol. I, H. Méthivier, *L'Ancien Régime* (Paris: P.U.F. ('Que sais-je?'), 1971); Méthivier, *La Fin de l'Ancien Régime*; Behrens, *The Ancien Régime*; A. Cobban, *A History of Modern France* (Penguin, 1961), 2 vols., Vol. I: *1715–1799*; Lough, *An Introduction*; R. B. Jones, *The French Revolution*; Ford, *Robe and Sword*; Gossman, *French Society and Culture* (Englewood Cliffs, New Jersey : Prentice-Hall, 1972).

2   The Writer and His Audience

In this traditionalist way of life must now be placed the writer, generally more critical of society than in the previous century, yet commonly inclined toward moderate reforms rather than direct subversion. Before trying to assess his social situation we should look first at the way he reached his audience and the problems he faced in doing so. The serious culture of the period is essentially a printed one,[1] but there are important oral aspects to be considered. One of the most prominent is an institution which the eighteenth century inherits but modifies: the salons, each one directed by a great lady whose word was law in her own domain.[2] Whether they had as much effect upon the development of *philosophie* as used to be thought is now questionable,[3] but the more serious ones frequented by writers must have provided a useful meeting-place, sometimes even every day (Mademoiselle de Lespinasse, for instance, received guests daily from five to nine pm for twelve successive years).[4] Furthermore, men of letters found that they were increasingly accepted on equal terms in these gatherings with the highest ranks of society. Duclos wrote in 1750 that 'Tous les jours, dans les cercles les plus brillants, les lettres rapprochent les conditions'.[5] Here too was an audience before which authors read their works aloud. Furthermore, salon hostesses like Madame de Tencin played an important part in the elections to the Académie Française of such as Marivaux in 1742. No account of literary life at this period can overlook the existence of such an institution. Less well organised, but possibly more influential because they were not exclusive nor subject to the whims of society ladies, were the cafés, resorts of increasing popularity. In the *Lettres persanes* (XXXVI), Montesquieu reports that 'Le café est très en usage à Paris. Il y a un grand nombre de maisons publiques où on le distribue. Dans quelques-unes de ces maisons, on dit des nouvelles; dans d'autres on joue aux échecs.' There were, according to one count, 380 in Paris in 1723 and 600 to 700 by 1782, though police reports, perhaps including analogous establishments that were not strictly cafés, put the figure as high as 1800 in 1788; almost all of them, it appears, carried the latest gazettes. Ordinances of Louis XVI in 1777–78 had allowed them an hour's extra opening time, till ten pm in winter and eleven pm in summer, a further proof of their success in fulfilling a public need. Care had to be taken over political discussion because of police informers, and Prévost paints a contrast with the more radical atmosphere prevailing in the London cafés; the Parisian coffee-houses would seem to have been wary of politics until the 1780s. But police records show that the conversation about religion was already of a radical kind before 1750. As the century advanced, cafés multiplied in the provinces also, especially from around 1770. Like the salons, the cafés played a rôle in broadcasting the ideas of the Enlightenment, though the precise extent of their importance would be difficult to evaluate.[6]

Clubs also played their part. An import from England, they drew their strength from an active membership of like-minded men. From the 1720s dates the most famous, the Club de l'Entresol, a discussion group of about twenty, particularly interested in social science and meeting weekly at the home of Président Hénault, where writers like Montesquieu and the abbé de Saint-Pierre met. As its secretary the marquis d'Argenson put it, 'c'était un café d'honnêtes gens'.[7] This body, though not at all revolutionary, was nevertheless too concerned with politics to be viewed with equanimity by the authorities, and in 1731 discreet pressure from Cardinal Fleury obliged it to disband. The heyday of the clubs was to come under the Revolution, when they had a prominent rôle in the general upheaval. The Jacobins, for instance, grew out of a group of Breton deputies who met daily in a café in 1789 to decide upon policy, the club acquiring its permanent name when it hired the disused Jacobin convent in the rue Saint-Honoré. Cobban estimates that there were 5000 to 8000 such clubs in France by 1793, with a total membership of half a million.[8] But these institutions, in some ways the forerunners of modern political parties, are of less direct concern for our present purposes. A similar purpose to the Ancien Régime clubs was served by the freemasons, who appeared in France in 1721 and by the Revolution possessed about 600 lodges and 20,000 to 30,000 members, according to Mornet.[9] Generally they were conservative in their social attitudes, but in their concern for promoting social welfare they coincided with the *philosophes*, and many of the latter (including Montesquieu, Voltaire and Condorcet) were masons; however, connections between the two movements were incidental and one may now confidently dismiss the long-standing belief that the *Encyclopédie* was a masonic conspiracy.[10]

In the provinces the more philosophical discussions would generally have gone on in the Academies. These bodies were less open than the Encyclopaedist group; dominated by the *parlementaires*, with a strong admixture of clergy, they excluded peasants, artisans and businessmen in all but exceptional cases. Yet the traditionalist emphasis was counteracted by the presence of intellectuals and provincial administrators and the existence of intellectual goals – the advancement of knowledge, especially scientific and technical. The Academies were taking on a new rôle. From a mere thirteen in 1715 for the whole of France, their numbers multiplied to 32 by 1789. More dramatic still was the increase in the essay competitions on cultural topics which they organised and supervised: from fewer than 50 in the first decade of the century to well over 600 in 1780–89.[11] Rousseau's two *Discours* are perhaps the best known of all such entries, being submitted for prize competitions organised by the Dijon Academy; the first, the *Discours sur les sciences et les arts* (1750) won him first prize and the beginnings of his literary renown, which he was never thereafter to lose.

Finally, any survey of the spoken word, however brief, must include some reference to theatre. Later we shall be examining some of the most important theatrical developments during the century. For the moment, let us simply consider the playhouse as an institution. The leading theatre, the Comédie Française, was dominated by aristocratic tastes and fashions, as the presence of spectators on the stage until 1759 and the creation of *petites loges* from mid-century make clear.[12] But the building as a whole was noisy and insalubrious, with primitive lavatories, poorly ventilated and insufferably hot in summer.[13] For those standing up in the *parterre* (about 550 to 600 people) theatregoing must have been a most uncomfortable business, especially as a typical performance lasted four to five hours, including one long and one short play. In addition, one suffered the indignity of having refuse showered on one's head from the boxes above. Conditions, in short, must have been such as would not be tolerated at a professional football match in Western Europe nowadays. Yet the bourgeoisie could not easily get seats even as late as the 1770s, according to Mercier, and the majority of those in the *parterre* would seem to have been bourgeois with some degree of culture. One wonders how French classical playwrights managed to convey even the slightest subtlety under such conditions. There must be astonishment too that people should willingly pay money to put up with so much inconvenience; presumably playgoing held as strong an attraction for the less wealthy who stood as for the élite who took their ease in their comfortable seats. Indeed, it seems that when conditions improved with the occupation of new quarters (first in the Tuileries in 1770 and then at the Odéon in 1782), a new plebeian element came into the *parterre* and taste declined. One writer suggested a remedy : 'Il y aurait un seul moyen d'amortir le tumulte du parterre, ce serait d'y admettre des femmes; la galanterie imposerait la décence....'[14]

For all its difficulties, however, the theatre offered a shared experience, and there were many, like Diderot and Rousseau, who saw (in very different ways) how public spectacles might unite and elevate the audience. The *drame bourgeois* was one such response to this challenge.[15] With the coming of the Revolution theatrical propaganda became more blatant still. The Comédie Française, under some duress, produced Marie-Joseph Chénier's *Charles IX* in November 1789 to great acclaim, and this play with its revolutionary sentiments inaugurated a new mood on the stage. In its condemnation of absolute monarchy, the clergy and the aristocracy, and in its demands for popular sovereignty, freedom of thought and progress through enlightenment it fitted the popular climate. Although the King eventually forbade its performance, Chénier managed to have censorship abolished and the play started a second run the following July. In 1791, the monopolies which the Comédie Française and the other royal theatres (the Opéra and the Opéra Comique, the latter having absorbed the Comédie Italienne in 1762) had enjoyed were abolished, an unlimited number of theatres was allowed and all authors given the right to negotiate their own terms with theatrical managements. The royal theatres had become associated with aristocratic reaction and now suffered the rivalry of more

radical houses; the Comédie Française troupe, indeed, only nar-
rowly escaped execution under the Terror. As tension mounted,
so the Paris theatre became more of a cockpit, reflecting the
struggles outside. But the new freedom also inspired tremendous
vitality. In 1793 over 40 theatres existed, putting on over 200
plays; 1500 new plays were produced in the decade after 1789.[16]
Unfortunately theatrical vigour did not necessarily connote cultural greatness. Doctrinaire attitudes hardened, many of the
Ancien Régime masterpieces like *Phèdre*, *Britannicus* and *Zaïre*
were ideologically suspect and therefore banned; only the most
thoroughgoing revolutionary plays were safe if political subjects
were raised (though non-political plays went on unimpeded).
After Robespierre's death, the pendulum swung towards anti-
Jacobin sentiments, but the ferment was already dying down,
and in the next few years many theatres disappeared; by 1797
only a score remained. The feeling was widespread that the abolition of controls on the creation of new theatres had inflamed the
political situation. A proposal in 1798 to limit the number to six
was not accepted, but it showed the way. In 1807 the maximum
of eight was decreed, by which time the Comédie Française,
Opéra and Opéra Comique had been re-established as national
theatres.[17]

A lively experiment seemed to have ended in an impasse, with
the *status quo* restored after twenty years. Yet the Revolutionary
history of Paris theatre is in some measure a logical culmination
of the attitudes to drama prevalent in eighteenth-century France.
Theatre was a strongly social phenomenon, responsive to the
public mood and theoretically capable of moulding it. We shall
need to bear this in mind when tracing the evolution of
eighteenth-century drama.

The theatre's rôle in spreading new ideas was, however,
necessarily restricted. The greatest stage triumph of the period,
Le Mariage de Figaro (1784), attracted only 97,000 spectators
(many of whom were presumably the same people seeing it more
than once) and no other play came near that record. Eighteenth-
century culture depended essentially on the printing-press. As
such, it was limited to those who could read, perhaps a quarter of
a million in all, and in reality to far fewer than this who could appreciate a serious argument. However, a printed page has perma-
nency, theoretically it can be read at any time and as often as one
wishes. So the growth of libraries becomes an important element.

From 1735 the Bibliothèque du Roi was open to the public, though only twice a week for two to two-and-a-half hours each time; other public libraries opened during the century and by 1784 a dozen were functioning in Paris. A multiplication of similar facilities was also going on in the provinces, particularly after 1770.[18]

As the age advanced, France also witnessed a proliferation of periodicals and, later, newspapers. Before 1720, the only important journals published in France were the weekly *Gazette*, an official paper which held the monopoly of political news, the monthly *Mercure de France* and the weekly *Journal des savants*, the last being the only one to deal with science, while also covering much else. None enjoyed a wide readership and little impact was made upon public opinion before 1750. Yet these remained the only officially recognised journals, and those who wished to start up competitors had to obtain special permission from the authorities, which involved *inter alia* the offering of a subsidy to one of the trio, generally the *Journal des savants*.[19] Their official status disinclined them from controversy; but if one wanted a livelier point of view it could be found in the Jesuit *Journal de Trévoux*, which lost much of its prestige with the suppression of the Jesuit Order in 1762 (though it continued to appear in various forms until 1778) or the *Nouvelles ecclésiastiques*, the Jansenist review begun in 1728. In the second half of the century other journals appeared, notably Fréron's *Année littéraire*, over which the editor, a famous anti-*philosophe*, retained sole control for over two decades until his death in 1776, or Pierre Rousseau's *Journal encyclopédique*, printed (like the Jesuit magazine) on safe territory outside French control. This latter periodical was the dominant champion of the *philosophe* cause throughout the 1760s, reaching a peak of popularity before declining in the 1780s in the face of more radical and outspoken, even scurrilous, works like Linguet's *Annales politiques, civiles et littéraires* (1777–92). With the coming of the Revolution established periodicals suffered from the new-found freedom, as permission to print and censorship were abolished in the great holocaust of feudal privileges on 4 August 1789; the *Journal encyclopédique*, relic of an outmoded world, ceased in 1793.[20] But the demand for periodicals had been increasing long before 1789. The *Mercure* was available in 26 towns in 1748 and in 55 by 1774.[21] The first French daily newspaper, the *Journal de Paris*, appeared in 1777. Two years later Paris had 35 newspapers and journals, while a rapid multiplication occurred in the provinces after 1770. When, therefore, freedom of the press was offered by the Revolution, a veritable explosion took place; at least 250 periodicals and newspapers were circulating in Paris alone by the end of 1789, and 350 the following year.[22] Journalism came of age in France under the Revolution and enjoyed great vitality in the early years before political repression grew, though as in the theatre cultural standards were far from the highest.

The essential medium of Enlightenment culture is however the book. Here too the scene is one of privilege and confusion. Privilege to print was conferred by the King through his ministers; but censorship could be exercised, not only by the government but also by the Sorbonne and the Paris *Parlement*. From the changing patterns produced by the various combinations of these three powers emerged arbitrary decisions according to the political atmosphere or the dominant figures of the time. Much jealousy existed, as might be expected, between government and *Parlement*, the latter being generally harsher in its punishments. The normal supervision of the book trade lay, however, with the *Chancelier*, the main law officer of the government, or the *Garde des Sceaux* (often the same person), under whom was a *Directeur de la librairie* responsible for censorship. Prosecutions against infringements of the law like the publication and sale of illegal books were directed by the *lieutenant général de police* (Chief of Police). The official punishment for clandestine printers was the pillory for the first offence and five years in the galleys thereafter, but following the great alarm caused in 1757 by Damiens's attempted assassination of Louis XV the death sentence, which had been abolished in 1728 for this offence, was reintroduced. Though these penalties were generally too draconian to be implemented, punishments continued to be severe, including imprisonment of indefinite duration and withdrawal of the official *maîtrise* to practise the trade. As late as 1768 Diderot wrote to Sophie Volland that a hawker selling copies of d'Holbach and Voltaire had been arrested with his wife and an apprentice, all three pilloried, whipped, and branded, the men sent to the galleys and the wife to prison.[23] However, the treatment of offenders seems to have been more lenient than in the previous century. Furthermore, many books did not conveniently fit into either the legal or illegal category. There were a great number to which the authorities were quite willing to turn a blind eye. So from 1718 onwards, but building up in large numbers only after 1750, there evolved a system of *permissions tacites*; the books which qualified were approved by a censor but no written permission was given. Others received a simple verbal (and unrecorded) *tolérance* from the police, which meant that they could be secretly printed and would generally be left alone provided they caused no public scandal. The advantage of these arrangements from the government's point of view was that they could be easily countermanded if necessary.

Without such compromises the regulation of the book trade, in an age when books were yearly growing more critical of political and religious orthodoxy, would surely have collapsed long before 1789; as things were, it survived in its piecemeal way into the beginning of the Revolutionary period. For the *privilège* to print was, like so many privileges under the Ancien Régime, monopolistic. It granted a particular bookseller the exclusive right to print and sell the book in question for a certain number of years. The system worked particularly in favour of a small number of wealthy booksellers in Paris;[24] the provincial booksellers were powerless against them and often resorted to counterfeiting in order to make a living. Malesherbes, the outstanding *Directeur de la librairie* of the century, tried during his years in office (1750–63) to help the latter in their fight against this restrictive monopoly, but he did not undertake any far-reaching reforms, probably because he knew that hopes of success along those lines were minimal. He worked on the basis that it was better to put up with small infringements of the law and reserve one's authority for the serious cases. Inevitably, as the number of critical works grew so did the business of censorship. In 1741 there were 77 official censors, and by 1762 the number had risen to 122. The task of arresting publishers and sellers of illegal books or of intercepting the large number of volumes being smuggled in from London, Switzerland and especially Holland likewise grew more rigorous. Even within the French borders there were problems of contraband. A favourite resort of printers, until its annexation by the French government in 1768, was the Papal enclave of Avignon. In 1754 30 printers were at work there, printing much of the time counterfeit editions with an easy outlet for them just across the border.[25] Like most procedures under the Ancien Régime control of publishing worked by rule of thumb and with increasing inefficiency. Illegal books from a well-known author simply cost more, so that after Rousseau's *Emile* (1762) had been condemned by both *Parlement* and Sorbonne and solemnly torn apart and burned by the hangman, it was fetching about 15 to 18 *livres*.[26] Indeed, the hangman often took care to substitute another book for the condemned one; such expensive volumes were not for burning.

It would seem, with hindsight, that the situation could not have been otherwise. The Ancien Régime did not command the repressive powers of a modern state, and the growing scepticism in French thought ensured a ready-made audience for the critical works that appeared; indeed one fed the other in ceaseless interaction. As we have seen, at first the censorship was relatively liberal under the Regent and thereafter mostly directed at Jansenism until the mid-1740s. The banning of Voltaire's *Lettres philosophiques* in 1734 was uncharacteristic for its time, and the reasons for this course of action are obscure;[27] but it was a harbinger of things to come. The liberalism of the early eighteenth century should however not be exaggerated. If the situation was still largely free from strife except on the Jansenist front, that was to some extent because critical works could hope for no accommodation with authority. One should not forget the large number of clandestine manuscripts, mainly on philosophical and religious themes, that still survive from the period before 1750. Of these, Jean Meslier's *Mémoire*, probably written in the 1720s, is the best known, because it is a most bitter denunciation of religion and society, and because Voltaire published an *Extrait* of it.[28]

But from about 1745 a new situation was being created as the Sorbonne intervened to defend the faith against the openly declared radicalism, examining Diderot's *Pensées philosophiques* (1746) and *Lettre sur les aveugles* (1749), Toussaint's *Les Mœurs* (1748) and Buffon's *Histoire naturelle* (which began appearing in 1749); the *Pensées philosophiques* had already been condemned by the *Parlement*. In this worsening situation the *Directeur de la librairie*, Maboul, gave sterner orders for the supervision of books, and a period of considerable persecution followed. Diderot was among those imprisoned; his offence was to have published the *Lettre sur les aveugles*, and he expiated it by a hundred days in the château at Vincennes. An air of crisis hung about the capital, the marquis d'Argenson being among those who predicted a revolution.

But this wave of arrests was to constitute the last important use of imprisonment by the State under the Ancien Régime against subversive writers. Periods of detention were imposed around 1760 upon various intellectuals, including Marmontel, Morellet, Mirabeau *père* and *fils*; Fréron had been gaoled in 1746 and 1757. But all these spells of imprisonment were of short duration, a few weeks at most, and for particular reasons such as (with Morellet and Fréron) excessively noisy indulgence in the war between the *philosophes* and their opponents. Only Linguet, who was sent to prison for twenty months in 1780–82, could be called a genuine victim amongst the intellectuals. With Malesherbes's term of office as *Directeur de la libraire* beginning in 1750 a more liberal régime was set up. Condemnation of books, publishers and sellers continued, but the new *Directeur's* firm belief in freedom of the press, allied to a flexible interpretation of the rules, meant that until 1758 many *philosophe* works, including the first seven volumes of the *Encyclopédie*, appeared without great difficulty.

The one exception, occurring in 1752, involved the *Encyclopédie* itself. A Sorbonne thesis by the abbé de Prades, after being successfully defended by its author, was later found to contain heretical propositions. The thesis was condemned to be burnt and the author fled the country. The danger for the *Encyclopédie* lay in the fact that he was a contributor. Enemies seized on the scandal, and the *Conseil d'État* was persuaded to suppress the two volumes that had already appeared (February 1752). But Malesherbes's intervention, both to protect the work against further attacks and also to ensure that under firmer control it would not provoke another scandal, led to the decree being quietly shelved. The privilege to print had not in any case been revoked, so no reversal of policy was needed to allow subsequent volumes to appear.

This apart, relative calm prevailed. Diderot, Rousseau, Maupertuis, Condillac, Buffon and d'Alembert, all actively publishing, were largely untroubled by authority during these years. But alarm was growing on the conservative side, a journalistic war was being waged against the *Encyclopédie*, and from 1757 the atmosphere began to deteriorate. Damiens's attempt upon the King led to a vigorous governmental reaction. Later in the year the publication of Volume VII of the *Encyclopédie* raised new controversies. D'Alembert's article 'Genève', advocating the establishment of a theatre in Geneva and praising its pastors for their deist sentiments, provoked a storm of protest, including Rousseau's *Lettre sur les spectacles*,[29] from within the city. To these troubled waters was added the explosive force of Helvétius's materialist essay *De l'esprit* (1758), which gained added notoriety from being approved by an unwary censor before its full implications were realised and it was condemned by *Parlement* to be burned. Denunciations of Helvétius's work flowed from all sides – the Queen, as leader of the devout party at Court, the Archbishop of Paris, the Sorbonne, the Jesuits, the Jansenists, the Pope. The unhappy author openly retracted which, added to the protection of powerful friends like Malesherbes, Choiseul and Madame de Pompadour, saved him from serious punishment.[30] But as Helvétius was associated with the Encyclopaedists his disgrace implicated them. This time Malesherbes had to bow before the storm, and in March 1759 the *privilège* was revoked by the Conseil d'État. However, work on the *Encyclopédie* still went on uninterrupted in Paris, and eventually, under the fictitious imprint of Samuel Fauche at Neuchâtel, it started reappearing with a *permission tacite* from Malesherbes, beginning with the volumes of plates (1762–72), then the remaining Volumes VIII to XVII of text in 1765.

The struggle was now joined. Voltaire's works appeared anonymously or under a fictitious pseudonym, generally first of all in Geneva. Rousseau, daring to put his own name on the title-page, incurred trouble in 1762 over *Emile*, which gave particular offence because of the deist *Profession de foi du vicaire savoyard* in Book IV. The work was condemned by the *Parlement* and Rousseau's arrest ordered, which forced him to flee from France, inaugurating a period of eight years of wandering that occasioned him considerable hardship, both physical and mental. Meantime, *Emile* had proved a success. As Belin says, the case epitomises the confused situation:

> Ce livre, imprimé par les soins du Directeur de la librairie, puis condamné par le Parlement, l'archevêque, la Sorbonne, et qui n'en était pas moins lu et goûté par tout Paris, est un des exemples les plus typiques des contradictions de l'ancien régime en matière de librairie et du progrès incessant que faisait la philosophie.[31]

Diderot, quite possibly as a consequence of his taste of gaol in 1749, preferred to keep his boldest ideas to his circle of friends, so works like *La Religieuse* (1760), *Le Neveu de Rameau* (1761–79), the

Rêve de d'Alembert (1769), the *Supplément au Voyage de Bougainville* (1772) and *Jacques le fataliste* (1773), all unpublished in his lifetime, were virtually unknown to his contemporaries at large. But in the struggle for freedom to print and publish the tide was by the 1770s flowing fast in the Encyclopaedists' favour, despite the continuation of stern edicts. Malesherbes had departed in 1763, but by then his protection was no longer so necessary.

No *philosophe* work of any importance was effectively suppressed. D'Holbach's *Système de la nature* (1770), atheist and materialist in outlook and rejecting the notion of freewill, showed how far irreligion had progressed; Voltaire now saw the danger from atheists as rivalling the perils of Christian fanaticism. The book could not but cause a scandal. It was banned by the government, denounced by the Pope, condemned to burning by the *Parlement*; that did not prevent anyone who wished from gaining access to it. Helvétius, after his troubles in 1758, took care not to publish his much sharper *De l'homme* in his lifetime. When it appeared in 1772, however, despite the almost ritual reaction from the *Parlement*, it had none of the impact of *De l'esprit*: thus far had ideas moved in fourteen years. The last serious attempt by authority to suppress a work of importance was made by Louis XVI upon Beaumarchais's *Le Mariage de Figaro* which took nearly six years to reach the public stage; but when it eventually arrived there in April 1784, the long wait and suspense only added to the brilliant success of the play. Without seeing the comedy as revolutionary, one may still conclude that the events surrounding it boded ill for the prestige of the monarchy. Under Louis XVI, much of the new journalism was to add a libellous factor not prominent before. This burgeoning group did not overlap with the Encyclopaedists, for whom it felt little but scorn and envy. When the Revolution came, it was the members of this Grub Street world who, now in power, took a leading part in destroying the Academies, salons and privileges of the Ancien Régime with which the leading members of the Enlightenment had often made accommodation even while opposing many aspects of their functioning. In a situation of increasing radicalism, the last word in the libertarian movement went to the revolutionaries, before the reaction set in around 1792 and political censorship again became the order of the day.[32] As for the system of *privilèges*, it survived until 1790. From 1777 authors had been given, by royal edict, the right to sell their own works, but only in 1793 did a decree of the Convention enable authors exclusively to retain and transfer their own literary property, thereby establishing at last firm legal safeguards of copyright.[33]

This last point is of fundamental importance in any discussion of the writer's material situation under the Ancien Régime. Unlike the position in England, where from Pope onwards authors were achieving financial independence, French men of letters during the eighteenth century sold their work in perpetuity to the publisher for one single and final payment. In consequence, despite the large market open to them not only in France but across Europe, they received only a small share of the revenue accruing. Official publishers were themselves plagued, as we have seen, by competition from counterfeiters, so the fruit of a man's intellectual labours went to support a large number of parasites. At a time when, in the 1720s, Pope was growing rich by his pen, writers like Le Sage and Prévost were barely making ends meet, despite the great amount of hack work which they undertook.[34] Dramatists encountered a similar system in the theatre, for they had to convince another privileged body, this time the Comédie Française (or on occasion the Comédie Italienne) that their plays were worth accepting and then submit to the modest payments meted out to them. One of Marivaux's most successful plays, the first *Surprise de l'amour* (1722), earned him less than 500 *livres* from the Italians, while the Théâtre Français paid him only 341 *livres* for the second *Surprise* (1727). Voltaire's *Mérope* (1743) achieved over 6000 *livres*, a record for tragedies at that date. As this sum was phenomenal it can be seen that one could not live off writing plays. Rousseau made only 600 *livres* from the *Discours sur l'inégalité* (1755), having received nothing for the *Discours sur les sciences et les arts* five years before. But the situation gradually improved. Rousseau himself obtained 6000 *livres* from his publisher for *Emile* (1762), and Diderot stated that he had gained 120,000 by his own pen in some 25 years. Gradually the writer was establishing a sort of independence. The market itself was growing; of the 44,000 volumes for which official approval was sought in 1723–89, 30,000 appeared after 1750. In 1777 Marmontel received, it appears, 36,000 *livres* for *Les Incas*, while Restif de la Bretonne earned 60,000 *livres* from his books in the 1780s. Similar strides were being taken in the theatre, where Beaumarchais successfully challenged the hold exercised by the Comédie Française, forming in 1777 the *Bureau de législation dramatique* to defend play-wrights' interests; but it was only after the Revolution that the law which in 1791 abolished the royal theatres' monopoly also gave dramatists the copyright of their own plays. Beaumarchais is, however, a sign of the times. His *Mariage de Figaro* brought him 60,000 *livres* in the three years after it opened – a far cry from the pittances paid to Marivaux and his playwright contemporaries a half-century earlier.

So unless writers were independently rich like Montesquieu, Helvétius, d'Holbach, or became rich by extra-literary means like Voltaire, they had to seek an alternative form of income. For some their regular livelihood was enough, which explains why so many were abbés: Saint-Pierre, Dubos, Morellet, even the vola-tile Prévost discovered in the ecclesiastical life security and calm; there were those abbés, like Condillac, who also did supplemen-tary teaching. Laymen writers often looked to education for their livelihood; Buffon and Daubenton taught at the Jardin du Roi, Rousseau gave music lessons. But there were many more who depended on patronage; Helvétius, Necker, Choiseul, and Vol-taire were among those who befriended struggling authors. Similar gifts were common from the royal household (although it is doubtful whether Louis XV or Louis XVI contributed as much to letters as did the Regent and his family).[35] Writers were often made substantial payments, for instance, when their plays were first performed at Court. The Imprimerie Royale would, on rare occasions, accord the distinction of printing literary works, as it did with Voltaire's *Poème sur Fontenoy* in 1745 and Crébillon *père*'s *Oeuvres* in 1750. But the most common form of royal patron-age was through a pension or sinecure. Voltaire's post of *historio-graphe du roi*, which he obtained in 1745 through the good offices of the duc de Richelieu, paid 2000 *livres* annually, with rooms pro-vided free at Versailles. After him it passed to Duclos and then Marmontel. Other monarchs, notably Frederick of Prussia and Catherine of Russia, offered larger rewards still. Besides Vol-taire, Frederick attracted writers as eminent as Maupertuis and La Mettrie to Potsdam. Amongst her many benefactions to French authors Catherine bought Diderot's library in 1765 for 15,000 *livres* and then made him its curator for life with a pension of 1000 *livres*, allowing him to spend his final years in comfortable circumstances and surrounded by his books.[36] Gusdorf speaks of the 'véritable marché des cerveaux' which affected the whole of

Europe, with sovereigns buying up writers as status symbols[37]. At least one royal servant in France felt that more should have been done in this direction. The Baron de Breteuil, in a work written probably about 1775, advocated a greater use of pensions, positions at Court, *brevets d'honneur* and other rewards, as a method of weaning authors away from attacks on government, religion and morality. Despite the impracticability of its hopes at this late date, the document is an interesting contribution to the history of literary patronage during the period.[38]

By 1775 patronage was not lacking, though most of it stemmed less directly from the King and rather more from the apparatus of government, with considerable advice tendered by the *philosophes*. Under the *Contrôleur général* pensions were allotted in the years just before the Revolution to Morellet, Marmontel, La Harpe, Chamfort and Saint-Lambert, all in good standing with the *philosophes*. The three official journals paid protection money for their monopoly and some of this went to writers named by the government. Journalism itself began to be very lucrative; Suard, as editor of the *Journal de Paris* in the 1780s, was reported to be earning 20,000 *livres* annually. The *Mercure de France* which, although the most widely circulated journal in Europe, never exceeded 7000 copies before Louis XVI, went up to 15,000 in the late 1780s. Much of the credit must go to the publisher Panckoucke, who proceeded to offer very generous payments to journalists from his arrival in Paris in 1762 onwards.[39] Faced with such rewards the *philosophe* party would obviously not wish to bring down the society that offered them. It is arguable that the group was effete by the 1780s, the great men dead, the epigones mere mediocrities interested, like Marmontel, in feathering their own nest.[40] But one must not forget that many writers were still vigorously productive, like Raynal, Morellet, Condorcet and Beaumarchais, some of whom welcomed the Revolution, at least in its early phases. As thinkers they could not rival the great *philosophes* but they do not suggest a played-out movement. If the majority of *philosophes* had never wanted to bring down the régime, there was much more to their attitude than complacent self-interest. Peter Gay sums up the dilemma:

> For many of the *philosophes*, enlightened absolutism was a refuge, a response to overpowering realities rather than a first preference, an imposed rather than a free choice ... [they] could either advocate a

new régime (which was a risky, and at best a utopian, venture), withdraw from politics as the arena of futility (which was a seductive
temptation), or work for specific changes without alienating the
powerful (which appeared to many of them the most promising
course).[41]

The material improvements were paralleled by the rise in
social status of the writer. Voltaire is, as so often, the best exemplar. The man who was imprisoned after receiving a beating
from the Chevalier de Rohan in 1726 eventually achieved an
apotheosis in his own lifetime when he returned to Paris just
before his death in 1778. As the century progressed, it seemed
that in terms of prestige France was a better place for authors
than England. Hume observed during his visit to Paris in 1765
that whereas in London a writer enjoyed little respect, in the
French capital 'a man that distinguishes himself in letters, meets
immediately with regard and attention'.[42] Arthur Young on his
travels in France in 1787–89 was surprised by the extent of this
renown: 'The society [in France] for a man of letters, or who has
any scientific pursuit, cannot be exceeded.... Persons of the
highest rank pay an attention to science and literature and
emulate the character they confer.' By contrast, a Fellow of the
Royal Society in London would not be received in a 'brilliant
circle'. In 1763 Gibbon had been irritated at being greeted solely
as an author in Paris, asserting that 'I did not want the writer to
eclipse the gentleman entirely',[43] an attitude strongly reminiscent of the one by Congreve that had displeased Voltaire.[44]
Even so, there were limits to the intimacy between writers and
high society. The monarchy had little use for writers. The only
author who received the honour of *gentilhomme de la chambre* during
this period was Voltaire, and even he did not derive much enjoyment from it, his relations with Louis XV always being strained.
If one applies the test of intermarriage between nobility and
bourgeois writers, perhaps the sternest of all criteria, the segre-
gation appears to be total except for the wedding of Diderot's
daughter to Monsieur de Vandeul.[45]
In matters of social esteem, nevertheless, we see the makings of
the modern French attitude towards its 'mandarins' of literature.
The reason for this surely lies, as John Lough suggests, in their
capacity to affect public opinion.[46] The French historian Rul-
hière in 1787 looked back to 1749 as the year when the *philosophes*

freed themselves from polite literature and acquired this hold.[47] The date, though too precise for such a general phenomenon, fits in with our earlier observations about the change in climate at around that time. Writers were now public figures, and writing a form of action: 'Le théoricien de l'inactuel est devenu un organis- ateur du réel'.[48]

And Paris was the stage on which to perform. Pottinger, taking 200 writers from each of the sixteenth, seventeenth and eight- eenth centuries and working from their places of birth and death, produces some interesting statistical tables. Whereas only 47 sixteenth-century writers born outside Paris died in the city, for the next two centuries the figures rise to 72 and 71 respectively.[49] Such limited information must obviously be treated with caution, yet the large increase would seem to be significant. The capital of France had begun exercising an attraction on the nation's writers that it has never since lost. Voltaire, the Parisian who spent almost all his last 28 years in exile, here seems the great exception; but he never lost touch with Paris, would surely have returned long before 1778 if he had been certain of immu- nity from arrest, and in the end was enabled to see it once more for three months before his death there.[52] Even Rousseau slipped back to spend his final years in Paris, despite all his love of iso- lated nature. Diderot came at the age of fifteen and never left again except on travel. Prévost, Le Sage, Vauvenargues, Saint- Lambert, Montesquieu, Condillac, Buffon, Crébillon *père* and *fils*, Restif de la Bretonne, Marmontel, Mirabeau, Condorcet were all provincials who settled in Paris or at least spent much of their life there. The *Encyclopédie* remained, despite strong tempta- tions to move elsewhere, a Parisian product from start to finish.[50] All the essential media were based on the capital. Indeed, the modern scholar may regret this overwhelming predominance, for it robs the cultural scene of much diversity. Despite excellent works of scholarship in recent years on provincial cities,[51] no French town outside Paris, regrettably, offers a culture sufficient- ly autonomous to merit attention in a general study of this kind. The only French-speaking city with enough vitality for our purpose is, significantly, Geneva.[52]

The writer, then, was clearly ascending the social hierarchy. Balzac's picture of the often frightening mobility open to men of talent in Restoration Paris could have been painted, albeit on a less heroic scale, before 1789. A Voltaire had shown the way to prosperity and fame, and after him the same path could be trodden by country boys of much humbler background like Diderot and Marmontel. The ladder could lead downwards too, especially after 1789. Marmontel, Morellet and Sedaine all lost their privileges in the Revolution; Sénac de Meilhan was forced from the highest administrative ranks into permanent exile under much reduced circumstances, while Chénier and Condorcet lost their lives. But the period 1789–1800 is culturally a hiatus. The *carrière ouverte aux talents* traces its origins in modern France to the Enlightenment, as does the rise of public opinion from which it drew its strength.[53]

NOTES

1. 'La culture intellectuelle de l'Europe moderne se présente, pour l'essentiel, sous la forme de l'imprimé', G. Gusdorf, *Les Principes de la pensée au siècle des lumières*, p. 466.
2. For a list of the most important salons of the century, cf. R. Niklaus, *A Literary History of France: The Eighteenth Century 1715–1789* (Benn, 1970), pp. 44–55.
3. See A. Adam, *Le Mouvement philosophique*, p. 13.
4. M. Glotz and M. Maire, *Salons du XVIIIᵉ siècle* (Paris: Hachette, 1945), p. 14.
5. Cited in Glotz and Maire, *Salons du XVIIIᵉ siècle*, p. 21.
6. Adam, *Le Mouvement philosophique*, pp. 16–18; C. Kunstler, *La Vie quotidienne sous Louis XVI* (Paris: Hachette, 1950), p. 318; D. Mornet, *Les Origines intellectuelles de la Révolution française (1715–1787)*, (Paris: Colin, 1933), pp. 123–5; G. Rudé, *Paris and London in the 18th Century: Studies in Popular Protest* (Collins, Fontana, 1970), pp. 45–6.
7. Cited in A. Soboul *et al.*, *Le Siècle des lumières, Vol. I, L'Essor (1715–1750)* (Paris: P.U.F., 1977), p. 607.
8. *A History of Modern France*, Vol. I, p. 173.
9. *Les Origines intellectuelles de la Révolution française*, p. 360. Cf. also Gusdorf, *Les principes de la pensée an siècles des lumières*, pp. 402–14, and Soboul *et al.*, *Le Siècle des lumières*, pp. 610–12.
10. R. Shackleton, ' The Encyclopédie and Freemasonry', *The Age of Enlightenment: Studies presented to Theodore Besterman* (Edinburgh/London: Oliver and Boyd, 1967), pp. 223–37.
11. D. Roche, *Le Siècle des lumières en province*, Vol. I, p. 325.
12. See below, pp. 136–7.
13. See H. Lagrave, *Le Théâtre et le public à Paris de 1715 à 1750* (Paris: Klincksieck, 1972), p. 106.
14. Fleury, *Mémoires* (c. 1782), edited by J. B. P. Lafitte (Paris, 1836–38), 6 vols., Vol II, p. 290; cited in J. Lough, *Paris Theatre Audiences in the Seventeenth*

and Eighteenth Centuries (Oxford University Press, 1957), p. 205 (this latter study provides a comprehensive account of the prevalent social conditions). See also C. Alasseur, *La Comédie Française au 18ᵉ siècle: étude économique* (Paris/ The Hague: Mouton, 1967).

15. See below, pp. 158–63.
16. R. Darnton, 'The High Enlightenment and the Low-Life of Literature in Pre-Revolutionary France', *Past and Present*, 51 (1971), p. 112 n.
17. See M. Carlson, *The Theatre of the French Revolution* (Cornell University Press, 1966).
18. Mornet, *Les Origines intellectuelles*, pp. 314–16.
19. R. Birn, 'The French-language press and the *Encyclopédie*, 1750–1759', *Studs. Volt.*, 55 (1967), pp. 263–86.
20. R. Birn, 'Pierre Rousseau and the *philosophes* of Bouillon', *Studs. Volt.*, 29 (1964).
21. N. Hampson, *The Enlightenment* (Penguin, 1968), p. 143.
22. G. Rudé, *Paris and London*, pp. 45–6; Mornet, *Les Origines intellectuelles*, pp. 343–9; Darnton, 'The High Enlightenment', pp. 112–13n.
23. Letter of 8 October 1768, Diderot, *Correspondance* (Paris: Editions de Minuit, 1955–70) 16 vols., Vol. VIII, p. 186; cited in P. Gay, *The Enlightenment*, Vol. II, p. 77. The same case is discussed by Bachaumont in his *Mémoires secrets*, where he comments on the harshness of the sentence (which had resulted from a decision of the Paris *Parlement*). See J. Lough, *Writer and Public in France from the Middle Ages to the Present Day* (Oxford: Clarendon Press, 1978), p. 182.
24. R. Darnton, 'Reading, Writing and Publishing in Eighteenth-Century France: A Case Study in the Sociology of Literature', *Daedalus*, 100 (1971), pp. 214–56.
25. See R. Moulinas, *L'Imprimerie, la librairie et la presse à Avignon au XVIIIᵉ siècle* (Grenoble: Presses Universitaires, 1974).
26. Hampson, *The Enlightenment*, p. 132.
27. Cf. my *Voltaire: A Biography* (Granada, 1981).
28. I. O. Wade, *The Clandestine Organization and Diffusion of Philosophic Ideas in France from 1700 to 1750* (Princeton University Press, 1938). The author found in all 392 copies, representing 102 essays, still extant. As for Meslier, see above, p. 34, note 36.
29. See below, Part II, Chapter 6.
30. See D. W. Smith, *Helvétius: A Study in Persecution* (Oxford: Clarendon Press, 1965), especially Part I.
31. J.-P. Belin, *Le Mouvement philosophique de 1748 à 1789* (Paris: Belin, 1913), p. 175.
32. See Belin, *Le Mouvement philosophique*; Darnton, 'The High Enlightenment'; Lough, *Writer and Public*, pp. 190–1; E. P. Shaw, *Problems and Policies of Malesherbes as Directeur de la librairie in France (1750–1763)* (State University of New York Press, 1966).
33. D. T. Pottinger, *The French Book Trade in the Ancien Régime, 1500–1791* (Harvard University Press, 1958), p. 237; Darnton, 'Reading, Writing and Publishing', pp. 230–1; R. Birn, 'The Profits of Ideas: *Privilèges en librairie* in Eighteenth-Century France', *Eighteenth-Century Studies*, 5 (1971–72), pp. 131–68.

34. Lough, *Writer and Public*, pp. 207–8; see also Darnton, 'The High Enlightenment', pp. 81–115.
35. A thorough survey of the writer's benefits from governmental patronage during the Regency has been undertaken by R. E. A. Waller, 'The Relations between Men of Letters and Representatives of Secular Authority in France, 1715–1723', D. Phil. thesis, Oxford, 1972. See also his 'L'Homme de lettres en France et en Angleterre (1700–1730)', *Dix-huitième Siècle*, 10 (1978), pp. 229–52.
36. See R. Desné, 'Quand Catherine II achetait la bibliothèque de Diderot', *Thèmes et figures du siècle des Lumières: Mélanges offerts à Roland Mortier*, edited by R. Trousson (Geneva: Droz, 1980), pp. 73–94.
37. *Les Principes de la pensée*, p. 484.
38. P. M. Conlon (ed.), Baron de Breteuil: 'Réflexions sur la manière de rendre utiles les gens de lettres', *Travaux sur Voltaire [Studs. Volt.]*, 1 (1955), pp. 125–31.
39. See S. Tucoo-Chala, *Charles-Joseph Panckoucke et la librairie française, 1736–1798* (Pau/Paris: Marrimpouey/Touzot, 1977); G. B. Watts, 'Charles-Joseph Panckoucke, "L'Atlas de la librairie française"', *Studs. Volt.*, 68 (1969), pp. 67–205.
40. See Darnton, 'The High Enlightenment'.
41. In *The Enlightenment*, Vol. II, p. 452.
42. Letter to Rev. Hugh Blair *et al.*, 6 April 1765, cited in Gay, *The Enlightenment*, II, p. 69.
43. A. Young, *Travels in France and Italy* (New York/London, 1915), p. 104; D. M. Low, *Edward Gibbon, 1737–1794* (London, 1937), p. 130; both cited in E. G. Barber, *The Bourgeoisie in 18th Century France*, (Princeton: Princeton University Press, 1955), pp. 132–3.
44. See below, p. 106.
45. E. G. Barber, *The Bourgeoisie*, pp. 133–4.
46. *Writer and Public*, p. 243. See also P. Bénichou, *Le Sacre de l'écrivain, 1750–1830* (Paris: Corti, 1973), especially pp. 11–62, in which he traces the origins and development of a 'lay priesthood' among men of letters in France during the latter half of the eighteenth century.
47. Gay, *The Enlightenment*, Vol. II, p. 83.
48. Gusdorf, *Les Principes de la pensée*, p. 481.
49. In *The French Book Trade*, p. 11.
50. See G. May, 'The Eighteenth Century: Paris in Literature', *Yale French Studies*, 32 (1964), pp. 29–39.
51. Perhaps the most outstanding example is L. Trénard, *Lyon: De l'Encyclopédie au Préromantisme* (Paris: P.U.F., 1958), 2 vols.
52. See J. M. Fahmy, 'Voltaire et Paris', *Studs. Volt.*, 195 (1981).
53. See below, Part II, Chapter 6.
54. The most useful summary of the writer's economic and social situation during this period is in Lough, *An Introduction to Eighteenth Century France*, pp. 231–76, and, more recently, his *Writer and Public in France*, pp. 164–274. Gusdorf, *Les Principes de la pensée*, pp. 466–515, also provides an illuminating account. In addition to the works cited incidentally, special mention should be made of P. M. Conlon, 'Voltaire's literary career from 1728 to 1750', *Studs. Volt.*, 14 (1961).

Part II
Case Histories

1 Aristocratic Reform Under the Regency: Montesquieu (1689–1755)

Lettres persanes (1721)

The *Lettres persanes* appeared early in 1721, having been written, it would seem, over a period between 1717 and 1720. They were immediately greeted by success, so much so that, according to Montesquieu himself, Dutch booksellers went around pleading with everyone they met, 'Monsieur, faites-moi des *Lettres persanes*'.[1] We have here then a work composed under the Regency and responding to the tastes of the Regency book-reading public. What were the elements of that success?

One of them must surely have been the age-old eagerness of people to read about themselves. The French being, as Montesquieu often makes clear, possessed of an avid curiosity, would have been more keen than most to hold up this mirror to themselves. They would hardly have been disappointed by the amount of information provided. For the moment, however, let us look at the initial impression created, the particular details Montesquieu chooses to emphasise in the very first letter XXIV) written by the Persian travellers from France. Given its position,[2] given that it is one of the longer letters, it will repay investigation.

The first and overwhelming impression to strike Rica on his arrival is movement: 'Nous sommes à Paris depuis un mois, et nous avons toujours été dans un mouvement continuel'.[3] Even the simple administrative matters of getting settled have required much scurrying to and fro. Compare the calm, ordered existence back home in Persia, where life was so much simpler! Not only are the two Persians rushing about, everyone else is too. No one walks, they all run; and in their haste they splash you from head

to foot (a detail Balzac was to use with telling significance about
the poor underdog a century later) or, if on foot, jostle you with
unspeakable rudeness. There is no room to walk, either; the
houses are so tall, the population so dense, that when all the
people pour into the streets you can hardly move. After this direct
visual observation Rica passes to more general matters. First, the
King, who is powerful, not through mineral wealth but because
he can exploit his subjects' vanity and sell off endless offices to
balance the exchequer. Further, he is a magician, for he can persuade the French to think as he wishes. Touching him for the cure
of evils is one such marvel; more subtle and significant is the way
he juggles with the currency, devaluing the coinage, causing in-
flation by mass issues of banknotes just as he pleases. There is an
even greater magician, the Pope, for he persuades people to
accept obviously incredible absurdities like the Trinity and the
Real Presence of the Eucharist. Besides, he has caused much
unrest with the Unigenitus Bull, which has provoked considerable opposition, especially from his 'ennemis invisibles', the Jansenists.

Much, if not most, of what is to come is foreshadowed in this
letter. French society has a vitality about it which can be extremely unmannerly and fatiguing to the outsider. There is a
hectic feverishness, a sense of instability; this is only increased by
governmental policies of a highly dubious nature, like watering
the currency. The King's 'magic' anticipates John Law, who will
rule 'l'empire de l'imagination', urging people to believe in
wealth that does not exist, like bills and notes, as here (CXLII)
Finally, the Church is equally metaphysical and equally subversive. It is not a comforting picture, yet there are other facets not
to be disregarded. For with the dynamic pace of life goes too a
sense of liberty, for all the authority of Church and State. Men
seem to believe that there is something worth hurrying for, even if
it be all too often pure material gain. More important, even
though King and Pope pronounce, they do not always win
unquestioned assent as they would have done in despotic Persia
(where the only alternative is outright and bloody revolt). The
Unigenitus Bull has raised serious objection, in particular – and
this is a highly significant detail – among women: 'Ce sont les
femmes qui ont été les motrices de toute cette révolte' (p. 66), for
the reason that they were forbidden by the Bull to read the Bible
It is an 'outrage fait à leur sexe' (p. 66), an assertion of feminine

inferiority. By distinguishing the feminist element in Jansenism
at this time, Montesquieu is able to include in this important
letter one of his central themes in the *Lettres persanes*, the situation
of women in society. He had already stressed the importance of
feminine liberty in Western Europe with his previous letter
(XXIII), which Usbek writes home from Leghorn. It is interesting to see that this, the very first despatch from Europe, should
give more prominence to the situation of women than to any
other aspect of society. By contrast, the next important letter
after these two (XXVI) is written by Usbek to the one woman in
the harem with any real sense of freedom, Roxane; and as we
shall see in the concluding letter of the book, Roxane can assert
her independence only in suicide.

The picture of French society is from the outset, then, an ambiguous one – so much life, so much movement, but also so many
absurdities and dangers. The problem lies in knowing how to
draw up the balance-sheet, for it is a complicated one compound-
ed of many details. The Frenchman is naturally a sociable
animal: 'il semble être fait uniquement pour la société'
(LXXXVII, p. 224); hence the multiplicity of institutions which
he has created for himself: the coffee-houses (XXXVI), journals
(CVIII), salons (LXXXII), theatre and opera (XXVIII),
country house suppers (CX) and parties (XLVIII). It is precisely this social intercourse that the Persian lacks; he meets his
fellows only on formal occasions, is a stranger to friendship, lives
isolated in his family. In Paris, by contrast, brilliance and rest-
lessness are the order of the day. There are men who 'collect'
births, deaths and honours, like the one whose epitaph reads:
'C'est ici que repose celui qui ne s'est jamais reposé' (LXXXVII,
p. 225). There are those who find the task of maintaining a reputation for wit almost impossible and who resort to prearranged
stratagems in order to avoid the ultimate indignity of being
thought a 'sot' (LIV). Some invent gadgets, to ward off age or
'preserve' virginity, others teach what they do not know (LVIII);
yet others try to display their brilliance in writing books (LXVI);
all are curious about the *dernier cri* (XXX), all are ruled by
fashion (XCIX) – indeed, the French pride themselves on
leading the world in clothing and cuisine, and care not a jot about
borrowing their laws from elsewhere (C). It is a splendid spectacle, not without charm. Paris is indeed a 'ville enchanteresse'
(LVIII, p. 151).

Yet charlatanry is never far away. Most of the frenzy is dictated by greed or pride. Men will go to absurd lengths, even to
practising alchemy (XLV), in order to acquire wealth. Ration-
ally, it does not make sense: 'Vous voyez, à Paris, un homme qui
a de quoi vivre jusqu'au jour du jugement, qui travaille sans
cesse, et court risque d'accourcir ses jours, pour amasser, dit-il,
de quoi vivre' (CVI, p. 269). In the hands of a speculator like
John Law such greed can lead to chaos and ultimate demoralisation. The social order is profoundly upset by the dizzying speed
with which fortunes are made and lost; lackeys, for instance, are
'un séminaire de grands seigneurs' (XCVIII, p. 248). 'Tous ceux
qui étaient riches il y a six mois sont à présent dans la pauvreté, et
ceux qui n'avaient pas de pain regorgent de richesses. Jamais ces
deux extrémités ne se sont touchées de si près (CXXXVIII, pp.
351–2), writes Rica in 1720.[4] It will not be long before the bubble
is to burst, and when it does it seems as if Law pulls the whole
edifice of State down about him. Montesquieu reserves his
most weighty strictures for this event. Law has done worse than
disservice to his king or ruin to the country. He has infected the
nation with dishonour, caused contracts to be broken, debts left
unpaid, families ruined. Nothing can be more fatal to a nation
than to destroy its moral sense: 'Quel plus grand crime que
celui que commet un ministre, lorsqu'il corrompt les moeurs
de toute une nation, dégrade les âmes les plus généreuses,
ternit l'éclat des dignités, obscurcit la vertu même, et confond
la plus haute puissance dans le mépris universel?' (CXLVI,
p.389).

Here speaks the true aristocrat. Contempt for mere wealth, a
sense of the social fabric being destroyed, a feeling that leaders
have a moral responsibility, that 'nobless oblige', all comes
through in these indictments. Many of the phrases have an aristocratic connotation: 'les âmes les plus généreuses ... l'éclat des
dignités ... la plus haute puissance'. To this we shall later return
when attempting to situate Montesquieu's social context more
precisely. For the moment it will be more relevant to look at the
other side of the coin; for the getting of wealth is only part of a
complex pattern that must be considered globally. The man who
goes on heaping up extra money when all his wants are cared for
may personally be a fool, but as a member of society he has
advantages to confer. For affluence encourages work, and with it
an industrious, expanding economy. Prosperity and liberty go

together; and freedom must be encouraged, for it is both natural and effective. Under a non-repressive government men look for ways and means of promoting their own interests. Where rewards are in plenty and punishments moderate and carefully proportioned to the crime, the motivating forces of human nature are brought into play. Furthermore, it is important that the incentives be diversified, not just coming from the King alone, as they do in Persia, where a man's whole fortune hangs upon whether he enjoys the despot's favour; such a man may easily fall overnight if all depends on the leader's caprice (LXXXIX). Already we see adumbrated the philosophy of institutional pluralism which will be spelt out at much greater length in *De l'esprit des lois* (1748).

These general principles are illustrated, as we have seen, by examples from French society, but above all by instances of feminine liberty. It is the situation of women which contrasts so markedly between France and Persia, and Montesquieu provides numerous occasions to underline the difference. The freedom of women, as we have seen, is one of the first things Usbek and Rica notice in both Leghorn and Paris. Thereafter this feminist theme is constantly appearing. Rica's second letter from Paris reports on a visit to the Comédie Française and the Opéra, but he appears scarcely to have noticed what was being performed on stage, so absorbed was he in the 'scènes muettes' (XXVIII, p. 75) being played in the *loges*; indeed, 'il semble que le lieu inspire de la tendresse' (p. 76). It is the same picture in the salons, so much so that Usbek has to be warned not to take the frivolity at face value and assume that marriages are never faithful (XLVIII). Even so, badinage is the general rule: 'Ce badinage ... semble être parvenu à former le caractère général de la nation' (LXIII, p. 161). Thus it is hardly surprising if marital infidelity is an accepted convention. There are, naturally, dangers attached to this liberty. One seduced actress speaks of her misfortunes (XXVIII), and a libertine 'homme à bonnes fortunes' confides to Usbek that his pursuit of pleasure is cold-blooded if not sadistic: 'je n'ai d'autre emploi que de faire enrager un mari, ou désespérer un père; j'aime à alarmer une femme qui croit me tenir...' (XLVIII, p. 125). Usbek is horrified and speaks passionately of how 'l'infidélité, la trahison, le rapt, la perfidie et l'injustice, conduisent à la considération' (p. 126). For once he seems to have a case when he contrasts these malpractices with the security Persian women enjoy. But these are the necessary evils of women's freedom, and it is up to the female sex to be prepared, for the credit side of the balance is so much more impressive. Perhaps the most important indication Montesquieu gives is in Letter XXXVIII, where Rica propounds a general truth: 'Il faut l'avouer, quoique cela choque nos mœurs: chez les peuples les plus polis, les femmes ont toujours eu de l'autorité sur leurs maris' (p. 101).[5] Feminine emancipation becomes one of the necessary elements of civilisation.

This is hardly surprising, given Montesquieu's belief that human nature can be fulfilled only in the enjoyment of freedom. Rica has to admit that 'je ne connais les femmes que depuis que je suis ici' (LXIII, p. 161). Despotism encourages dissimulation, only free women are unafraid of revealing their character. One feels that Usbek has never learnt this lesson until he receives Roxane's final tragic letter. The difference between French and Persian women is well summed up in two antithetical statements. Writing to her about Western women, Usbek tells Roxane of 'le désir continuel de plaire qui les occupe' (XXVI, p. 73). This is an open, freely directed activity. By contrast, he has in the previous paragraph just indicated Roxane's prisoner-rôle: 'je ne puis pas m'imaginer que vous ayez d'autre objet que *celui de me plaire*' (my italics). Women of East and West alike are concerned with exploiting their personal attractions, as the deliberate parallelism of Montesquieu's language makes clear; but how different is the end in view! The contrast is the more piquant because, ironically, Usbek is writing to the one member of his harem who has a Western sense of independence and does not accept his assumptions. Compared to the active, self-confident lives of French society women, Persian women are sacrificial victims, liable to be killed if there is any suspicion that their honour has been tarnished (XLVII), humiliated in their person by the eunuch's examination on their entry into the harem (LXXIX), constantly subject to terror and punishment. Since they are not to know the joys of freedom, it seems logical to imprison them as early as possible: 'On ne saurait de trop bonne heure priver une jeune personne des libertés de l'enfance' (LXII, p. 159). For it will be much harder to stamp out this natural inclination for liberty once it has taken root. As it is, lacking liberty they turn to perverse pleasures like lesbianism and mutual denunciation.

They are indeed sub-women, as the eunuchs who guard them

are sub-men. Montesquieu establishes early an analogy between the two groups. Fatmé writes to Usbek: 'Vous [vous autres hommes] êtes charmés que nous ayons des passions que nous ne puissions pas satisfaire' (VII, p. 23). In similar terms two letters later the Chief Eunuch, recounting his castration, tells how 'on éteignit en moi l'effet des passions, sans en éteindre la cause' (IX, p. 26). The number of letters devoted to eunuchs indicates Montesquieu's fascinated horror at their situation; a castrated man is a living paradox, 'toujours prêt à se donner, et ne se donnant jamais' (LIII, p. 137). Sexual activity is a fundamental good, losing it is second only to losing life itself. The Chief Eunuch, with simple eloquence, says that his master 'm'eut obligé ... de me séparer pour jamais de moi-même' (p. 26). There is nothing left but to channel sexual energy into the power-drive: 'il me semble que je redeviens homme, dans les occasions où je leur [aux femmes] commande encore' (p. 27).

All Montesquieu's humanity comes through here. Despite the problems posed by individual freedom, it is the cornerstone of every valid philosophy. Montesquieu's faith in human nature is in line with the contemporary tendency towards attenuating the doctrine of Original Sin. Happiness and virtue must go hand in hand, as they do for the Troglodytes. Justice is based on universal criteria applicable to Persian and Frenchman, male and female, alike; it is not the product of local conventions, as Hobbes would have us think. Men are naturally gregarious. That is why, whatever his foibles and faults, a Frenchman is essentially right in his sociable behaviour: 'c'est l'homme par excellence' (LXXXVII, p. 224). There is no higher virtue than *bienfaisance*: 'Tout homme est capable de faire du bien à un homme: mais c'est ressembler aux dieux que de contribuer au bonheur d'une société entière' (LXXXIX, p. 229). It is an essentially secular quality, by contrast with charity and its religious overtones.[6] Indeed, Montesquieu's whole work is characterised by a strong secular intention, as his critic, the abbé Gaultier, perceptively noted in his reply, the *Lettres persanes convaincues d'impiété* (1751), when he pointed out that 'dans les principes de l'auteur, la société est la fin de l'homme'.[7] The criterion of social utility is the determining one in Montesquieu's judgments of contemporary France and Persia.

By this criterion the Church fails badly. The picture presented in the *Lettres persanes* is one of quarrels and divisiveness: 'il n'y a

jamais eu de royaume où il y ait eu tant de guerres civiles, que
dans celui de Christ' (XXIX, p. 79). In particular, the disputes
between Jesuits and Jansenists occupy Montesquieu's attention.
While he shows some sympathy for the Jansenists in their opposition to the Unigenitus Bull, there is, as Robert Shackleton says,
'no trace of enthusiasm for Jansenist doctrine'.[8] Churchmen are
an embarrassment to the State because of their trouble-making
(LXI). Montesquieu makes clear his strong dislike of religious
intolerance, pleading for a country where different religions
would live in peace side by side (LXXXV); he hopes that the
Regency is already fostering this spirit in its new policy of toleration towards Jews and Protestants.[9] Nor are Christian doctrines
especially to be venerated. Montesquieu comments on them ironically (XXIV), or compares Christianity with Mohammedanism
on the same footing, showing that both are inferior to the pagan
religion of Rome because they encourage depopulation (CXIV-
CXVII). In this latter respect, Catholicism is plainly suicidal:
'J'ose le dire: dans l'état présent où est l'Europe, il n'est pas possible que la religion catholique y subsiste cinq cents ans' (CXVII,
p. 296). So much for the True Apostolic Church! No sentence in
the *Lettres persanes* illustrates more clearly Montesquieu's audacity in applying non-transcendental questions to transcendental
subjects.

He is nonetheless a sincere deist, and his views on natural religion are as respectful as those on Christianity are sceptical. The
sublime Cartesian vision of the universe, built on the simplest
physical laws, in itself explains his respectful awe at the Creation
(XCVII). Such a Creator, working through invariable and
eternal principles, must necessarily be just: 'La justice est un
rapport de convenance, qui se trouve réellement entre deux
choses: ce rapport est toujours le même, quelque être qui le consi-
dère...' (p. 213). This *rapport*, in Mark Waddicor's words, 'is a
normative as well as a descriptive concept'.[10] Justice is enshrined
in the hearts of men, and men have to be impelled by some
motive to do evil. The law of inertia, as it were, is to act virtuously: 'nul n'est mauvais gratuitement'.[11] Despite the relativi-
stic views expressed elsewhere, on the question of natural law
Montesquieu is firmly rationalist. Both Shackleton[12] and Starobinski[13] detect, with reason, an uneasiness over this question.
May not the uneasiness however be related to an attitude more
profoundly personal than either of them suggests? There are indi-

cations in this letter that if Montesquieu were deprived of this firm belief in the immutability of justice, the consequences would be almost too awful to contemplate. Having asserted that 'la justice est éternelle, et ne dépend point des conventions humaines', Usbek briefly considers the alternative hypothesis, adding quickly: 'ce serait une vérité terrible, qu'il faudrait se dérober à soi-même' (p. 214). A few lines later, after invoking the consolation that justice is a principle in men's hearts, he continues: 'Sans cela, nous devrions être dans une frayeur continuelle; nous passerions devant les hommes comme devant les lions; et nous ne serions jamais assurés un moment de notre bien, de notre bonheur, et de notre vie'. The ironic mode has entirely disappeared; one feels that for Montesquieu the Hobbesian theory is diabolic, to be rejected at all costs. There is an affective need of faith in absolutes if the abyss is not to yawn under one's feet.

So the wise man betakes himself to natural religion, whose precepts, beyond the one metaphysical assumption we have been considering, are essentially social: 'dans quelque religion qu'on vive, l'observation des lois, l'amour pour les hommes, la piété envers les parents, sont toujours les premiers actes de religion' (XLVI, p. 115). He will seek out civilised pleasures, like the pursuit of science. Montesquieu is entirely of his age in his fascination for scientific experimentation. One paragraph in Letter XCVII enumerates a series of problems, seemingly a random selection but in fact based on considerable knowledge of recent discoveries, as Vernière's edition usefully makes clear.[14] It is highly significant that in one of the earliest letters Usbek, long before he reaches Europe, talks of his interest in science. The discrepancy with his Persian background is patent. Pierre Barrière plausibly suggests an autobiographical element here.[15] Equally interesting is the terminology used. Tired of life at Court, Usbek decides to escape into scientific study: 'Je feignis un grand attachement pour les sciences; et, à force de le feindre, il me vint réellement' (VIII, p. 24). The analogy with the Pascalian *pari*, with those who, pretending to believe, come to do so, seems highly likely, and deliberate.[16]

But one cannot so simply escape; one must live in the world. The world, as we have seen, is one of unbridled greed, heading for destruction. Yet there might be hopes of a remedy, if only the rulers would apply it. After Louis XIV's death the Regent quickly replaced the system of government through ministers by government through Councils, seven in all, each consisting of ten members, mostly nobles. It was an attempt to withdraw authority from the Crown and restore it to the nobility; but the experiment was shortlived, the Councils apparently ruining it by their own shortcomings, and in 1718 they were suppressed. John McManners suggests that they were anachronistically thinking in terms of the last Regency under Louis XIV and the Fronde (1648–53).[17] (Interestingly, Montesquieu includes one letter (CXI) which is a humorous *pastiche* of the *Mémoires* of the Cardinal de Retz, a leading Frondeur, that had appeared in 1717). He himself does not at all yield to the temptation of casting the *Parlement* in the sanguinary rôle it had played during the minority of Louis XIV. But he feels that the *Parlements* have an important political function, like the *Conseils* (whose abolition he regrets as premature – CXXXVIII). At first the Regent saw the *Parlements* as a legitimate ally (XCII), but this reversal of policy was not maintained, and in less than five years we are witnessing the exile of the Paris *Parlement* to Pontoise. Montesquieu's attitude is unambiguous. The *Parlement* has suffered because it dared to speak the truth. In fragmentary form we already see the outlines of the *thèse parlementaire* which is developed at greater length in *De l'esprit des lois*.[18] If there existed an opposition party to check the Crown's excesses, if the *Parlements* acted as a *dépôt des lois* with proper respect for the sanctity of laws, changing them, if at all, only 'd'une main tremblante' (CXXIX, p. 325), for they are 'la conscience publique' (p. 326), then perhaps the excesses of a man like John Law might be curbed.

For monarchy seems clearly indicated to Montesquieu already as the most useful and relevant form of government. As the Troglodyte episode shows, it makes allowance for human weakness. It allows men freedom to follow their bent, it encourages them through incentives rather than coercion, through stable laws and moderate punishments, to seek the good of themselves and others at one and the same time. It provides for a pluralist society, so that not every mark of favour and prosperity has to depend on the king. It alone gives a suitable framework to Montesquieu's concept of tolerance, *bienfaisance* and general humanitarianism. But alas! monarchies are not self-perpetuating institutions. The balance is too delicate: 'C'est un état violent, qui dégénère toujours en despotisme, ou en république' (CII, p. 257). The melancholy of these lines foreshadows the final *débâcle* with which we take leave of Paris.

How pessimistic are the *Lettres persanes*? It is hard to pronounce a valuation, because they are so close (particularly the final ones) to the events they describe. Montesquieu concluded on a crisis whose consequences were still obscure when the work appeared some months later. In the circumstances, his only general deduction from events can be to suggest the more useful policies that might have been followed. There is some reason, however, for believing that we should consider the collapse of Law's system with as much apprehension for France as the downfall of Usbek for his harem. An unpublished fragment relating to May 1720 makes the comparison clearer than the letters we have in the work itself. The writer paints an apocalyptic picture of France: 'Toute la nation *est en larmes. La nuit et le deuil* couvrent ce malheureux royaume: il ressemble à une ville prise d'assaut ou ravagée par les flammes ... *J'habite ici le pays du désespoir*' (p. 408). In similar terms Roxane writes to Usbek: '*L'horreur, la nuit et l'épouvante* règnent dans le sérail: *un deuil affreux* l'environne ... nous n'avons plus rien de libre que les pleurs' (CLVI, p. 399). Zachi's letter is in similar vein: 'j'ai du moins la consolation de *verser des larmes*: ... et *je tombe dans le désespoir*' (CLVII, p. 401). Solim too speaks of '*l'affreux désespoir* où je suis' (CLIX, p. 402) (my italics throughout). For the time being, in both places, the light has gone out of the world. By a carefully organised analogy with his fictitious model in Persia, Montesquieu has given full weight to his perception that traditional French culture is on the brink of disintegration.

The *Lettres persanes* were so successful because they appealed to their audience on many levels. Their ironic observations, their basic humanity, their attacks, with varying degrees of force, upon the religious and political institutions of France, all these factors would recommend them widely. Besides, the manner in which they were written – lucid, graceful, witty, full of paradox and antithesis – was most beguiling; they are, as Charles Bruneau suggests, a classic example of the *style coupé*.[19] The lightness of touch conceals the formidable erudition, which the critical editions of Adam and Vernière have fully displayed. The sensibility, especially in the letters from the harem women, would increase further their popularity. Their strong support for the feminine cause would win an important constituency of the French eighteenth-century reading public.[20] Indeed, it is possible that the delicate eroticism they occasionally contain would endear them to women as much as to men, if we are to believe Madame de Lambert when she claims that it is the feminine taste in reading which has led to more candid literature.[21] Montesquieu's frankness is in any case always prudently controlled. According to Jean Buvat's *Journal de la Régence*, 'les harengères de la halle' thought that the régime's banknotes were fit only to 'torcher leurs derrières'.[22] However profound Montesquieu's disgust for the financial system, he would never have turned to expressions so alien to his whole style of writing. Yet his readers could recognise a contempt of equal proportions behind his refinement.

Montesquieu had relied upon a host of sources for his work[23] and it can scarcely be said to create a new *genre*. Nonetheless, no one before had applied the mode with such comprehensive range or radical effect. The work was to go on to influence the Enlightenment, of which it would form an integral part, and to increase an awareness of the break-up in ordered French society which it dramatically revealed. Indeed, Lanson's famous remark about Voltaire's *Lettres philosophiques*, that they were 'la première bombe lancée contre l'Ancien Régime', could more properly be applied to the *Lettres persanes*. Voltaire looked to them for his *contes*, notably *Zadig* (1747) and *Le Monde comme il va* (1748). The discussions of depopulation and its causes inspired Hume and Beccaria. More widely, the Letters strengthened the tradition begun by Fontenelle, but going back to roots in Descartes and even beyond, of couching bold ideas in a literary form.

The *Lettres persanes* spring directly from the Regency. True, more than half the letters are dated before Louis XIV's death, but their whole trend is towards the *dénouement* at the height of the Regency; besides, the earlier letters are generally the less comprehensive, and it is the post-1715 ones which contain the bulk of the serious discussions. Most important of all, the work was begun long after Louis XV had succeeded to the throne. To their date of publication under the Regency we owe their openly censorious views on religion and society. It could even be argued that Voltaire's *Lettres philosophiques*, thirteen years later, constituted a work less critical of French institutions. In any case, the tolerance towards radical opinion shown by the Regent is clearly demonstrated in this instance; whereas Voltaire had to flee to avoid arrest in 1734, Montesquieu could publish with impunity, albeit anonymously and abroad. We have seen contemporary evidence of the freedom which publishing obtained under the duc d'Orléans.[24]

At the same time, it must be borne in mind that Montesquieu's radicalism is wholly aristocratic in tone and attitude. The refinement of style fits with the benevolent outlook on human society, the view that rulers should possess moral fibre before all else, the opinion that a *Parlement* of nobles like Montesquieu himself is the best guarantor of liberty. There is no sense of existential choice in the *Lettres persanes*. Roxane, it is true, speaks of sacrifice at the end, but there is no alternative for her any longer. Montesquieu espouses the belief dear to Shaftesbury that private and public interest can go hand in hand without causing conflict. The catastrophes in the *Lettres persanes* are the result of bad institutions turning men into evil ways. We see the basically good Usbek forced to play the role of despot called for by his situation. If John Law is an evil force, the fault lies essentially in banks and bills of exchange. For Montesquieu, too, 'le peuple' does not exist, except as the vaguest of backgrounds. The obscenities of 'harengères' are excluded, and the 'harengères' too. Marivaux, as we shall see, had not omitted 'le peuple' from his much briefer essay a few years earlier on 'les habitants de Paris'.

These limitations help paradoxically only to show the work's strengths; for if Montesquieu had been merely defending the aristocratic cause it would not have enjoyed its enduring success. For all its partialities and occasional inconsistencies, the *Lettres persanes* constitutes one of the major statements of the early Enlightenment.

NOTES

1. Robert Shackleton, *Montesquieu* (Oxford University Press, 1961), pp. 27–8.
2. The anachronistic date of the letter (4 June 1712, but referring to the promulgation of the Unigenitus Bull in 1713) suggests that Montesquieu may have moved forward this letter from a later date that it originally had. This would only strengthen the case for seeing it as carefully chosen to create the maximum effect at the outset of the letters from France.
3. *Lettres persanes*, edited by A. Adam (Geneva: Droz, 1954). Unless otherwise indicated, all subsequent references will be to this edition.

4. See Barbier's entry in his *Journal* for 22 December 1720:

> L'on est bien accoutumé au luxe et au plaisir dans cette ville!...
> Malgré la misère générale où l'on est, je n'ai jamais vu un spectacle plus
> rempli et plus superbe qu'hier, mercredi, à l'Opéra ... pourtant il n'y a
> pas un sol dans les meilleures maisons, et la circulation des choses néces-
> saires à la vie et à l'entretien ne se fait que par le crédit.

E.-J.-F. Barbier, *Journal d'un bourgeois sous le règne de Louis XV*, edited by P.
Bernard (Paris: 10/18, n.d.). p. 34.

5. It would seem that Montesquieu is here drawing on a feminist work by
Poulain de la Barre, *De l'égalité des deux sexes* (1673). See B. Magné, 'Une
source de la Lettre persane XXXVIII?' *Revue d'histoire littérarie de la France*
(hereafter *RHL*) 68 (1968), pp. 407–14; D. Williams, 'The Politics of
Feminism in the French Enlightenment', pp. 336–8.

The complexity of Montesquieu's attitudes towards women, in which he
seeks a balance between feminine liberty and masculine superiority, has
been brought out at length by J. G. Rosso, *Montesquieu et la féminité* (Pisa:
Goliardica, 1977). pp. 270–444. See also P. Hoffmann, *La Femme dans la
pensée des lumières* (Paris: Ophrys, 1977), pp. 324–51.

6. The abbé de Saint-Pierre, who apparently created the term *bienfaisance*,
specifically designated it to fill this gap:

> Depuis que j'ai vu que parmi les chrétiens on abusait du terme de charité
> ... j'ai cherché un terme qui nous rappelât précisément l'idée de faire du
> bien aux autres, et je n'en ai pas trouvé de plus propre pour me faire
> entendre que le terme de bienfaisance. S'en servira qui voudra, mais il
> me fait entendre et il n'est pas équivoque.

Cited in P. Hazard, *La Pensée européenne au XVIIIe siècle* (Paris: Boivin, 1946),
3 vols., Vol I, p. 233.

7. See p. 82; cited in *Lettres persanes*, edited by P. Vernière (Paris: Garnier,
1960), p. 246, note 1.

8. *Montesquieu*, p. 39. Montesquieu by his attitude reveals that sympathy for
the *Parlements* does not have to go hand in hand with Jansenist attitudes.
'Certainly the Jansenists were *parlementaire* in politics; it does not necessarily follow that the *Parlements* were Jansenistic in religion' (R. S. Tate,
'Petit de Bachaumont: his circle and the *Mémoires secrets*', *Studs. Volt.*, 65
(1968), p. 205).

9. This letter is dated 1714, but as Adam points out (Adam edition, p. 155,
note 2), it clearly refers to the period following Louis XIV's death. The
mistake reveals that Montesquieu's main interest is in Regency affairs, even
though most letters antedate that period. This point is demonstrated stati-
stically by J. Ehrard, 'La Signification politique des *Lettres persanes*', *Archives
des lettres modernes*, 116 (1970), pp. 34–7.

10. *Montesquieu and the Philosophy of Natural Law* (The Hague: Nijhoff, 1970), p.
187.

11. Adam edition, p. 213. Herein lies the cardinal error of the Inquisition: 'ils
croient les hommes mauvais' (XXIX, p. 80).

12. *Montesquieu*, p. 42.
13. J. Starobinski, *Montesquieu par lui-même* (Paris: Seuil, 1953), p. 77; see also his edition of *Lettres persanes* (Paris: Gallimard, 1973), pp. 7–40.
14. See p. 202, note 1.
15. 'Les éléments personnels et les éléments bordelais dans les "Lettres persanes"', *RHL*, 51 (1951), p. 22.
16. Rhédi similarly finds emancipation through the study of art and science in Venice: 'enfin je sors des nuages qui couvraient mes yeux dans le pays de ma naissance' (XXXI, p. 84).
17. 'when the nobility did have their chance to share in the government of the state under the Regency, they failed miserably. Their financial manoeuvres, their foolish disputes over precedence and their general selfish incoherence reveal what their idea of government really was; it was of the last Regency and of the Fronde that they were thinking,' J. McManners, 'France', in *The European Nobility in the Eighteenth Century*, edited by A. Goodwin (Black, 1953), p. 28.
18. Montesquieu, however, refrains from taking a wholly partisan line on behalf of the *Parlements* in *De l'esprit des lois*. He is concerned not so much to safeguard aristocratic rights as to ensure that the *Parlements* perform the national duty expected of them, challenging the King in the name of law so as to defend civil liberties.
19. *Petite Histoire de la langue française* (Paris: Colin, 1958–61), 2 vols., Vol I, pp. 250, 254–5.
20. How far removed this attitude was from the legal position may be seen in the fact that in 1731 the Paris *Parlement* passed an ordinance affirming the authority of husband over wife and depriving women of equality before the law. See D. Williams, 'The Politics of Feminism', pp. 337–8.
21. *Réflexions sur les femmes* (1730), cited in Atkinson and Keller, *Prelude to the Enlightenment*, p. 45.
22. *Journal de la Régence*, edited by E. Campardon (Paris: Plon, 1865), 2 vols., Vol II, pp. 280–1.
23. For details, see the Vernière edition, pp. xvii–xxviii.
24. See above p. 10.

2 The Individualist Approach: Marivaux (1688–1763)

Lettres sur les habitants de Paris (1717–18); La Double Inconstance (1723); Le Prince travesti (1724); L'Île des esclaves (1725); L'Île de la raison (1727)

Marivaux's position in society was less assured than Montesquieu's. The latter was born into the *noblesse de robe* and retained a secure position in it all his life. Marivaux, by contrast, though no *déclassé*, came of less distinguished parentage. His father belonged to the ranks of royal administrators, rising eventually to the Directorship of the Mint in Riom in 1701 (when his son was thirteen years of age) and remaining there till his death. He felt frustrated by the cramping mediocrity of his situation,[1] which, furthermore, was so ill-paid that the family could apparently afford neither servants nor property.[2] This atmosphere of constantly renewed struggle against financial hardships while keeping up respectable bourgeois appearances must have been the climate in which Marivaux spent his formative years, which should in itself give pause to those who would see his work as composed of aristocratic arabesques unrelated to the world of real events. Yet he managed to escape from this provincial drudgery, perhaps because of help from a well-connected maternal uncle, the architect Pierre Bullet.[3] The other extrinsic event of significance for an understanding of Marivaux's work occurred in 1720, when John Law's financial system collapsed and with it Marivaux's investments, which well-meaning friends had prevailed upon him to commit to Law's speculations in hopes of a quick profit.[4] How much he lost is not known, and it would in any event be unwise to assume that he was obliged by his financial losses to take to writing; for the chances of living by one's pen, especially in early eighteenth-century France, were remote if not impossible.[5] For those who tried to make a livelihood out of Grub Street the situation was precarious and squalid in the extreme.[6] Marivaux's earnings appear to have been small,[7] and it required political patronage for him to maintain even a modest financial standing. In short, we have here a man who, quite unlike Montesquieu, was rarely free from financial need throughout his life. At the same time, thanks probably to his links with Fontenelle,[8] he became an *habitué* of the salons, especially that of Madame de Tencin who was instrumental in getting him elected to the Académie Française ahead of Voltaire in 1742. The Modernist sentiments of his acquaintances at this salon (and at that of Madame de Lambert, which he also frequented) fitted in with Marivaux's own emphasis on literary originality and the avoidance of imitation.[9] He would have been naturally well disposed towards the unorthodox and adventurous approach of the Comédiens Italiens when they returned to Paris at the Regent's request in 1716 – one more sign, incidentally, that the age of Louis XIV, who had expelled them in 1697, was at an end. Unlike Voltaire, whose more conservative taste was affronted by the Italians,[10] Marivaux followed their progress with eager curiosity, and he was the first important dramatist to write full-length plays for them.[11]

This conjunction of circumstances helps to explain, so far as social situations ever can, the peculiar flavour of Marivaux's plays. Before coming to a selection of them, however, let us briefly look at an early work, the *Lettres sur les habitants de Paris* which, like Montesquieu's *Lettres persanes*, observes and reflects on the reality of the world around and is inspired to some extent by the same sources, notably La Bruyère's *Les Caractères* (1688) and Dufresny's *Amusements sérieux et comiques* (1699). The *Lettres sur les habitants de Paris*, nonetheless, antedate Montesquieu's creation, appearing originally in the *Mercure* in 1717–18. It is a much briefer collection of letters than the *Lettres persanes*, less ambitious and lacking any real sense of unity; but in it Marivaux may be said to come of age as a writer. Here he enters into his true domain, the observation of man in his contemporary reality, discovering within himself 'ses dons, ses pouvoirs et ses armes'.[12]

A number of observations testify to Mairvaux's sharp eye. He gives an amusing description of the 'provincial, nouvellement débarqué dans Paris', so overwhelmed by the courteous attentions of the saleswoman that he cannot escape without buying something.[13] He shrewdly notes the mixed motives of people attending an execution, feeling curiosity and compassion at the same time.[14] Like Montesquieu, he is impressed by the gallantry of Parisian women, though he specifically limits his comments here to the bourgeoisie (pp. 18–20). He refers to translators (whom he castigates as not being original enough to think for themselves), philosophers and geometricians (pp. 33–4). It is recognisably the same world as that of the *Lettres persanes*.

But the differences are more important than the similarities. As we have noted, Marivaux devotes a section specifically to a social class ignored by Montesquieu, 'le peuple' (pp. 10–14). The view is a detached and rather unsympathetic one, but the significance lies rather in Marivaux's choosing to portray the masses at all. He does so for the same reason as he portrays everything else in these *Lettres*. Since he is especially fascinated by psychological motivation, the lower classes are for that purpose as interesting as the upper. The sight of the audience at an execution attracts Marivaux essentially because it reveals the inconsistencies of human nature: 'Je gagerais que le peuple pourrait, en même temps, plaindre un homme destiné à la mort, avoir du plaisir en le voyant mourir, et lui donner mille malédictions' (pp. 12–13). When he dwells upon a class distinction, as between the nobility and the bourgeoisie, it is primarily in order to indicate the way their affiliations reveal themselves in human behaviour. You cannot, he says, distinguish them by their houses, furniture or general 'dépense', but one thing tells them apart – the 'certain air subalterne' which the bourgeoisie invariably carries with it (p. 14). This is the view of a man whose social philosophy will always move from the individual person to the general truth. Social forces interest Marivaux, but only in so far as they are motivated by and affect human beings each one of whom is unique. Much of his unpopularity with his own age may stem from this. Funck-Brentano claimed that 'individuals did not exist' in the Ancien Régime; Ogg, citing this assertion, supports it: the individual 'was not yet considered a personality, distinctive and unique'.[15] Marivaux gives the lie to this generalisation.

So one naturally finds Marivaux's gaze turning more keenly to women than to men, because women are more vulnerable, and one discovers that he is especially taken by what is acquired, not natural, in their ways. In particular he studies the aristocratic woman, for here is the summit of refinement and therefore of affectation: 'Grâces ridicules aux gens raisonnables … inimitables aux bourgeoises ... peut-être le chef-d'œuvre de l'orgueil' (pp. 26–7) – manners both magnificent and foolish in the highest degree. All is studiedly artificial: 'l'habillement, la marche, le geste et le ton' (p. 26) – developed by parental vanity and the examples set by other gracious ladies, and consummated through personal study in this particular domain. Marivaux is struck by the magnificence of the paradox: so much effort and style, all deployed to serve the ends of folly. The play-element is fundamental to their code of behaviour: 'tout est jeu pour elles; jusqu'à leur réputation' (p. 27) – a striking observation which throws light upon the refined class of any age who are imprisoned by gratuitousness and irresponsibility, even at the most serious moments of their lives. (One thinks of Mathilde de La Mole in Stendhal's *Le Rouge et le noir* striving to escape from such a world into the perils and joys of commitment.)

Everything for these women is ritual, courtship above all; and the garment most proudly worn is the slightest, the *négligé*, because it is the equivalent of nakedness, pretending to do without extra charms but pretending falsely (p. 28). It is 'une abjuration simulée de coquetterie; mais en même temps le chef-d'œuvre de l'envie de plaire' (p. 28). It has the simplicity of modest clothes but is itself immodest, the product of the lubricious vanity that invented it. Not that the unchastity is itself deliberate, adds Marivaux, for the motive force is a feeling of complaisance for one's own charms; but the end result is the same. Women dressed in a *négligé* exclaim: 'Laissez-moi ... je me sauve, je suis faite comme une folle'. But in reality they are thinking the very opposite: 'Regardez-moi, je ne suis point parée comme les femmes doivent l'être ... tout naît de moi, c'est moi qui donne la forme à mon habit, et non mon habit qui me la donne ...' (p. 29). The apparent rejection of coquettish aids proves to be the highest form of coquetry; the female form, barely clad and accessible to furtive glances in the boudoir, is at its most erotic. It is the world of Fragonard. These women are full of hypocrisy in their language too. The spoken word may well be the opposite of the true thought (p. 29).[16] Women are by their very situation wearers of masks: 'Une femme qui n'est plus coquette, c'est une femme qui a cessé d'être' (p. 28).

This alertness to the vagaries of human behaviour is omnipresent in Marivaux's journals and drama; the plays, however, which are of most interest to us here are those which set that awareness in a precise social situation containing matter for comment and interpretation. *La Double Inconstance* (1723) has always been eminent in this group, for the tale of a prince who abducts a poor peasant girl to his palace in order to alienate her affections for her rustic lover might well, on the face of it, be seen as nothing less than the account of a crime.[17] At Court the Prince can count on the unfailing support of his courtiers, simply because he is the holder of patronage and fortune; Trivelin, Flaminia, Lisette all have the strongest incentives to help him win over Silvia. But the privileges of Court at first have no effect on Silvia and Arlequin. Arlequin explicitly disdains 'honneurs ... richesses ... belles maisons ... magnificence ... crédit ... équipages' (I, 4); Silvia would do the same. Gradually, however, a way is found to suborn them. Both are open to flattery; in addition Arlequin is greedy for fine food and Silvia for fine clothes. Every man, however simple and honest, would seem to have his price. The picture of Court life has that same ambivalence which appears in the portrait of the aristocracy emerging from the *Lettres sur les habitants de Paris.* Its sophistication is attractive. Silvia remarks in wonderment: 'Je n'ai jamais vu de femmes si civiles, des hommes si honnêtes, ce sont des manières si douces, tant de révérences, tant de compliments, tant de signes d'amitié...' (II, 1). But she is not deceived by this façade. The good manners signify nothing on the moral plane. Honesty, loyalty, good faith are wholly absent: 'ils ne savent ce que c'est que tout cela, c'est tout comme si je leur parlais grec' (II, 1).

This theme of social prestige and authority rises to its climax in Act III. Arlequin, though now well on his way to exchanging Silvia for Flaminia and thereby satisfying the Prince's wishes, remains impervious to the offer of nobility. Aristocratic rank is a useless present to Arlequin; what could he do with it? The Seigneur who is making him the offer argues that he will be more feared and respected. This makes no sense to Arlequin; he simply wants to be loved for his own sake. As for the idea that aristocracy carries obligations of honour which might require revenge for an insult, that has no attraction for one who makes no secret of his cowardice! Nor does Arlequin see the merit of returning evil for evil (III, 4). The concept of nobility seems totally irrelevant to a man without pride about his social station. This, however, is merely a prologue to the more important following scene between Arlequin and the Prince. For here Arlequin invokes feudal convention, claims that the Prince should be his protector but instead is stealing from him the one precious thing he has. To this the Prince can make no sort of reply. He is genuinely in love, genuinely suffering, and no politician. Eventually Arlequin recognises the Prince's good qualities, and it is this recognition which prompts him to concede Silvia's hand, a concession which neither authority nor bribery could have obtained.

Simplistic assertions about the tragic dimensions of this play are all too easy to make. The situation is in reality a long way short of tragedy or even pathos. By the time the scene just discussed takes place, Arlequin can envisage the loss of Silvia without great pain. Marivaux has made sure that Arlequin should lay no claim to the status of tragic hero.[18] Nor have the affections of Arlequin and Silvia for each other been alienated against their will. Love arises by consent, not force.[19] The two 'victims' grow in moral experience, and one might argue that it is rather the Prince, blind to himself till the end,[20] who is the one most to be pitied.[21] Marivaux is interested primarily in love; the social situation is only a means to that end. The Court is not well-defined in time or place, its activities, merits and defects are traditional. Yet the circumstances are arresting. Dangerous as speculations about hypothetical situations in literature are, one cannot help wondering what would have happened if Silvia had not conveniently fallen in love with the Prince, or Arlequin with Flaminia. Even if he stops short of describing actual injustices, Marivaux sketches the apparatus of power and the nature of social inequality with enough detail to make us fully aware of them. Even so, the response, here as elsewhere, is one of acquiescence. The true revenge of the underdog is to outdo his master in goodness. Marivaux typically emphasises the individual and the moral aspects. Seen through such a prism, aristocratic privilege seems indefensible; no one in this play who attempts an apology for it succeeds. But one must accept that this is how the world is, and Marivaux, despite the radical questions he puts into Arlequin's mouth, ends with a conservative answer, on the social plane at least. One symbolic detail may serve to conclude. When Arlequin writes to the Prince's Secretary of State to say that he wants to go home, he characteristically gets the title wrong, addressing him as 'Monsieur' instead of 'Monseigneur' (III, 2).[22] In line with his farcical rôle, Arlequin is indifferent: 'Mettez les deux, afin qu'il choisisse'. But when, later on, he is engaged in

his serious discussion with the Prince, he chooses the correct title
unbidden. Perhaps the distinction is trivial, but Arlequin has
learnt it, one more element in his education, and he will know
how to use it when he wishes to be taken seriously. The simple
peasants emerge as more worthy than their masters; but they will
not be interested in making a political issue of it.

Many of these themes are present again in *Le Prince travesti*
(1724), in more serious form. Here the arbitrariness of royal
power is more directly conveyed. The Princess, in pursuit of her
own selfish ends, arrests Lélio without formality. The courtier
Frédéric is a much nastier specimen of his tribe than anyone in *La
Double Inconstance*, pliable as he is with all those in power and mer-
ciless with unfortunates.[23] Most interesting of all is the seriousness with which the love affair between Hortense and Lélio is
depicted. In pointing out to Lélio that she cannot accept his love
because both of them are dependent upon the Princess ('et il n'y a
point de remède à cela'), Hortense reminds us that even the
deepest love must take due note of the social realities (II, 7). For
his part, Lélio dares to evoke the possibility that the people might
disobey their sovereign lady, albeit 'par amour pour elle' (II, 8).
The play has, it is true, a happy ending, but this is contrived with
almost indecent haste; the brusque change to benevolence in the
Princess is unconvincing, while Frédéric's fate is left completely
open. The dilemmas propounded by the play have not been entirely dissipated. Furthermore, Hortense's profession of love is,
as Frédéric Deloffre says, an 'admirable cri de passion',[24] a revelation in French comedy where perhaps the only comparable
antecedent is Dona Elvire in Molière's *Dom Juan*.

This individualist sympathy for people not their own masters
is continued in *L'Île des esclaves* (1725), perhaps the most interesting of all the early plays from the social point of view. On this
island slaves and servants (no clear distinction is made) wish to
destroy the barbarism in their masters' hearts and restore them
to the ranks of humanity. Candour being one means to this end,
Arlequin and Cléanthis recount their masters' faults with great
enthusiasm and no small penetration. Cléanthis, for the greater
confusion of her mistress Euphrosine, tells of an evening when
the latter had used all the tricks of coquetry to conquer her *cava-
lier*. Having damned a rival with faint praise, Euphrosine had
pretended not to notice when her lover 'offrit son cœur'. 'Continuez, folâtre, continuez, dites-vous, en ôtant vos gants sous pré-

texte de m'en demander d'autres. Mais vous avez la main belle; il la vit, il la prit, il la baisa...' (Scene 3).[25] In the same scene Euphrosine adorns herself with her *négligé* in exactly the way Marivaux had described in the *Lettres sur les habitants de Paris*: 'Regardez mes grâces, elles sont à moi, celles-là.... Voyez comme je m'habille, quelle simplicité! il n'y a point de coquetterie dans mon fait.' By contrast, the servants have to endure the constant insults and capricious tempers of those on whom they wait. Yet Arlequin, though lacking all the social graces, is 'un homme franc ... un homme simple ... un bon cœur' (Scene 7). There is no correlation at all between success and virtue. If now, on this island the rôles of servants and masters are inverted, that is mere chance. But chance rules the world anyway, as Cléanthis asserts: 'n'est-ce pas le hasard qui fait tout?' (Scene 6). Figaro's monologue in Beaumarchais's *Le Mariage de Figaro* makes the same point 60 years after. Cléanthis herself stresses her meaning a little later: 'Fi! que cela est vilain, de n'avoir eu pour tout mérite que de l'or, de l'argent et des dignités!' (Scene 10).

On this island, however, the erstwhile lords and ladies must be brought to an honest avowal of their faults as the first step on the road to recovery. The process is painful, but like recovery from a bad fever (Trivelin, the master of ceremonies, says that they are 'nos malades' – Scene 2), with sympathetic help and the right advice they stand a good chance of success. Before that happens Arlequin and Cléanthis themselves have much to learn. While their desire to unmask their masters is quite understandable in view of their past sufferings, they for their part must rid themselves of the desire for revenge. If they achieve this, it is because their natural moral qualities are sensitive to genuine appeals for humane treatment. Arlequin leads the way; he pretends to love Euphrosine in order to vex her, but the pretence breaks down when she throws herself on his mercy (Scene 8). In the following scene he recognises, like Arlequin in *La Double Inconstance*, that a victory in these circumstances is sterile. Despite his master Iphicrate's abusive ways in the past, Arlequin sees that he himself must have the larger heart – 'car il y a plus longtemps que je souffre' (Scene 9). But Arlequin is not some kind of noble savage; rather he is an individual whose nature, fragile as is all human nature, has not had to undergo testing by the demoralisation that comes from possessing power: 'si j'avais été votre pareil,' he says to Iphicrate, 'je n'aurais peut-être pas mieux valu que vous'

(Scene 9). So he accepts his master's repentance and urges Cléanthis, who is less charitable, to do likewise: 'quand on se repent, on est bon; et quand on est bon, on est aussi avancé que nous' (Scene 10). True advancement can be measured only in moral terms. The servants, as in the earlier plays, accept that there are rich and poor. Trivelin sums it up: 'La différence des conditions n'est qu'une épreuve que les dieux font sur nous' (Scene 11). The *status quo* must be accepted.

If then the play is radical, the radicalism is moral and religious rather than social and political. Self-knowledge is gained through suffering and forgiveness; the prescription sounds more like Dostoevsky than Voltaire. The servants, for all their strongly characterised individuality, belong to the traditional comic mould. There are none of the lackeys here that Montesquieu had claimed were forming 'un séminaire de grands seigneurs'.[26] The test of candour through which Iphicrate and Euphrosine are put at the beginning has links with the confessional;[27] the marquis d'Argenson made the shrewd remark in his contemporary review that Trivelin 'fait ici la fonction d'un véritable directeur des consciences'.[28] As in *La Double Inconstance* and *Le Prince travesti*, it is impossible to be sure whether those in power have really learnt anything. They seem genuinely touched,[29] but then they are about to return to their former demoralising situation of privilege. More important, if one sees the play as a spiritual progress, is the advance made by Cléanthis and more particularly by Arlequin, who reminds Cléanthis to go down on her knees before Euphrosine even as the latter is asking forgiveness (Scene 10).

As a reformist statement, *L'Île des esclaves* offers little. Marivaux's detached view about human nature[30] and resignation to the existence of social inequity belong to a man who believes that the true kingdom is not of this world. Even so, the bold portrayal of aristocratic corruption and deceit deserves notice, especially as it is appearing on a public stage, not simply being read by private individuals.[31] Marivaux does after all dare to assert that all men are equal,[32] and the *Mercure* reviewer was not keen on the *divertissement* at the end where apparently slaves sang with joy at having their chains broken.[33] In other respects too this play belongs to and promotes the climate of the day. Like the earlier ones we have considered, but to a greater degree, it is redolent of sensibility, especially in Arlequin's scene with Euphrosine; furthermore, this aspect was seized upon by contemporary reviews. La Barre de Beaumarchais, describing the play as 'un petit bijou', added: 'les huit premières scènes auront beau vous divertir, vous aimerez encore mieux les pleurs délicieuses que vous arracheront les sentiments généreux qui brillent dans les trois dernières scènes'.[34] The *Mercure* also gave attention to this aspect in its generally favourable review.[35] We are on the threshold of Nivelle de La Chaussée's success in the theatre with his *comédies larmoyantes* that will open the way to the *drame bourgeois*.[36]

In comparison with this poignant play, *L'Île de la raison* (1727), though a more elaborate reworking of the same basic theme, is somewhat disappointing. Here too, on a shipwrecked island, the new arrivals have to learn to be reasonable, modest, self-aware. Once again the servant class is more quickly converted than its superiors, though in this play a further dimension is introduced with the two cultural representatives, the Philosopher and the Poet, who prove quite intractable. The Comtesse, like Euphrosine in *L'Île des esclaves*, is vain and spiteful. The servants, though as penetrating in their remarks as in the earlier play, show no malicious pleasure in revealing their masters' shortcomings; to that extent they are dramatically less interesting. On the other hand, the motif of conversion through humility carries the same Christian overtones, and these are reinforced by the joy of the 'saved'.

L'Île de la raison, however, advances a step further in its treatment of the rôle of women. One of the island's rules is that only women may make declarations of love. Men become the passive element, sought out only when the women want them, and obliged to play the reluctant rôle until the alliance is assured. The dramatist fully exploits the comic possibilities of this neat reversal, since the shipwrecked party (and, characteristically, the aristocrats most of all) are slow to adapt to these new conventions. But there is a serious side to this idea. Blectrue, one of the islanders, is horrified at European courtship customs ('Que deviendra la faiblesse si la force l'attaque?' – II, 3) which he argues are the consequence of men's vicious inclinations. By contrast, on the Island of Reason men help to save women against themselves: 'L'homme ici, c'est le garde-fou de la femme' (II, 7). This feminist paradox may well owe something to the *Réflexions sur les femmes* (1727) of Marivaux's friend Madame de Lambert.[37] Like Montesquieu, Marivaux is of his time in this respect, and with greater depth and incisiveness, as the range and detail of the feminine characterisation in his plays bear ample witness. Indeed, as his theatre develops, so too does the strength of feminist assertions,[38] and the marquis d'Argenson will find Araminte's decision to marry her *intendant* Dorante in *Les Fausses Confidences* (1737) positively indecent.[39] Clearly Marivaux is trying to isolate the 'pure' woman, free of prejudices arising from convention, by creating a hypothetical model. He carried out a similar experiment some years later in *La Dispute* (1744).[40]

One final point about this play merits notice: the contemptuous treatment of Poet and Philosopher. Marivaux's attitude towards the Poet would seem to be directed more against his vanity than his trade, for he speaks favourably of poetry in the *Lettres sur les habitants de Paris* (to the disadvantage, precisely, of philosophers). But the *philosophe*, hero of the Enlightenment, is no more than a pedantic bore, as Marivaux had long ago made clear in these *Lettres*: 'un pédagogue qui vous régente durement'.[41] The Philosopher in *L'Île de la raison* is a physicist, interested in optics (I, 2), which was itself one of the most developed branches of physical science in the eighteenth century (thanks largely to Newton's discoveries, published in his *Optics* (1704) and translated into French by Coste in 1720). Marivaux, by demonstrating the contemptibility of his Philosopher, is reacting against the passion for science of his age. He is not, of course, denying science its validity in its proper realm and his own works will often, as here, contain the elements of a scientific approach;[42] but he is inveighing against the tendency to see the philosopher-scientist as necessarily the highest amongst human creatures. As ever with Marivaux, a man's moral qualities are his most important.

In 1727 more than half of Marivaux's drama was still unwritten. He went on producing plays with great regularity right up to the 1740s, and his two major novels, *La Vie de Marianne* (1731–41) and *Le Paysan parvenu* (1734–35), were still to be written. As these works appeared, certain lines were drawn with greater firmness. The question of social prestige was interwoven more subtly with erotic psychology in *Les Fausses Confidences*, money played a central rôle in *Le Legs* (1736), woman's social and personal situation was delineated with insight and delicacy in *Le Jeu de l'amour et du hasard* (1730) and *L'Epreuve* (1740), the nature of 'natural' man considered in *La Dispute* (1744). But the guidelines were already laid down by the time of writing *L'Île de la raison*. Roman-

tic and realistic elements already coexisted. The aim continued
to be to seek personal happiness (through marriage, in most
cases) rather than to dwell on social revolt or class conflict.

In some ways Marivaux's relationship to his own age is more
complex than Montesquieu's. The former writer pursues his path
with considerable indifference to or even distaste for many of the
contemporary fashions. As we have seen, he sought out the
Italian players at a time when the weight of prestige rested firmly
with the Théâtre Français. Already in the *Lettres sur les habitants de
Paris* much space is given to describing 'l'auteur supérieur' who,
aware of his own great qualities, is not deflected by current opin-
ions. Although his individualist tastes fitted in more with the
Moderns than the Ancients, Marivaux claimed to belong to
neither: 'je ne suis d'aucun parti: *Anciens* et *Modernes*, tout m'est
indifférent'.[43] '...écrire naturellement ... n'est pas écrire dans
le goût de tel Ancien ni de tel Moderne, n'est pas se mouler sur
personne quant à la forme de ses idées, mais au contraire, se ressembler fidèlement à soi-même...'[44] This aim he carried out.
There is no space to dwell here on the accusations of preciosity
directed for the most part by an uncomprehending public who
did not appreciate the wealth of suggestiveness and subtlety in
his dramatic dialogue or his narrative and discursive styles.[45]
Whereas Fontenelle, Le Sage, Montesquieu, and Voltaire never
forgot the prime claims of clarity, Marivaux accepted that
complex phenomena might need complex expression to do them
justice. This point is firmly asserted in a short article written
for the *Mercure* in 1719, 'Sur la clarté du discours'.[46] As the
editors point out,[47] this attitude calls in question the whole
doctrine of classicism and outlines an 'esthétique de la sugges-
tion'.

Yet Marivaux's individualism belongs to the early Enlightenment. The critical but moderate attitude towards social and political institutions, the feminist tendencies,[48] the contempt for
money, the belief that nobility is a moral order before it is a social
one, these views are not so far removed after all from Montesquieu's, any more than the sensibility which often underlies the
spectacle of human suffering. Even Marivaux's Christianity is of
its time, for despite its obvious sincerity it is moral rather than
metaphysical in its content. He has ultimately far more in
common with his enemy Voltaire than either had with Pascal.
Furthermore, in presenting new ideas on stage, he too popu-

larised and thereby contributed to the philosophic evolution of the century.

NOTES

1. M. Gilot, 'Maître Nicolas Carlet et son fils, Marivaux', *RHL* 68 (1968) pp. 489–91.
2. Gilot, 'Maître Nicolas Carlet', p. 486.
3. L. Desvignes-Parent, *Marivaux et l'Angleterre* (Paris: Klincksieck, 1970), p. 47, note 83. G. Bonaccorso, *Gli Anni difficili di Marivaux* (Messina: Peloritana, 1964, p. 44, n. 7), is much more tentative in his conclusions, however.
4. See letter to Lesbros de la Versane, cited in E. J. H. Greene, *Marivaux* (University of Toronto Press, 1965), p. 47.
5. See above, p 48.
6. See R. Laufer, *Lesage ou le métier de romancier*, pp. 125–6. Darnton (in 'The High Enlightenment') rightly stresses the appalling conditions of hack writers at the end of the century and sees this as an important factor in provoking the Revolution. It is as well to remember, however, that similar conditions existed a half-century earlier without stimulating similarly radical reactions.
7. Nevertheless, Marivaux was more popular in the eighteenth century than is generally realised. If one totals the spectators attending his plays at both the Théâtre Français and the Théâtre Italien during the period 1720–50, he comes a close second to Voltaire alone. See H. Lagrave, *Marivaux et sa fortune littéraire* (Saint-Médard-en-Jalles: Ducros, 1970), pp. 42–4; and Lagrave, *Le Théâtre et le public à Paris de 1715 à 1750*, pp. 605–7.
8. See Bonaccorso, p. 70. L. Desvignes-Parent (*Marivaux et l' Angleterre*) is highly informative on this early period (pp. 21–54).
9. On this general question, see the useful article by L. Gossman, 'Literature and Society in the Early Enlightenment: The Case of Marivaux', *Modern Language Notes*, 82 (1967), pp. 306–33.
10. 'moi qui n'aime point du tout ces pantalons étrangers', letter to marquise de Bernières, [17] September [1725], Best. D 249. Cf. also letters to Mademoiselle Quinault, 16 August [1738], Best. D 1590, and to comte d'Argental, 30 October [1748], Best. D 3800. (Best. D refers to the relevant number of the letter in the definitive edition of the Voltaire Correspondence by T. Besterman, in *The Complete Works of Voltaire*, Vols. 85–135 (Geneva, Banbury and Oxford: 1968–77). All subsequent references to Voltaire's letters will take this form.)
11. Regnard and Dufresny had offered them isolated scenes for interpolation into conventional Italian pantomime and farces: F. C. Green, *Minuet: A Critical Survey of French and English Literary Ideas in the Eighteenth Century* (Dent, 1935), p. 154. The 'Italian' influence on Marivaux's drama should not

however be seen as decisive. For a judicious discussion of his debt to French and Italian comic theatre, see V. P. Brady, *Love in the Theatre of Marivaux* (Geneva: Droz, 1970), pp. 65–76.

12. M. Gilot, *Les Journaux de Marivaux: Itinéraire moral et accomplissement esthétique* (Paris: Champion/Université de Lille III, 1975), 2 vols., Vol. I, p. 127.

13. *Journaux et Oeuvres diverses*, edited by F. Deloffre and M. Gilot (Paris: Garnier, 1969), p. 16. All textual references will be to this edition.

14. (p. 12).The editors point out (p. 556, note 12) a similar passage in Diderot's *Jacques le fataliste*; the resemblances are close enough to make one suspect that Diderot was directly influenced by Marivaux's observations.

15. D. Ogg, *Europe of the Ancien Régime, 1715–1783*, pp. 37–8. The quotation from Funck-Brentano appears in the latter's *The Old Régime in France* (1929), p. 34.

16. This discrepancy is used for ironic purposes throughout Marivaux's drama, and not only in portraying women. According to d'Alembert, Marivaux requested of the actors that they 'ne paraissent jamais sentir la valeur de ce qu'ils disent, et qu'en même temps les spectateurs la sentent et la démêlent à travers l'espèce de nuage dont l'auteur a dû envelopper leurs discours' ('Eloge de Marivaux', *Oeuvres complètes* (Paris, 1821–22), 5 vols., Vol. III, p. 582).

17. As indeed one of Jean Anouilh's characters in *La Répétition* (1950, Act I) sees it.

18. The contemporary reviewer for the *Mercure* indicates that the audience was not unduly moved, though he appears to consider this a defect rather than a virtue: 'Cette scène aurait fait un plus grand effet sur les spectateurs, si Arlequin leur eût paru uniquement occupé de Silvia', Marivaux: *Théâtre complet*, edited by F. Deloffre (Paris: Garnier, 1968), 2 vols., Vol. I, p. 249.

19. For a fuller discussion of this problem, see the author's 'Cruelty in Marivaux's Theatre', *Modern Language Review*, 62 (1967) pp. 238–47.

20. While pleading his own cause most vigorously with Silvia, he claims that his reply to her question about whether to leave Arlequin is given as an 'homme sincère' (III, 9). In Marivaux's theatre, anyone asserting his own sincerity is *ipso facto* suspect.

21. "*La Double Inconstance* n'est ni une tragédie de l'amour ... ni une comédie satirique sur les moeurs des courtisans. Elle est le récit quasi objectif d'une *éducation sociale*: celle de Silvia et d'Arlequin,' Marivaux: *Théâtre*, edited by B. Dort (Paris: Club Français du Livre, 1961–62), 4 vols., Vol. I, p. 290.

22. A similar mistake drew down upon Hennin, the French *Résident* in Geneva, a sharp rebuke from the maréchal de Richelieu some years later, the latter refusing to reply to Hennin until he had written again in the proper mode of address. Voltaire, acting as intermediary, came close to overstepping the mark for sarcasm when he wrote to Richelieu: 'J'avoue Monseigneur que l'impertinence est extrême' (9 September 1767, Best. D 14413).

23. M. Deloffre appositely quotes a passage from *Le Spectateur français, 22ᵉ feuille*, written at about the same time as this play (cited in *Théâtre Complet*, Vol. I, p. 1062, n. 34):

je ne comprends rien à eux [les courtisans], ni à la passion qu'ils ont pour le rang, pour le crédit, pour les honneurs, car cette passion là suppose des cœurs orgueilleux, avides de gloire, furieux de vanité; cependant ces gens si superbes et si vains ont la force de fléchir sous mille opprobrès qu'il leur faut souvent essuyer; le droit d'être fier et de primer sur les autres, ils ne l'acquièrent, ils ne le conservent, ils ne le cimentent qu'au moyen d'une infinité d'humiliations dont ils veulent bien avaler l'amertume: quelle misérable espèce d'orgueil!

24. *Théâtre complet*, Vol. I, p. 324.
25. Sartre depicts a similar scene in *L'Être et le néant* in demonstrating a 'conduite de mauvaise foi'. The woman, ardently pursued by her suitor, enjoys the situation because she can temporarily put off any decision and pretend to a belief in platonic love. When he takes her hand, 'la jeune femme abandonne sa main, mais *ne s'aperçoit pas* qu'elle l'abandonne' (Paris: Gallimard, 1943), p. 95: my italics. Marivaux is more indulgent in his comment but no less observant.
26. See above, p. 62.
27. *Théâtre complet*, Vol. I, p. 1078, n. 12.
28. *Théâtre complet*, Vol. I, p. 512.
29. Iphicrate makes vague promises of better treatment to Arlequin (Scene 9). Euphrosine goes further and promises to share all her worldly goods with Cléanthis (Scene 10). It would seem, however, that both Arlequin and Cléanthis will go on being servants.
30. This should not be exaggerated, however. While believing that man's pride is basic to his nature, Marivaux also regards him as naturally inconsistent ('nous sommes des esprits de contradiction' – *L'Indigent Philosophe*, 7ᵉ *feuille*, in *Journaux*, edited by Deloffre and Gilot, p. 321) rather than naturally wicked ('la nature ... a de quoi tromper celui qui la veut voir mal, comme elle a de quoi éclairer celui qui la veut voir bien', *'Indigent Philosophe*, 5ᵉ *feuille*, p. 306). A belief in Original Sin as being a necessary part of man's make-up seems to be inherent in Marivaux's philosophy, along with a firm conviction that men have a conscience.
31. It did not go down well at Court; see T. S. Gueullette, *Notes et souvenirs sur le Théâtre-Italien au XVIIIᵉ siècle*, edited by J. E. Gueullette (Paris, 1938), p. 105.
32. *Théâtre complet*, Vol. I, p. 510.
33. *Théâtre complet*, Vol. I, p. 515.
34. *Théâtre complet*, Vol. I, p. 511.
35. *Théâtre complet*, Vol. I, p. 515.
36. See below, pp. 158–63.
37. *Théâtre complet*, Vol. I, p. 1087, note 43.
38. See Desvignes-Parent, pp. 317–24, who traces the pattern up to *Le Préjugé vaincu* (1746), though without at this point making reference to *L'Île de la raison*. Earlier the author had claimed that Marivaux obtains the idea of women pursuing men from Book III of Swift's *Gulliver's Travels* (pp. 120–3).
39. Lagrave, *Marivaux et sa fortune littéraire*, p. 49.
40. See the excellent discussion of the ideas in this play in W. H. Trapnell, 'The "Philosophical" implications of Marivaux's *Dispute*', *Studs. Volt.*, 73 (1970), pp. 193–219; the article usefully relates the play to contemporary social philosophy.
41. In *Journaux*, edited by Deloffre and Gilot, p. 34. It has often been suggested

that the poet is Voltaire, though E. J. H. Greene disagrees (*Marivaux*, p. 108). Possibly both Poet and Philosopher draw upon Voltaire; the Philosopher had left France to avoid the Bastille, while the Poet had written scandalously against a powerful man (I, 8); both details relate to Voltaire's life. Although, as Greene argues, Marivaux felt an aversion for personal satire, Voltaire constituted a special case: 'Si Marivaux a jamais montré du fiel et même de l'injustice, ç'a été contre un seul homme...' (d'Alembert, *Eloge de Marivaux*: cited in *Théâtre complet*, Vol. II, p. 1022). Greene's statement that the hostility between Marivaux and Voltaire dates from later than 1727, according to the evidence available to us, is correct; but this does not of course exclude the possibility that the quarrel had earlier origins.

42. Jacques Roger accords Marivaux high praise in this respect: 'Jamais écrivain n'a ressemblé plus que lui à un naturaliste.... Il est toujours resté ... l'observateur de ces animaux étranges que sont les hommes...,' *Les Sciences de la vie dans la pensée française du XVIII* siècle*, p. 777.

43. *Le Spectateur français, 7* feuille*, 21 August 1722, in *Journaux*, edited by Deloffre and Gilot, p. 147.

44. *Le Spectateur français, 8* feuille*, 8 September 1722, in *Journaux*, edited by Deloffre and Gilot, p. 149.

45. The classic reference work here is F. Deloffre, *Une préciosité nouvelle: Marivaux et le marivaudage*, 2nd edition (Paris: Colin, 1967).

46. *Journaux*, edited by Deloffre and Gilot, pp. 52–6.

47. *Journaux*, p. 49.

48. For a discussion of the scope and limitations of Marivaux's feminist ideas, see the author's 'Women in Marivaux: Journalist to Dramatist', *Women and Society in Eighteenth-Century France: Essays presented to John Spink* (Athlone Press, 1979), pp. 42–54.

I am indebted to the editors of *Woman and Society in the Eighteenth-Century France: Essays in Honour of John Stephenson Spink* (Athlone Press, 1979) for kindly allowing me to cite certain material used in my article 'Women in Marivaux: Journalist to Dramatist' for that volume.

3 Money and the Establishment: Prévost (1697–1763)

Manon Lescaut (1731)

The Chevalier des Grieux sums up most pertinently the inherent paradox in the *Histoire du Chevalier des Grieux et de Manon Lescaut*[1] that gives it its special ambiguity. He has just told us once again how the whole world is as nothing beside Manon's presence and love: 'Je la tiens du moins, disais-je; elle m'aime, elle est à moi. Tiberge a beau dire, ce n'est pas là un fantôme de bonheur. Je verrais périr tout l'univers sans y prendre intérêt. Pourquoi? Parce que je n'ai plus d'affection de reste.' Though beautifully expressed, this is the basic stuff of the traditional romance. *Manon Lescaut* combines it with a further dimension. The Chevalier continues:

> Ce sentiment était vrai; cependant dans le temps que je faisais si peu de cas des biens du monde, je sentais que j'aurais eu besoin d'en avoir du moins une petite partie, pour mépriser encore plus souverainement tout le reste. L'amour est plus fort que l'abondance, plus fort que les trésors et les richesses, mais il a besoin de leur secours; et rien n'est plus désespérant, pour un amant délicat, que de se voir ramené par là, malgré lui, à la grossièreté des âmes les plus basses.[2]

Amor vincit omnia; but ... On the one side, we find a worship of Manon that is idolatrous. Des Grieux knocks on the door of the house where she is 'avec le respect qu'on a pour un temple' (p. 140); her face is 'capable de ramener l'univers à l'idolâtrie' (p. 178);[3] at her death he describes her as 'l'idole de mon cœur' (p. 200). It may not be too fanciful, bearing in mind that

Manon's name is a derivative of Marie, to compare his adoration with the cult of the Virgin. Constantly opposed to this ethereal sentiment, however, is the desperate need for money which overrides all. As Lionel Gossman puts it, 'Worldly values and the social persona are ... in theory insubstantial in Prévost's novel ... in practice, the values of the world and the social persona alone have the force of reality'.[4]

This unremitting struggle against insolvency is well understood by des Grieux's creator. Though the abbé Antoine-François Prévost's money worries were mainly ahead of him when *Manon Lescaut* appeared in May 1731, the instability of character that was largely responsible for them is well attested by this date. Two periods of military service and two periods of noviciate instruction with the Jesuits were already completed when, in 1720 at the age of 23, he sought to bury himself away from the world (he himself refers to it as a 'tombeau') in a Benedictine monastery in Normandy (pp. xxiii–xxv). Despite some success in his new profession, he was called to Paris in 1727, in part at least because 'il y serait moins dangereux qu'ailleurs' (p. xxxv). In that same year he commenced his literary career, and beginning also to lead a social life, asked permission of Rome to be translated to a less austere Benedictine congregation; but for reasons still obscure the concession was delayed, and characteristically impetuous, Prévost took matters into his own hands by fleeing the monastery in October 1728 into exile, physically in England and spiritually in Protestantism. It was possibly during this stay that *Manon Lescaut* was written, while Prévost was acting as instructor to the son of Sir John Eyles (pp. xlviii–xlix). Not long after its publication, the turbulence and disorder of des Grieux's existence were reflected in Prévost's own life: the departure for Holland in 1730 because, apparently, he promised to marry Sir John's daughter and was dismissed by the displeased father (p. lii),[5] the encounter with Lenki Eckhardt who was to exercise over him the same dominion as Manon over the Chevalier, the onset of serious financial troubles leading to a flight from his huge debts and back to England in January 1733, the forging of a bill of exchange drawn on Sir John Eyles's son (an offence punishable by death – luckily for Prévost, Francis Eyles withdrew his complaint),[6] and a return to France in 1734 and a monastic position, but not without grave difficulties and some considerable string-pulling.[7] Many years were yet to pass before life became easier for

him financially. In 1738–40 he was still waging unavailing struggles against bankruptcy; yet Prévost had been paid at least 3500
livres in 1740, which can be compared with the 2500 *livres* that
Diderot was to receive in 1755, at a time when the latter's life was
beginning to be less precarious.[8]

It is hardly surprising, then, to find that money functioning as
an obstacle plays a central role in *Manon Lescaut*. We do not know
the colour of Manon's eyes or hair but we are informed of every
detail about des Grieux's financial vicissitudes, and these details
link up to form a totally coherent pattern.[9] The Homme de
Qualité gives des Grieux four *louis* (about 140 *livres*) on their first
meeting (p. 14), the Chevalier and Manon have about 150 *écus*
(450 *livres*) between them when they flee from Amiens (p. 22)
and of this sum twelve to fifteen *pistoles* (120–150 *livres*) remain a
month later in Paris, according to des Grieux's calculations (p.
27). By contrast, the sums promised and provided by, or stolen
from, Manon's lovers are astronomical; 60,000 *livres* from
Monsieur de B. (p. 48), a permanent credit of 10,000 *livres* from
the young G. M. (p. 131), plus assorted supplementaries like
jewels on the first occasion, or a furnished house, carriage and
servants on the second. Yet there are moments of poverty
stricken despair: after Manon's escape from prison the Chevalier
spends his last six *livres* on a hired coach ride (p. 108); at Le
Havre after selling his horse he has seventeen *pistoles*, enough to
provide Manon with 'quelques soulagements nécessaires' and
themselves with a pittance towards their establishment in
America (p. 183). What is the difference between misery and
bliss? Initially, it would seem, 6000 *livres* a year; according to the
Chevalier, it would give them 'une vie honnête, mais simple' (p.
49). By that he means the Opéra twice a week, a carriage and
limited opportunity for gambling. (Turgot in 1764 was to consider an income of 6000 *livres* decent but by no means rich.) But
as that soon turns out to be inadequate, one must presumably
think of a much larger sum as necessary, something like the
15,000 *livres* which Turgot estimated to be the minimum income
if one wished to be considered wealthy in Paris.[10] It is indicative
of the peculiar quality of this novel that one can actually put a
price on what would give consummate joy to the Chevalier des
Grieux's soul: the ownership, say, of land worth 75,000 *livres*
regularly yielding five per cent interest.

This is one of *Manon Lescaut*'s most spectacular innovations. In some respects the novel bears comparison with *La Princesse de Clèves* and is in the line of French classical taste, yet the notion of Madame de Clèves having to worry about money problems is ludicrous. By contrast, in *Manon Lèscaut* we even know the price of a common whore in Paris: three *livres* an hour (p. 177). Nor is the realism limited to financial detail. The whole seamy side of Regency Paris[11] stands revealed: prostitution, card-sharping, theft, murder and, most of all, prisons. Places like cafés, *cabarets*, and a *friperie* (second-hand clothes shop), which, if respectable, are hardly elevated in nature, all make their appearance. The forces of 'law and order' are much in evidence, from the brutal, mercenary bully-boys who form the King's Guards to the *guet royal* and various *archers* and *exempts* of the police and assorted 'domestiques', 'portiers' and 'concierges' at the different gaols, not to mention the Father Superior at Saint-Lazare whose kindnesses the Chevalier repays so cruelly.

In brief, this is a harsh and sordid world, motivated almost universally by money. It is characteristic that the only time des Grieux makes any money, he does so by systematic cheating at cards. (Regular employment is of course debarred to him as an aristocrat, except in the Church, the Army or the Law, all of which are out of the question so long as he is on bad terms with his father.) One of the main games played at the hôtel de Transylvanie is *pharaon* (p. 63), which is itself outlawed, as Buvat makes clear in his *Journal de la Régence* for December 1719.[12] Interestingly enough, Buvat's next entry speaks of 'le prix excessif auquel les denrées et les marchandises de toutes sortes étaient montées depuis quelque temps' as a result of the turbulence caused by Law's System. The swift changes in des Grieux's financial position symbolise the evanescence of fortunes of which Montesquieu had written. So he justifies his own conduct to his father with the claim, astonishing even by what we know of Regency immorality, that 'les deux tiers des honnêtes gens de France' keep a mistress (p. 163).[13] For those unfortunate enough to be without money or protection matters were very different. Manon's despair at being imprisoned for immorality (p. 102) finds an echo in the anonymous painting at the Musée Carnavalet (reproduced by Deloffre and Picard) of prostitutes being picked up by the police and despatched to prison, which shows, as the editors put it, a kind of 'accablement général' (p. 309). At least Manon had been interned on a charge of some substance.

Often the *archers* charged to arrest vagabonds exceeded their competence, fired by zeal as a result of the *pistole* per head which the
Compagnie des Indes offered them for bringing in recruits; Buvat
tells of the riots caused in 1720 by such criminal enthusiasm,
which had led to the death of more than a score of these militia-
men.[14]

This sense of arbitrary and unequal justice comes through
clearly once the couple in *Manon Lescaut* get into trouble. Both are
imprisoned after stealing from the elder G.M., but whereas the
Chevalier is sent to a gentlemen's prison run by missionaries at
Saint-Lazare, Manon is offered no such indulgence and incar-
cerated in the *Salpêtrière* at the *Hôpital*.[15] They are there in consequence of *lettres de cachet* signed by the *lieutenant général de police*
(Chief of Police) at G.M.'s instigation. Des Grieux fears that he
will be whipped on entering gaol (p. 80) but there is never any
question of it. He goes on to enjoy a privileged relationship with
the Father Superior, has no difficulty in obtaining a pistol for his
escape (p. 95), and later finds that the good Father has concealed
from the public all news of des Grieux's murder of the porter
(p. 113); it is a revealing picture of aristocratic immunities. Even
so, on this occasion Manon too enjoys some privileges, being
lodged in the least rigorous part of the prison and well looked
after. It might have been much worse. Manon could have been
sent to the gallows for theft.[16]

But she will not enjoy any particular favours the next time.
Although des Grieux is now sent to the same prison as she (the
Petit Châtelet), he is able to purchase a 'chambre proprement
meublée' for himself and, he hopes, one for Manon too (p. 158).
He is allowed to write to his father (p. 159) and generally treated
like a gentleman. Within a couple of days he is taken to the Chief
of Police (p. 160). Since the latter was responsible for the 'netteté
et sûreté de la Ville [Paris]' (p. 160, note 1), since his duties included 'the suppression of crime, fire prevention, lighting, street-
cleaning, the supervision of lodging-houses, cafés, clandestine
printing-presses, gaming-houses',[17] the special interest taken in
the Chevalier by an official so busy and so authoritative was a
signal favour. He treats des Grieux indulgently, as befits a young
man still sowing his wild oats. For the official it is mainly a
squabble between two noble families; and once the elder G.M.
and des Grieux's father go together to see him and ask for the
Chevalier's release the problem is resolved. It is true that the

Chevalier would be heading for serious trouble if he continued along the same path. His father warns him that he could finish up on the Place de Grève (p. 161) (where in March 1720 after a notorious murder the comte de Horn and the capitaine de Mille were broken on the wheel[18]). But, as we have seen, his most serious crime of murder had been covered up.

For Manon, on the other hand, 'd'une naissance commune' (p. 22), there is to be no remission. When the Chevalier tries to intercede for her with the Police Chief it is treated as a joke; and once the two fathers ask that she be transported to America all hope is lost. It is the triumph of authority, judicial, parental, social, against those without power, more particularly against a woman of humble origins once she has put herself on the wrong side of the law. It is imaginative of Prévost to devise a punishment that does not simply condemn Manon to death or let her rot in prison, as would have been entirely in keeping with reality,[19] but instead banishes her from France to a world where, by contrast with Old World corruption, there may paradoxically yet be hope of a better order. Justice will fail, however, in the New World too because power is once more subverted to serve personal ends.

Yet the conclusions to be drawn from this novel are not, it would seem, didactic or reformist. One has only to compare Voltaire's *L'Ingénu* (1767), which also gives a central place to the arbitrariness of imprisonment, to see that, by comparison, *Manon Lescaut* reveals a resignation to the social order. True, there may well be an aristocratic disdain for the sordid world of commerce and finance, not only on the part of des Grieux but of the author himself, who had emerged from the new *noblesse de robe*,[20] but this involves no programme of social change as it had with Montesquieu. Like Rousseau later, Prévost considers that 'les grandes villes ne sont point un séjour favorable à la vertu',[21] explicitly disagreeing with Saint-Evremond, who had maintained (in a letter of 1676) that 'un honnête homme doit vivre et mourir dans une capitale'.[22] Jean Sgard sees him as torn by contradictions, born to a firmly established social situation, yet fated to break with it: 'Il a réellement appartenu à deux mondes, à un monde ancien, catholique, hiérarchisé, classique et à un présent libertin, individualiste et sentimental'.[23] Hence the ambiguities, precluding any fixed social outlook.

Manon Lescaut, nonetheless, holds an important position in the development of the novel in France. It is, as its title announces, an 'histoire', whose aim is to tell a story about people in a private situation, like the seven 'histoires' in Robert Challe's *Illustres Françaises* (1713) to which Prévost's novel appears to owe a debt.[24] The aim is now to convey, through the first-person narrator, a familiarity with the reader which, allied to precision of detail, will provide a sense of directness and reality. The technique had evolved from the third-person *nouvelle historique* of which *La Princesse de Clèves* is the masterpiece, with its stress on brevity and tragic dignity. By uniting the realism of writers like Challe with the qualities handed down by Madame de La Fayette, Prévost was remaining firmly within the French tradition. The fact that Voltaire paid him the tribute of saying that he could have written tragedies[25] is both a supreme compliment from the most fastidious of critics in this field and also an indication of Prévost's essentially orthodox taste. The novel has the elevated tone of classical tragedy – 'c'est parfois Phèdre en prose'.[26] Prévost's realism is strictly limited: 'le réel ... n'est pas décrit pour lui-même, mais en tant qu'élément dramatique'.[27] The setting does not depend on minutiae, but on sparing use of detail; as Vivienne Mylne points out in her excellent appraisal of *Manon*, clothes are never described for their own sake, any more than are Paris or the countryside.[28] English Showalter acutely observes that the eighteenth-century novel, even when it deals with money, declines to show money being made, whether it be in law office, bank, or merchant's headquarters. For these novelists, 'the daily concern of a man to earn his living held no interest... Even *Manon* is no exception.'[29] Money, though an obstacle to the true life, is not of interest in and for itself to Prévost. It required the arrival of a Balzac to conceive of the matter differently in France. However, within the period of our study, we shall later see some steps being made towards a new approach in Sedaine's *Le Philosophe sans le savoir*.

Yet Prévost's narrative makes a radical departure in one respect. Through his stay in England the novelist had acquired from English literature the confidence to write of extravagant passion and low life. Unlike Voltaire, who never accepted Shakespeare as more than a brilliant barbarian, Prévost was delighted by works like *Hamlet*, and for him English tragedy was unsurpassed by either French or Greek.[30] He probably knew tales of bandits and criminals by Defoe.[31] Some years before Voltaire,

Prévost was importing a fashion for England, and particularly for English taste, into France. Yet in *Manon Lescaut* the wild romantic drama is subordinated to chaste language, and the brutal detail is consigned to the background or quickly passed over, as with Lescaut's death. Georges May rightly points out that it would be a grave error to see Prévost as a forerunner of the populist novel.[32]

Furthermore, Prévost helps to accelerate a change of taste that is already proceeding in France. *Manon Lescaut*, like his other works, is a lachrymose book. Swoonings and tears are frequent and fit well with the confessional tone. The Homme de Qualité serves as the ideal father-figure for these revelations, a sympathetic listener and a helpful friend in need, so different from des Grieux's own father, and a surrogate for the absent mother.[33] That the Chevalier might have poured out his troubles in a real confessional is never considered. The nearest to it is the recurrent pattern of confidences shared with Tiberge, but these are generally deceitful and offered with the intent of gaining something, usually money, from him. Despite frequent references to Christian concepts like grace the author pursues a line of conduct that is secular, even pagan.[34] The main and almost the sole representative of the Church, Tiberge, is naïve, wearisome, even suspect in the degree of his attachment to the Chevalier. Des Grieux, so far as he has a philosophy, is more of a *libertin* than anything else: 'De la manière dont nous sommes faits, il est certain que notre félicité consiste dans le plaisir; je défie qu'on s'en forme une autre idée' (p. 92). So hedonism is the way of life to follow, and virtue, which is 'sévère et pénible' (p. 93), is incompatible with pleasure. In this affirmation des Grieux fully admits the immorality of his conduct: 'je reconnais ma misère et ma faiblesse' (p. 93); but he persists in it, even glories in it, for he detects not only 'misère' in himself but 'grandeur' too. He is doubly an aristocrat: by his birth, and by his capacity for feeling:

Le commun des hommes n'est sensible qu'à cinq ou six passions, dans le cercle desquelles leur vie se passe, et où toutes leurs agitations se réduisent. Otez-leur l'amour et la haine, le plaisir et la douleur, l'espérance et la crainte, ils ne sentent plus rien. Mais les personnes d'un caractère plus noble peuvent être remuées de mille façons différentes; il semble qu'elles aient plus de cinq sens, et qu'elles puissent recevoir des idées et des sensations qui passent les bornes ordinaires de la nature; et comme elles ont un sentiment de cette grandeur qui les élève au-dessus du vulgaire, il n'y a rien dont elles soient plus jalouses (p. 81).

Similarly, Voltaire envisages the possibility, in *Micromégas* a few years later, that superior men (or giants) from other planets may be endowed with more senses. Robert Tate, in making the link, indicates the Lockean influence common to both. For Locke's assertion, in Book II of his *Essay Concerning Human Understanding* (1690), that ideas come from sense-impressions (though he himself insisted on the importance of reflection in ordering those impressions), was destined to enjoy great success in eighteenth-century France and to give a philosophical support to the wave of sensibility that is increasingly evident in literature from about 1690.[35] All des Grieux's faults are in his own view redeemed by the nobility of his heart; the essential part of him, his true self, is untouched by a corrupt world, and in America he and Manon are able to reach and exploit what is best in them so long as society allows it.[36]

This alliance between love and nature, the insistence upon the goodness of emotionality, have much to recommend them to an age which is eager to see the advantages of the passions; it will become a commonplace to stress their utility.[37] Novels will be full of tales proclaiming the innocence of love, thereby justifying all kinds of excesses.[38] Already in 1733 Mathieu Marais, though finding the novel 'abominable', had to admit that 'on y courait comme au feu'.[39] As Françoise Weil concludes from her research on contemporary reactions to the novelist, 'Une des raisons du succès de Prévost est certainement cet art de faire pleurer';[40] she adds that she has discovered only one unfavourable judgement on *Manon Lescaut*. Montesquieu's attitude was however detached and cynical: 'Je ne suis pas étonné que ce roman, dont le héros est un fripon, et l'héroïne, une catin ... plaise; parce que toutes les mauvaises actions du héros ... ont pour motif l'amour, qui est toujours un motif noble, quoique la conduite soit basse. Manon aime aussi; ce qui lui fait pardonner le reste de son caractère.'[41] For all the purity with which Prévost describes the Chevalier's love, *Manon Lescaut* would seem to have had a considerable influence upon the evolution of the erotic novel, preparing the way for love affairs less and less subtly portrayed, opening on to unashamed pornography, which reaches a climax in the late

1740s.[42] But by the seductive quality of his young lovers and the tenderness with which their relationship is narrated, Prévost manages to relegate the sordid qualities to the background as regrettable accidents and leave one with only the lasting memory of des Grieux's faithfulness and Manon's beauty. *Manon Lescaut* is a moral novel if truth to psychological detail is what counts; but if one concludes that the murder, thefts and treacheries are to be glossed over and excused by a shining love, then there is much to be said for Picard's view that it is 'l'un des romans les plus immoraux de la littérature française'.[43] Nonetheless, the confessional approach, the indulgence in sentiment prepare the way for Rousseau's *La Nouvelle Héloïse* (1761) and beyond it the autobiographical elements so strongly represented in novels as different as Chateaubriand's *René* (1802) and Constant's *Adolphe* (1816).

One cannot conclude an account, however cursory, of *Manon Lescaut*'s relationship to the social conditions of the time without some reference to the circumstances of its publication. The novel first appeared in Amsterdam in 1731. But despite success to the point of being sold out in Holland and England, and further acclaim in Germany, where it was published in translation in 1732, it attracted no attention in France, and until very recently 1733 was still being advanced by reputable critics as the publication date.[44] It is now clear beyond a shadow of doubt that the book first saw the light of day in 1731, and numerous references and reviews have been uncovered by Deloffre to attest it.[45] The novel however remained unknown in France until June 1733, when a new edition from Amsterdam was sold in Paris, attracting almost immediate interest from the *Journal de la Cour et de Paris*; a month later Voltaire knew of it.[46] The success of the work built up, as we have seen from Marais's remark, and on 5 October the syndics charged with the task of examining new publications seized copies on sale, apparently for two reasons, according to the *Journal de la Cour et de Paris*: 'Outre que l'on y fait jouer à gens en place des rôles peu dignes d'eux, le vice et le débordement y sont peints avec des traits qui n'en donnent pas assez d'horreur'.[47] In 1735 another seizure was ordered. Prévost himself was, however, left in peace, and there seems little evidence that he suffered in any way from these governmental initiatives. If anything, the novel benefited all the more from this excellent publicity, and the fact that a particularly fine edition was published in 1735 seems to bear this out. In keeping with the paradoxical nature of the book censorship in eighteenth-century France, the privilege to print (which had originally been obtained for the whole of the *Mémoires d'un Homme de Qualité* in 1728) was renewed without apparent difficulty at the end of 1736; and at least a dozen editions, some legitimate, some pirated, appeared between 1738 and 1753.[48]

Although the reason for official hostility to *Manon Lescaut* seems clear, the total silence in France for two years after its original publication has perplexed scholars. Henri Roddier argued that in 1731 Prévost was anxious to establish himself as an historian and so played down all publicity about the novel.[49] While this thesis seems perfectly valid, it does not appear to be sufficient on its own to account for such widespread silence, and Georges May has offered another explanation which not only complements Roddier's but appears more satisfactorily wide-ranging.[50] In *Le Dilemme du roman* May had revealed the existence, hitherto only barely suspected, of a proscription laid upon novels by the Chancelier Daguesseau from the time he became *Garde des Sceaux* in 1737, resulting in a dramatic fall in the proportion of new novels published in France. He now traces the argument back a few years, claiming that Daguesseau was already making it difficult several years earlier for novels to appear and that he was perhaps responsible for ensuring the silence in the French press over *Manon Lescaut*, as he was apparently to do for the last three parts of Marivaux's *La Vie de Marianne* when they appeared in 1742. Daguesseau had already, according to Chamfort, given permission to print the first volumes of Prévost's *Histoire de M. Cleveland* in 1731 only on condition that Cleveland would become a Catholic by the end of the work. According to May's hypothesis the Chancelier, annoyed at Prévost's publishing *Manon Lescaut* abroad, reacted by clamping down on all reviews and then by seizing the copies that were circulating in 1733. (The entry of the 1731 edition into France had also been strictly forbidden.)[51] The conjecture seems highly plausible, though it leaves unexplained why Daguesseau should not have intervened to prevent renewal of the privilege in 1736.

Despite the fragility of these theories, the general picture is clear. *Manon Lescaut*, as a novel, was a dangerous work in the eyes of the Establishment. We see here a good example of 'le dilemme du roman'. If the novel chose to be realistic, it incurred charges of immorality; so it was essential to claim, as did Prévost in the

'Avis de l'auteur' preceding his work, that it was morally edifying. The further charge, which often ran counter to the first, was
that the novelist was telling lies.[52] No wonder that May entitles
one chapter of his book 'Charybde et Scylla'; either way it seemed
that the novelist could not win. Yet despite all the opposition, the
genre continued to increase in realism, especially when, after the
appearance of Richardson's *Pamela* (1740), a way out of the
impasse appeared whereby morality and truth could go hand in
hand.[53] But the degree of social realism is limited, as we have
seen. Far from taking delight in representing low life, as does
Marivaux in the *Lettres sur les habitants de Paris* and again in the
famous quarrel scene between the *cocher* and Madame Dutour in
La Vie de Marianne, Prévost restricts it to what is essential for
rounding out the situation in which des Grieux's passion for
Manon develops. There is the same aristocratic disdain for
money-making as in the *Lettres persanes*, the same concern for
noble language; and it is arguable that the author completely
sympathizes with his hero's claims to special treatment based on
aristocratic rank. One finds it hard to see a direct correlation
between *Manon Lescaut* and the growth of the bourgeois spirit
which is generally held to be responsible for the rise of the novel.
As Vivienne Mylne puts it, 'although Prévost's novels evince a
preoccupation with winning the reader's belief by realistic narrative methods, it is in the last resort the 'truth' of character which
has kept this one story alive'.[54] In the process of describing the
obstacles to the Chevalier's love Prévost has made important
advances in the evolution of the novel in France. For all that, its
ultimate aim and achievement, in literary terms, seem aristocratic and conservative. On the social plane, it criticizes the existing
state of affairs but offers no suggestions for improvement. In this
respect it is clearly contemporary with Marivaux and, despite the
more positive sociological concerns of the *Lettres persanes*, not far
removed in spirit from Montesquieu's work either.

NOTES

1. Only the full title does justice to the work, by stressing first of all that it is an
   'histoire' (see p. 120), and then by giving pride of place to the Chevalier des

Grieux before Manon. For the purposes of simplicity, however, further references will be to the more convenient and popular formulation, *Manon Lescaut.*

2. Edited by F. Deloffre and R. Picard (Paris: Garnier, 1965), pp. 108–9. All textual references will be to this edition. This may be the most suitable occasion to express one's gratitude for the editors' masterly piece of scholarship; the numerous references to it in themselves bear witness to its great value for this chapter.

3. In their edition Deloffre and Picard point out that this phrase was sufficiently striking to be singled out by a contemporary reader, Mathieu Marais, who otherwise found everything in the novel antipathetic (p. clxiii).

4. 'Prévost's *Manon*: Love in the new world', *Yale French Studies*, 40 (1968), p. 95. See also M. Kusch, '*Manon Lescaut*, ou voyage du Chevalier des Grieux dans la basse Romancie', *Studs. Volt.*, 143 (1975), p. 152: 'the novel is as much a financial statement as a sentimental story, as much a bankruptcy as a "tragedy"'

5. For a fuller account of this episode see F. Deloffre, 'Les "fiançailles" anglaises de l'abbé Prévost', *L'Abbé Prévost: Actes du Colloque d'Aix-en-Provence, 1963* (Aix-en-Provence: Annales de la Faculté des Lettres, 1965), pp. 1–9.

6. The possible reasons for this change of heart are discussed by Deloffre, 'Les "fiançailles" anglaises', p. 8.

7. J. Sgard, 'L'Apostasie et la réhabilitation de Prévost', *Actes du Colloque d'Aix*, pp. 11–22.

8. J. Sgard, *Prévost romancier* (Paris: Corti, 1968), p. 402.

9. Roger Laufer has established a list of words relating to money in the novel, from which it emerges clearly how frequent and diverse they are. He enumerates 35 terms in all, headed by 'argent' (used 34 times), 'pistole', 'bourse' (fourteen each), 'richesses' (eleven) and 'francs' (ten): *Style rococo, style des 'lumières'* (Paris: Corti, 1963), p. 88.

10. E. Showalter, Jr., 'Money matters and early novels', *Yale French Studies*, 40 (1968), p. 121. See also his *The Evolution of the French Novel 1641–1782* (Princeton University Press, 1972), especially pp. 154–7.

11. The book is easily dated to a brief period in 1719–20 during which prostitutes were deported to the French colony of Louisiana (Deloffre and Picard, editors, pp. ix, xii).

12. 'On publia une autre ordonnance qui fit défense, sous peine de désobéissance et de trois mille livres d'amende, de jouer à aucun jeu de dés et de cartes, surtout aux jeux de hoca, biribi la dupe, pharaon et la bassette...', J. Buvat, *Journal de la Régence*, Vol. I, p. 475. But such was the passion for gambling during the Regency that the regulation proved quite ineffectual. See also J. Sgard, 'Tricher', *Le Jeu au XVIII siècle* (Aix-en-Provence, 1976), pp. 251–8.

13. Barbier, however, writes that 'De vingt seigneurs de la cour, il y en a quinze qui ne vivent point avec leurs femmes et qui ont des maîtresses' (*Journal d'un bourgeois*, edited by Bernard, December 1750, p. 236). Given what we know of the Chevalier's capacity for twisting the facts to suit himself, it does not require much effort to extend this limited observation to cover all the 'hon-

nêtes gens' in France.

14. *Journal de la Régence*, Vol. II, pp. 77–8. The *archers* were not lacking in arms, since they carried a rifle, a sword, a bayonet and two pistols: C.E. Engel, *Le Véritable Abbé Prévost* (Monaco: Editions du Rocher, 1957), p. 166. See also C. Kunstler, *La Vie quotidienne sous la Régence*, pp. 132–3.

15. Thomas Pennant visited the *Salpêtrière* on his Continental tour in 1765: 'a sort of workhouse for girls and women, of which there are in the house 7500'. He was allowed to visit all parts of the prison, even the lunatic asylum, except for the area allocated to 'women of the town of the lowest order', of whom there were, he said, '8 or 900': *Tour on the Continent 1765*, edited by G. de Beer (London: Ray Society, 1948), p. 24.

16. D. Guiragossian, '*Manon Lescaut* et la justice criminelle sous l'ancien régime', *Studs. Volt.*, 56 (1967), p. 681.

17. F. C. Green, *The Ancien Régime*, p.30. Guiragossian, '*Manon Lescaut* et la justice criminelle', quotes an even longer enumeration of duties (pp. 685–6).

18. See Buvat, *Journal de la Régence*, Vol. II, pp. 503–10.

19. 'On n'était jamais absolument sûr d'en [de prison] sortir quand on y entrait. Mille causes entravaient le retour à la liberté. Souvent, durant leur détention, des prisonniers contractaient des dettes vis-à-vis des géôliers, surtout pour frais de nourriture. Une fois libérables, s'ils ne s'acquittaient pas, les concierges . . . les empêchaient de sortir.': R. Anchel, *Crimes et châtiments au XVIII⁺ siècle* (Paris: Perrin, 1933), p. 90.

20. 'Son père . . . acheta la charge de conseiller du Roi, qui conférait la noblesse à titre personnel . . .' (Deloffre and Picard, editors, p. xiv).

21. *Le Pour et Contre* (Paris: Didot, 1733–40), 20 vols., Vol II, no. 18, p. 60; cited in Atkinson and Keller, *Prelude to the Enlightenment*, p. 148, note 23.

22. Cited in Atkinson and Keller, *Prelude to the Enlightenment*, p. 150, note 25.

23. *Prévost romancier*, p. 16.

24. See Deloffre and Picard, editors, pp. lxxvi–lxxxiii.

25. Letter to Thieriot (28 December 1735), Best. D 973.

26. Deloffre and Picard, editors, p. cxxxiv; this follows a succinct account of the tragic elements in the novel.

27. Sgard, *Prévost romancier*, p. 254.

28. *Prévost: Manon Lescaut* (London: Arnold, 1972), p. 42. See also P. Stewart, *Imitation and Illusion in the French Memoir–Novel, 1700–50* (Yale University Press, 1969), p. 164. Laufer points out that technical terms, apart from those related to money, are few: *Style rococo, style des 'lumières'*, p. 88.

29. 'Money matters and early novels', p. 132.

30. *Mémoires d'un Homme de Qualité*, Book V; cited in Sgard, *Prévost romancier*, p. 264.

31. Sgard, *Prévost romancier*, p. 266.

32. *Le Dilemme du roman au XVIII⁺ siècle: étude sur les rapports du roman et de la critique (1715–1761)* (Yale University Press, 1963), p. 193.

33. Atkinson and Keller point out Prévost's preoccupation with a mother-figure and give examples (pp. 39–41).

34. See Deloffre and Picard, editors, pp. cxxvii–cxxix, which argues that the notion of fatality is essentially a pagan one.

35. '*Manon Lescaut* and the Enlightenment', *Studs. Volt.*, 70 (1970), p. 20.

36. See L. Gossman, 'Prévost's *Manon*', p. 96.
37. See, for example, the characteristic examples quoted by Tate (supra, note 35) p. 20, from Diderot, Helvétius and Voltaire.
38. L. Versini, 'Quelques thèmes empruntés à Prévost par le roman français au dix-huitième siècle', *Actes du Colloque d'Aix*, pp. 244–5.
39. Cited in Deloffre and Picard, editors, p. clxiii.
40. 'Les premiers lecteurs de Prévost et le "Dilemme du roman"', *Actes du Colloque d'Aix*, p. 227.
41. *Mes pensées, Oeuvres complètes de Montesquieu*, edited by R. Caillois (Paris: NRF, Bibliothèque de la Pleiade, 1949–51), 2 vols., Vol. I, p. 1253.
42. G. May, *Le Dilemme du roman*, pp. 60–1.
43. Deloffre and Picard, editors, p. clv.
44. See, for example, C. E. Engel, *Le Véritable Abbé Prévost*, pp. 116–27.
45. Deloffre and Picard, editors, pp. lxi–lxiii, clvii–clxi.
46. Letter to Thieriot [28 July 1733], Best. D 640.
47. Deloffre and Picard, editors, p. clxii.
48. M. Brun, 'Contribution à la vie d'un roman: *Manon Lescaut*', *Actes du Colloque d'Aix*, pp. 211–15.
49. 'La "Véritable" Histoire de *Manon Lescaut*', *RHL*, 59 (1959), pp. 209–10.
50. 'Nouvelles Conjectures sur la date de la première édition de *Manon Lescaut*', *Actes du Colloque d'Aix*, pp. 207–10.
51. M.-R. de Labriolle, 'Le *Pour et Contre* et son temps', *Studs. Volt.*, 34 (1965), p. 34, note 34.
52. See V. Mylne, *The Eighteenth-Century French Novel: Techniques of Illusion* (Manchester University Press, 1965), especially Chapters I–II.
53. G. May, *Le Dilemme du roman*, pp. 102–5.
54. *The Eighteenth-Century French Novel*, p. 103.

4 Luxury in a Secular Civilisation: Voltaire (1694–1778)

Lettres philosophiques (1734); Le Mondain (1736); Défense du Mondain (1737)

If Voltaire wrote an equivalent of the *Lettres persanes*, it is not his *Lettres philosophiques*; the closest analogy is probably with *Le Monde comme il va*.[1] The *Lettres philosophiques* point in a different direction. Instead of having the exotic foreign visitor come to Paris, as in Montesquieu's work, the Parisian visitor goes to London. The essential reason for the originality of Voltaire's *Lettres* lies in this change of setting and perspective.

> By the end of 1725 Voltaire, then just over thirty, had the world at his feet, being already recognised as the standard bearer of French letters. He was happy in love, or at least successful. He was the intimate of the learned and the great. Three of his plays were performed at court . . . he had fame, security, money . . .[2]

A quarrel with the scion of one of the proudest families in France, the Chevalier de Rohan, was to change fundamentally this comfortable existence. Voltaire might mingle with the aristocracy, even modify from 1718 on his family name Arouet into an aristocratic form (Arouet de Voltaire). He remained nonetheless of bourgeois origins, even though Arouet *père* was a highly-placed civil servant. As the family was well connected Voltaire had a good start in society; but faced with a leading aristocrat he was to discover unambiguously in a moment of crisis what his true social standing was. The squabble, occurring in early 1726, led to a beating which the Chevalier ordered his servants to inflict humiliatingly upon the writer. Voltaire, not one to take lightly such a wanton piece of violence, sought revenge, even considering apparently whether to call upon the help of the King's Guards,[3] much as the Chevalier des Grieux might have done. Whether such rumours were correct, he was clearly heading for disaster, and the decision to intern him in the Bastille was as much for his own good as in the name of public order. He was released only on the condition that he live at least 50 leagues' distance from Paris.

Voltaire chose to go to England; and in due course the discovery he made of a very different civilisation during the next two-and-a-half years was to flower in the *Lettres philosophiques*, published long after his return to France. Here is not the place to analyse that work at length,[4] but rather to insist on one aspect of English life which figures prominently, the respect generally accorded its men of letters. Not only was Sir Isaac Newton demonstrably a great man; it was to England's honour that she had recognised this greatness while he lived, so that his funeral was of truly royal proportions.[5] By contrast, France was implicitly a nation where a Voltaire would always be humiliated by a chevalier de Rohan. Whereas the Court of Louis XIV displayed an interest in culture, no longer was this the case. But in England things were different – 'communément on pense' (II, p. 119); so one finds aristocrats cultivating literature, like John Hervey, Rochester, Waller and many others. On the other hand, Voltaire is somewhat annoyed with Congreve for priding himself more on being a gentleman than a writer (Letter XIX). For he sees the importance of an enlightened social élite, making culture respectable 'aux yeux du peuple, qui en tout a besoin d'être mené par les Grands' (II, p. 129). In England culture spreads downwards from the top, whereas in France it flourishes only amongst the professional bourgeoisie and in the Church ('nos Magistrats, nos Avocats, nos Médecins, et beaucoup d'Ecclésiastiques': II, p. 120) – social groups which need an educated mind in order to carry on their daily work. English men of letters tend to be appointed to official posts: Addison, Newton, Congreve, Prior, Swift. While this path was not open to a Catholic like Alexander Pope, he too flourished, since the high esteem for literature allowed him to grow rich on his translations of Homer (II, p. 158). Voltaire, following Pope's example, made money (probably in the region of 30,000 *livres*) from the English edition of his epic poem *La Henriade* (1728), where the impressive subscription list was headed by George I and Princess Caroline.[6] France was superior only in its institutional encouragement of the arts and sciences through the Academies, one more legacy of that enlightened monarch Louis XIV; but even here Voltaire had reservations and by the 1748 edition of the *Lettres philosophiques* he had considerably modified his praises (II, p. 170,n).

John Lough points out that this account of English writers is not strictly accurate, as the political patronage which Voltaire mentions had long since disappeared; but the latter is nearer the mark in seeing Pope's independence as indicative of real progress. English writers continued to enjoy more favoured conditions than their French colleagues throughout the century.[7] Though mistaken in his belief that State patronage of writers had been widespread under Louis XIV, Voltaire discerned rightly that official support would continue to be relevant; as we have seen, it remained common practice for the rest of the century.[8] (As for himself, he had already realised that intellectual freedom required financial security independent of the State, and on his return from England he had set about making money through financial speculations.[9]) Although less well off than English writers, French men of letters saw a gradual improvement during the period, both in fortune and in prestige; Voltaire's beating at the hands of Rohan's henchmen was the last notorious example of its kind.[10]

Yet his relationship with authority was never to be smooth, and he lived his life under the threat of persecution. The *Lettres philosophiques*, once published, were publicly torn apart and burned in Paris and an order was issued for their author's arrest. He escaped just in time, taking refuge at the château of his mistress Madame du Châtelet at Cirey in Champagne until the storm died down. In 1736 the appearance of his poem *Le Mondain* caused a further scandal and a period of voluntary exile for some months in the Low Countries. *Le Mondain*, an apology for worldly affluence, continues the theme set out so clearly in the *Remarques sur Pascal* which had formed a supplement to the *Lettres philosophiques*. Like the *Remarques*, it is a firm indictment of the spirit that prompts austerity, frugality and self-sacrifice. Every *honnête homme* cares for 'La propreté, le goût, les ornements' (v. 11).[11] The paradox of luxury is summed up in the poem's most famous line 'Le superflu, chose très nécessaire' (v. 22). By contrast, rude nature did not know the concept of personal property; primitive peoples had no wine or silk or gold, they were unacquainted with either hard work or soft ease. This was not virtuous living; it was 'pure ignorance' (v. 43). Voltaire then proceeds to turn the polemic into scandal by citing a privileged example of the simple life – Adam and Eve in the Garden of Eden. Our forefathers, it soon appears, had not been living in a Paradise before the Fall; they were simply a dirty, crude pair, little better than animals, wretchedly eking out a mere subsistence.

No; the true good life is that of the *honnête homme* in Paris, London, Rome, surrounded by works of art, sculpture, silver-ware, tapestries. He moves in a brilliant society enhanced by gilt carriages, gleaming mirrors, perfumed baths, enjoys rendez-vous with delicious actresses, attends the Opéra, finishing the day with exquisite suppers and champagne. The ending to the poem is trenchant. Voltaire bids the primitivist ascetics keep their Golden Age. For me, he concludes, 'Le Paradis terrestre est où je suis'.

When the poem was published in Paris, contrary to its author's intentions, the condescending portrait of Adam and Eve promptly aroused hostility. Having fled to Holland, Voltaire composed there the *Défense du Mondain*, sending a copy to Frederick of Prussia in January 1737. A tone of *badinage* is still to be found in this latter poem, but the approach is different, for this time Voltaire has, as the title indicates, a thesis to justify. As he told Frederick in a letter accompanying the poem, luxury is not just delightful, it makes good *economic* sense: 'Je crois qu'on peut enrichir un état en donnant beaucoup de plaisir à ses sujets'.[1] The poem begins pungently with the satiric portrait of a boring misanthropic Jansenist who tells Voltaire he will surely to to Hell for having written *Le Mondain*. This character begins to hold forth against the evils of luxury but has to stop every so often to moisten his throat, parched from the monologue, with a magnificent and expensive wine; the comic irony, unperceived of course by him, is worthy of Molière.

However, the bulk of the poem is taken up with the author's reply to this grotesque figure. Luxury is shown to be socially and economically beneficial:

Le riche est né pour beaucoup dépenser;
Le pauvre est fait pour beaucoup amasser.

....

Ainsi l'on voit en Angleterre, en France,
Par cent Canaux circuler l'abondance.
Le goût du Luxe entre dans tous les rangs;
Le Pauvre y vit des Vanités des Grands ... (vv. 57–8, 67–70)

Voltaire goes on to praise Louis XIV's minister Colbert for encouraging affluence and, looking back to Biblical times (but this time to praise and not to mock), he extols Solomon, 'Roi philosophe' (v. 114), who used cedarwood, gold and silver for embellishment.

Le Mondain essentially stresses the moral arguments in favour of luxury; the *Défense*, by contrast, concentrates on economic aspects. In the former Voltaire elevates hedonism into a new moral code. As Jean Starobinski puts it, pleasure is no longer seen by the Enlightenment as dissipation but as the awakening of a consciousness, the hope of a world rebuilt according to Nature and Reason.[13] *Le Mondain* is a plea for civilised Epicureanism; but the implications of such an existence for the society in which one lives are not developed. The *Défense*, in this respect, shows a clear shift of emphasis. Furthermore, that shift is in line with the thinking of the age as affluence increases. Trade with the East Indies (referred to in *Le Mondain*) became particularly active after the East Indies Company abandoned Louisiana in 1731.[14] Between 1715 and 1750 French foreign trade almost tripled;[15] it almost quadrupled by 1788.[16] Luxury ceased to be a sign of status, became a matter for debate as eighteenth-century France gradually moved away from a subsistence economy. The luxury of public ostentation was gradually replaced by a greater insistence upon private enjoyment of the comfortable.[17] With the general economic boom in agricultural prices that began around 1730 and went on for a half-century landed proprietors could indulge their new-found wealth in wider consumption. Until a new recession occurred around 1778, the French people were, generally speaking, progressively better off than their fathers throughout this period. Despite the many restrictions on transport and industry, like the numerous internal tolls and customs barriers, despite widespread misery and the many occasions when a harvest failed in some region or other, despite an industrial growth vastly inferior to Britain's, the country was growing visibly richer all this while. One index of this which survives to the present day is the quantity of fine houses and squares built all over France during the eighteenth century.[18]

But the new luxury posed moral problems. How should a civilisation be measured if its prosperity was based on selfish or at least amoral impulses? Wealth had been attacked as socially poisonous by Fénelon in his *Télémaque* (1699). Montesquieu's *Lettres persanes*, in their account of the Troglodytes, reveal the same nostalgia as Fénelon for a golden age of natural simplicity. The author himself seems to incline in favour of an affluent society in Letter CVI, but this is in reply to one attacking it, so the ultimate attitude remains uncertain, in keeping with the ambiguity of the overall social position displayed in the work. But as the century advanced, the luxury argument moved away from a defence of frugality for its own sake and into a wider discussion of the uses and abuses of affluence. Voltaire's own intervention in the debate may well have had a decisive effect. Few after 1736 continued endorsing limitations upon production as a good thing in itself; even Rousseau did not feel that the answer lay in that direction. At the same time the argument in favour of total enjoyment regardless of the consequences also came to seem outmoded. Voltaire's own hardening resistance to this point of view between *Le Mondain* and the *Défense* foreshadowed the turn in the debate. For Diderot, Beccaria, Montesquieu (in *Del l'esprit de lois*), Helvétius, Condillac, Saint-Lambert it was a matter of distinguishing between the good and evil uses of luxury and of harnessing the former for the public welfare.

'A comprehensive analysis of the debate on luxury could only be produced after years of work by an economic historian who was also a sociologist and a literary critic', asserts Richard Fargher with some justification.[19] The subject, with all its complex ramifications, awaits an authoritative statement.[20] Meantime, we may note that in two poems of just 128 lines each Voltaire had encapsulated so much that prevailed in the climate of his age: a *badinage* and its subsequent apology, which count among the most important poems of the Enlightenment.[21]

NOTES

1. See the discussion of this *conte* in my edition of *Zadig and Other Stories* (Oxford University Press, 1971), pp. 33–6.

2. T. Besterman, *Voltaire* (Longman, 1969), p. 106.
3. Best. D 268.
4. See the discussion of the *Lettres philosophiques* in my *Voltaire* (Hutchinson, 1975), pp. 109–24. I have also treated the English visit at some length in *Voltaire: A Biography* (Granada, 1981).
5. G. Lanson, editor, *Lettres philosophiques*, revised by A.-M. Rousseau (Paris: Didier, 1964), 2 vols., Vol. II, p. 2. All subsequent textual references will be to this edition.
6. O. R. Taylor, editor, *La Henriade, The Complete Works of Voltaire* (Geneva: Institut et Musée Voltaire, Vol. 2, 1970), pp. 65–75. However, see also A.-M. Rousseau, *L'Angleterre et Voltaire*, Studs. Volt., 145–7 (1976), p. 154, n.
7. *An Introduction to Eighteenth Century France*, pp. 233–4.
8. See above. pp. 48–50.
9. *Voltaire: A Biography*.
0. Lough, *An Introduction*, p. 263.
1. A. Morize, *L'Apologie du luxe au XVIIIe siècle et 'Le Mondain' de Voltaire* (Paris: Didier, 1909), p. 133. All references to the two poems will be taken from this edition.
2. Best. D 1251.
3. *L'Invention de la liberté, 1700–1789* (Geneva: Skira, 1964), p. 54.
4. Morize, *L'Apologie du luxe*, p. 142, n. 12.
5. P. Sagnac, *La Formation de la société française moderne* (Paris: P.U.F., 1945–46), 2 vols., Vol. II, p. 12.
6. Lough, *An Introduction*, pp. 71–2.
7. See the excellent chapter by G. Gusdorf on luxury in *Les Principes de la pensée au siècle des lumières*, pp. 444–61.
8. See Lough's authoritative survey, *An Introduction*, pp. 64–97.
9. *Life and Letters in France*, p. 35.
0. Useful contributions are however beginning to appear; in addition to those already mentioned; see, for example, R. Galliani, 'Le Débat en France sur le luxe: Voltaire ou Rousseau?', *Studs. Volt.*, 161 (1976), pp. 205–17; H. Kortum, 'Frugalité et luxe à travers la querelle des anciens et des modernes', *Studs. Volt.*, 56 (1967), pp. 765–75; H. C. Payne, '*Pauvreté, misère* and the aims of enlightened economics', *Studs. Volt.*, 154 (1976), pp. 1581–92; Payne, *The Philosophes and the People* (New Haven and London: Yale University Press, 1976).
1. I have treated the subject in more detail in 'Voltaire's Poems on Luxury', *Studies in the French Eighteenth Century presented to John Lough* (University of Durham, 1978), pp. 108–22.

5 The Rise of Technology: *L'Encyclopédie* (1751–72)

The Planches

When one looks at the eleven volumes of plates which accompany the seventeen volumes of text in the *Encyclopédie*, one is struck perhaps above all by two things: first, as with the *Encyclopédie* articles, by the great range and quantity (there are nearly three thousand plates in all),[1] second, the technical accuracy and loving care for detail brought to this daunting task. The plates are mainly devoted to illustrating articles on the arts and crafts, though they also take in sciences and engineering and even on occasion fields wholly outside the artisan's world. Successful drawings require the utmost clarity, and this requirement has generally been met. One notes with admiring pleasure, for instance, the careful portrayal of the finger positions in the tapestry-weaving at the Gobelins[2] or the extensive detail in a picture showing how cardboard is made and the many tools involved.[3] For this work Diderot called on the help of craftsmen, many of them engravers or designers, like Goussier (his chief assistant on this side), Cochin *fils* (*garde des dessins du cabinet du roi*) or Soubeyran (who ran a drawing school in Geneva).[4] Goussier and Lucotte (another designer) did the drawings for more than 1500 plates between them. Although at least 40 designers and engravers were involved in the fabrication of the plates, only seven were employed regularly, and this probably explains the high degree of consistency which reigns throughout.[5] Many drawings, however, owe much to those which Réaumur had been preparing for publication under the aegis of the Académie des Sciences since 1711, and accusations of plagiarism were quickly flung at the *Encyclopédie* editors. While the charge is not wholly baseless, it should not be exaggerated. A very large part of the plates is based on original work, and even when this is not the case, an effort is made to go further than merely reproducing the borrowed illustration.[6]

In any case, what we have here is a wide record of eighteenth-century technology, described so that an intelligent layman can follow it without undue difficulty. There are detailed pictures of mining, glass-making, work with leather or textiles, on the land or in the iron foundries. Some of the heavy industries like mining were hard on health, dangerous, and exhausting. By contrast, at the other end of the spectrum the trade of silversmith and goldsmith was among the most privileged, limited to a very few ancient guilds in Paris, enjoying monopoly and royal protection in a way guaranteed to make Paris the jewellery and fashion centre of Western Europe. Glass-makers also were held in high esteem, the leading artisans even attaining to noble rank as 'gentilshommes – verriers'; the blowing of crown glass in particular was restricted to four Norman families who had held the privilege since the fourteenth century. The numerous excellent plates devoted to glass reveal one of the most successful areas of *Encyclopédie* investigation into arts and crafts, following up an article extending to no less than 64 pages in folio which gave an historical account of glass though the ages and then detailed the various methods, processes and tools of glass-working. The silk industry is another one commanding prestige and careful attention.[7] But inevitably the results are uneven and some areas are inadequately covered – Gillispie mentions the humbler side of the textile trade and parts of the iron industry as cases in point (p.xxii).

Two impressions make themselves irresistibly clear. The first destroys any myth of a pre-industrial craftsman's paradise. The slate-quarrymen carrying blocks weighing 200 pounds up the steep, narrow and uneven mine-shaft[8] seem no less alienated from any sense of humanity than their unfortunate descendants in the mills and foundries of the nineteenth century. But the illustrator attempts to make no case for them. He portrays them didactically, with total detachment, leaving it to us to see, if we wish, the dignity or the wretchedness of their toil. The second conclusion borne in upon the reader is that this world belongs irrevocably to the farther side of the Industrial Revolution. These machines, however complex, generally do no more than extend the power and skill of human hands. There is no awareness of the vast developments which steam will effect, giving a new power of its own beyond the mechanics operated by human energy or water power. The steam engine makes an appearance but is accorded only five plates, a derisory number compared with that lavished on, say, glass.

The technical articles and illustrations form a substantial, indeed essential part of the *Encyclopédie,* as its subtitle makes clear: it is a 'dictionnaire raisonné des sciences, des arts et des métiers'. As Diderot put it in the *Prospectus* to the *Encyclopédie*: 'On a trop écrit sur les sciences; on n'a pas assez bien écrit sur la plupart des arts libéraux; on n'a presque rien écrit sur les arts mécaniques'. The conclusions to be drawn seemed obvious: 'Tout nous déterminait donc à recourir aux ouvriers'. This they have done:

> On s'est adressé aux plus habiles de Paris et du royaume; on s'est donné la peine d'aller dans leurs ateliers, de les interroger, d'écrire sous leur dictée, de développer leurs pensées, d'en tirer les termes propres à leurs professions, d'en dresser des tables, et de les définir, de converser avec ceux de qui on avait obtenu des mémoires, et (pré-caution presque indispensable) de rectifier dans de longs et fréquents entretiens avec les uns, ce que d'autres avaient imparfaitement, obscurément, et quelquefois infidèlement expliqué.

They have proceeded methodically with their technical studies, as d'Alembert indicates in the *Discours préliminaire*: each article considers (1) the location of the subject, manner of preparation, qualities, kinds, operations; (2) the objects made from it; (3) the tools and machines employed; and gives (4) a precise definition of the technical terms. Like Descartes in his *Discours de la méthode,* the illustrators have worked from the simple to the complex in their designs, gradually constructing the most intricate machin-ery by the continuous assembling of the diverse elements.

The first volume of the plates did not appear till 1762 (the full eleven volumes came out in the next ten years), but the idea of including them in the *Encyclopédie* goes back to the early planning stages. At first, it would seem, the technical illustrations and probably the relevant articles too were to be derivative from such works as were available on the question. But by 1748 the new policy of direct observation in the workshops had been decided; and in 1750 when Diderot's *Prospectus* appears a minimum of 600 plates was promised. Many of the visits were lengthy and exhaus-tive, like Goussier's six-week stay at Montargis, 100 kilometres from Paris, to study the paper-making industry at the large l'Anglée factory there. Such an outlay became possible as the scope and capital investment developed, along with the mounting revenues from subscriptions.[9]

Why was so much attention paid to arts and crafts in the *Encyclopédie*? The answer is simple. If one were to offer a truly comprehensive account of the current state of human knowledge this side could no longer be neglected. In the past, says Diderot in the article 'Art', a distinction has been made between liberal and mechanical arts to the detriment of the latter: 'Cette distinction, quoique bien fondée, a produit un mauvais effet, en avilissant des gens très estimables et très utiles'. Since we accord greater status to liberal arts we encourage idleness and fill our towns with 'contemplateurs inutiles' and our countryside with petty tyrants. The balance must be redressed: 'aux yeux du philosophe il y a peut-être plus de mérite réel à avoir fait naître les Le Brun, les Le Sueur et les Audran, peindre et graver les batailles d'Alexandre, et exécuter en tapisserie les victoires de nos généraux, qu'il n'y en a à les avoir remportées'. The paradox is remarkable: 'nous exigeons qu'on s'occupe utilement, et nous méprisons les hommes utiles'. It follows that England, economically more advanced than France, is to be admired; Diderot repeats Voltaire's praise for England in the *Lettres philosophiques* as the land where merit and skill are properly rewarded, but in doing so he extends it to include English respect for French inventors of machines like the stocking frame (see the article, 'Bas').

Diderot does not pretend to originality in this approach. He ascribes the honour to Francis Bacon, comparing the latter's zealous empiricism with the unscientific scepticism of Montaigne and Descartes in practical matters: 'Bacon regardait l'histoire des *arts mécaniques* comme la branche la plus importante de la vraie philosophie' (see the article, 'Art'). Equally foresighted in Diderot's eyes was Colbert who, in Louis XIV's reign, established factories under royal protection. It was Colbert who had charged the *Académie des Sciences* in 1675 with the task of undertaking a systematic study of French industry, and not his fault if the project lost its impetus; Réaumur, as we have seen, had collected a large number of plates but published nothing on the subject before his death in 1757.[10] But there were other predecessors of equal significance whom Diderot does not mention: Fontenelle, important not only because as a true *philosophe* he had

ever since the *Entretiens sur la pluralité des mondes* (1686) practised
the art of popularising difficult scientific material, but because in
his rôle as permanent secretary of the Académie des Sciences
since 1697 he had supervised the publication of *Histoire et
Mémoires* by the Académie at the rate of about one volume a year,
editing and condensing with uncommon skill such works as
Réaumur's *L'Art de convertir le fer forgé* from 566 pages to sixteen;[11]
Locke, who had advocated technical schools in 1697; the abbé de
Saint-Pierre, who had advanced similar suggestions in 1728; the
founders of training establishments like the *Ecole des ponts et
chaussées* (1747), the *Ecole du corps royal du Génie* (1748), and the
Ecole royale militaire (1751). Public opinion was already quite
favourable to the new technological atmosphere.[12] Yet the *Encyclopédie* was the first publication in France to declare unambiguously how indispensable the artisan was to society. As F. G.
Healey points out, *homo faber* emerges as a true Enlightenment
archetype, working upon his material environment, aided by his
senses, necessity and reason, usefully employed and untrammel-
led by metaphysical considerations.[13]

One problem was immediately evident to Diderot and his colleagues. To use a machine with skill and to explain how one uses
it are two very different accomplishments. Hardly a dozen out of
a thousand men, says d'Alembert in the *Discours préliminaire*
know how to express themselves clearly about their work. The
Encyclopaedists found themselves with 'la fonction pénible et
délicate de faire accoucher les esprits'. The only solution was
often to obtain the machine oneself and learn the job on it. In so
doing they discovered another area of darkness, the vast ignorance of terminology which even the most literate man possessed
The task of acting as intermediary between worker and reader so
as to make the one intelligible to the other was enormous. Diderot
and his colleagues were facing the new methodological problem
of turning technology into literature so that it could be easily assi-
milated by the lay reader. Predecessors like Thomas Corneille
and Fontenelle had used technical terms, but not, as did the *Encyclopédie,* to describe the technique themselves or marry the explanations to the illustrative plates. As he makes clear in the article
'Encyclopédie', Diderot is aware of the changes taking place in
linguistic usage; vocabulary is becoming increasingly technical
and will continue to develop along these lines: 'la langue, même
populaire, changera de face'. The technical articles seek to define

the details of their subject as never before, according to a new mode that is not the incomprehensible jargon of the specialists but a style wherein 'l'objet se fait voir sans réfraction appréciable'.[14] Jacques Proust considers that Diderot may have done more for the progress of technology by the form of these articles than by their contents.[15]

The Encyclopaedists wished to learn one particularly important aspect of their artisans' work: they sought to unveil any trade secrets they could find. For if these productive forces were to be properly released for the good of the community, such jealously guarded strong-boxes must be sprung open. The enemy was the corporative guild system, backed by the weight of tradition and vested interests. Once again Diderot was in the van of the attack. In 'Chef-d'oeuvre' he criticises the institution of 'masterpieces' by whose technical quality was judged the capacity of journeymen to be received as full members, and points out the injustices we have already noted about these examinations. The article 'Maîtrises' (by Faiguet de Villeneuve) reinforces the point, arguing that so many who are bandits and idlers are potentially useful citizens whom the corporations have rejected. Elitism creates a dispossessed class, whereas a society open to talent would be hard-working and prosperous. So it was in accordance with their hostility to this closed system that the Encyclopaedists publicised, with full illustration, such prized details as for example those of blowing goblets,[16] the finest product of the glass industry and a very lucrative trade. One may easily guess the irritation of the goblet craftsmen! The *Encyclopédie* group were not always so successful, however. They did not discover, for instance, from the tinners what secret ingredient the latter added to make their molten tin stick on the sheet iron when applied to it. The reason for this may be found in another aspect of the guild's fight against outsiders. Civil war may often have existed within a guild, but in face of the growing entrepreneurial competition from without masters and journeymen necessarily found themselves on occasion in alliance against the aristocratic investors and the merchant-manufacturers who were seeking to free the labour market. As might be expected, circumstances often dictated a rearguard action from all ranks against wealthy bourgeois and noblemen outside.[17]

But despite all the attacks on vested interest and privilege the *Encyclopédie* should not be seen in crude Marxist terms as campaigning for the proletariat against the bourgeoisie. The aim is certainly to give greater recognition to 'the working class', but the term is anachronistic if it is thought of as connoting mass action. The time simply was not ripe. For all the increase in industrial production during the eighteenth century, there was very little concentrated factory work. Textile production, for instance, was almost wholly a rural craft, organized and dominated by merchant capitalists, leaving the town artisans at a very serious disadvantage.[18] So it is hardly to be wondered at that in the anonymous article 'Manufacture' the author's interest and sympathy are much more attracted to cottage industry ('manufactures dispersées') than to centralisation ('manufactures réunies'). One of the reasons given for this preference briefly anticipates the problems of the next century. The larger establishments encourage impersonality and harsh treatment: 'A la grande *manufacture* tout se fait au coup de cloche; les ouvriers sont plus contraints et plus gourmandés. Les commis accoutumés avec eux à un air de supériorité et de commandement, qui véritablement est nécessaire avec la multitude, les traitent durement et avec mépris....' But when we find the author arguing that it is dispersal, not concentration, of industry which makes for greater economy, we realise how far the assumptions governing his view are removed from ours. The *Encyclopédie*, in this as in other respects, was no pioneer in the technological realm. Yet, as Proust makes clear, Diderot and his colleagues are not backward-looking, they are basing their views on reality:

> Il est prouvé depuis longtemps que ce qu'on a appelé la grande industrie avait été au XVIIIe siècle une création exceptionnelle, et surtout artificielle, soutenue le plus souvent par le trésor royal, seul ou venant en aide à des capitaux privés. L'auteur de l'article *Manufacture* l'a fort bien montré, ce soutien ne pouvait s'admettre que dans l'industrie de luxe, eu égard à la perfection de ses produits.[19]

If the steam-engine plays such a small part in the *Encyclopédie* illustrations the reason is clear. Such engines as existed were more interesting than useful, and only a half-dozen were to be found in France. Diderot shows his fascination for this machine but not unnaturally fails to see its wider possibilities.[20] Even in England, where there were 20,000 spinning jennies by 1789, the use of steam power was barely getting under way (Hargreaves' spinning jenny dates from 1766, Arkwright's water-frame for spinning, which facilitated the change to factory production, from 1769). Diderot and his colleagues are concerned not with urban masses but with what they call 'artistes', a word well chosen to bring out the elements of individual skill, intelligence and technique involved. As was mentioned earlier, however, the attitude of the illustrators seems to be one of detachment. None of the plates appears to try to evoke compassion for the worker's lot; if anything, the somewhat antiseptic air of the plates often ignores some of the most frightful aspects of the job. The drawings of the blast furnace suggest an operation of almost ideal efficiency – it requires imagination to realise the filth and heat that would have been constant companions; it needs further information for us to know that the life of a blast furnace was short and full of menace for its workers, since explosions could happen at any time, with all the terrors wrought by flying pieces of iron, both solid and molten. Now this is not to argue a want of sensibility on the illustrators' part. The dangers of blast furnaces are in any case conveyed in the text. The *Encyclopédie* is not seeking to arouse pity for these artisans, whatever the private feelings of the artists drawing the pictures. It wishes to inform on the strictly technical aspects, and by informing to win respect for the seriousness and social utility of these workers' lives.[21]

It is therefore not surprising that the workers who helped Diderot and his team with their investigations have remained largely anonymous. Only a few are named amongst the collaborators and they almost all come from prestigious crafts like silk-weaving and watch-making, luxury industries. The other main group involved from the industrial world came from a higher stratum – factory owners and investors who moved in the best society and often had aspirations to the nobility. As Daniel Roche puts it of these collaborators as a group, 'Leur participation traduit plus une réhabilitation intellectuelle des arts manuels qu'une exaltation de la condition ouvrière ou artisanale':[22] The ordinary worker is as absent from the pages of the *Encyclopédie* as the ordinary peasant.[23]

Our rather special approach to the *Encyclopédie* therefore leads us to the same conclusions about social orientation as do the more 'philosophical' articles. It is a production essentially by and for the bourgeoisie. In the article 'Représentants' (by the baron d'Holbach) there is a strong plea for greater political participation by 'le peuple', who are described in phraseology reminiscent of Voltaire's in the *Lettres philosophiques* as 'la partie la plus nombreuse, la plus laborieuse, la plus utile de la société'; but it quickly emerges that what the writer has in mind is the enlightened property-owning bourgeois: 'des citoyens plus éclairés que les autres ... que leurs possessions attachent à la patrie'. In 'Le Peuple' the Chevalier de Jaucourt takes a somewhat more democratic line. Accepting that the only true candidates for membership of 'the people' are 'les ouvriers et les laboureurs', he permits himself to imagine what their daily existence is like. Here we see a humanitarian sympathy for the humble people who are so much subject to a hard life of poverty, as the chevalier enters a passionate protest against the taxes which are largely responsible for such misery. But one must note the limits to his plea. He is seeking to ameliorate the economic conditions of their lives; there is no indication that he wants them to play a more active political role in the nation.

Yet we must discriminate more closely in calling the *Encyclopédie* a bourgeois document. The mere fact that the last two articles are associated with aristocratic pens should in itself give us pause. The collaborators to the *Encyclopédie* formed an apparently heterogeneous group, as Proust points out.[24] Most of the 137 known authors listed in the Inventory of the *Encyclopédie*[25] belong to the *Tiers État*, but some, as we have seen, come from the nobility and there were a few clergy too. The *Parlements* and the Army were both represented. Some Encyclopaedists were rich, others poor. Perhaps the key to their unity lies in what they oppose; Diderot's words will serve for them all:

> 'Nous avons eu pour ennemis déclarés la cour, les grands, les militaires, qui n'ont jamais d'autre avis que celui de la cour, les prêtres, la police, les magistrats, ceux d'entre les gens de lettres qui ne coopéraient pas à l'entreprise, les gens du monde, ceux d'entre les citoyens qui s'étaient laissé entraîner par la multitude.[26]

They were opposed in general to those who upheld traditional hierarchies and values. While giving space, for instance, to articles and plates on armaments and war ('Armurier', 'Arquebusier', 'Militaire', for instance) they tended to share Diderot's view that craftsmen were more valuable than soldiers. The Encyclopaedists were on the whole modernists,[27] generally arrayed against long-standing privileges like the arbitrary taxation system, the forced conscription of the poor into the militia, the guilds, an unlimited monarchy, the authority of the Church.[28] They invoked the principles of experimental enquiry in pursuit of knowledge. Jean Ehrard usefully indicates how a belief in technical progress must underlie any hope of a more general advancement: 'Ceux qui savent l'importance des techniques de production dans l'organisation du bonheur social sont seuls en mesure de penser vraiment la condition humaine dans le futur'.[29] For d'Alembert it is this spirit of observation allied to rigorous experiment which distinguishes the moderns from the ancients (see the article, 'Expérimental'). The Encyclopaedic group drew heavily upon administrators, scientists, artists, men of letters, doctors, teachers, Academicians. By contrast business and commerce (unlike industry) are not represented. Quite surprisingly, the merchant capitalists who were playing such an important part in the most progressive sector of the economy[30] do not appear: could this be due to the influence of Physiocratic opposition to trade and finance? The *Encyclopédie* has its roots in the bourgeoisie, but in only a limited part of it, for the most part composed of property-owners comfortably off; the petty bourgeoisie is largely absent.

Despite some curious exceptions, the most striking aspect of this group is its association with creative enterprises, the modern sector of French society that saw progress in terms of a more productive economy, freed from the restrictive practices in the social, political, economic and philosophical domains that flourished under the Ancien Régime. By the nature of things they were in conflict with the Government. What they sought was a reformist policy under a hereditary monarch, but one whose power was limited as in Britain by the separation of powers which Montesquieu had discerned (see the article, 'Monarchie limitée', by Jaucourt). The King needed to be advised by men chosen as representatives of all interests in the nation – not only the clergy and nobility, but the judiciary, industry, commerce, agriculture; all are 'des hommes également nécessaires' (see the article, 'Représentants'). In the economic realm the *Encyclopédie* is equally liberal in acting as a home for Physiocrats like Quesnay, who claim that as agriculture is the only sector increasing the national wealth (since it alone achieves a clear profit) the government should free it of all restraints. These views were not

always compatible with the support for industrial enterprise tha
we have seen in the technological parts of the *Encyclopédie*, and
Diderot for one wavered in his views on Physiocracy,[31] but both
attitudes coincided in demanding greater liberty from th
Government. The Encyclopaedists did not desire or seek to
promote the Revolution of 1789, but they helped to pioneer, fo
all their limitations of foresight, the technical and industrial rev
olution that made its impact by the middle of the nineteenth
century.

The readers of the *Encyclopédie* seem to have come from broadly
the same social classes as its writers, with appreciable reinforce
ments from groups that had hung back from writing for it, such
as civil servants and the clergy. The work cost 980 *livres* in its orig
inal edition, with binding for the whole set of volumes adding a
further 160 *livres*.[32] That immediately made it prohibitive to
people of modest means, even if paid for over twenty years.[3]
Later editions were cheaper but still an expensive luxury. Yet the
work was a commercial success. The first edition attracted some
4000 subscribers; by the Revolution there were probably four o:
five times that number of copies available, perhaps half of them
in France.[34] The publishers made a profit of about 2,400,000
livres on the original edition alone.[35] It was indeed a large capital
ist enterprise; accordng to Voltaire its publication gave work to a
thousand men for more than 25 years[36]. So it is piquant to se
that when in March 1759 the *Conseil d'État du Roi* revoked the of
ficial privilege to print and forbade sale and distribution of the
volumes already published, the publishers' threat to take the
Encyclopédie abroad was itself enough to persuade the *Directeur d*
la librairie, Malesherbes, to give the work a *permission tacite* ir
order to continue appearing.[37] The forces of modernism had sym
bolically triumphed over the Establishment, and precisely fo
those economic reasons which the Encyclopaedists were putting
forward in their work.

The official ban on the *Encyclopédie* in 1759 sufficiently indicates the degree of opposition it encountered. The receptior
accorded the work in the press was at first almost wholly hostile
often virulently so. The Jesuit *Mémoires de Trévoux* began attacks
in 1751. Part of the reason was that their *Dictionnaire de Trévoux*
was being plagiarised by the *Encyclopédie,* but the attack turned
essentially upon a defence of the Christian religion. The Jansenist journals, notably *Les Nouvelles ecclésiastiques,* were more sple-

netic, in part perhaps because members of their faction like Chaumeix saw the need for preventing the Jansenist opposition to the Government from being bracketed with the Encyclopaedists. No French review acted, or could dare to act, as a staunch defender of the work (though the *Mercure* remained mildly sympathetic); its only allies were the *Journal encyclopédique*, which began appearing on foreign soil from 1756, and Grimm's *Correspondance littéraire*, which was a confidential news-sheet intended only for subscribers and not for general distribution.[38] The scandal which arose over the abbé de Prades's Sorbonne thesis in 1752 because of its inclinations towards natural religion spilled over onto the *Encyclopédie*, on which he had collaborated, and this led to the first royal edict forbidding printing and sale. But that prohibition lasted only three months and no further crisis occurred till 1757. It now seems evident that after 1752 Malesherbes officially discouraged further attacks on the dictionary.[39] But in 1757 the unlucky combination of Damiens's attempt upon the life of Louis XV, the appearance of d'Alembert's article 'Genève'[40] and, the following year, the publication of Helvétius's radical *De l'esprit* led to the stoppage in 1759 and definitive withdrawal of the official privilege to print. During this difficult time press attacks, notably from Fréron in *L'Année littéraire*, intensified the hostility. Polemical tracts were also appearing from enemies like Palissot, Chaumeix and Moreau, the last aping Voltairean satire in representing the Encyclopaedists as Cacouacs. Yet when the *Encyclopédie* resumed publication in 1762 with the first volume of the plates, the hostility was no longer so lively.[41] The *Encyclopédie* had been more an object of controversy in the 1750s. By the following decade its ideas did not appear so provocative. Nor should one read the story of the opposition too pessimistically; as Jacques Proust makes clear, the hostile attacks proved to be excellent publicity.[42]

The *Encyclopédie* was in its contents no revolutionary work but a summation of knowledge at mid-century and a body of ideas which, though sometimes contradictory because of the wide range of collaborators and the free hand given them by the editors, were generally liberal in temper. However, the principle behind the work was not yet a matter of universal agreement.[43] Diderot was well aware of the task he had undertaken, as his key article 'Encyclopédie' shows. The intention was to present as comprehensive a body of knowledge as a 'société de gens de lettres' could procure, positive knowledge not metaphysical spe culations, and centred on man, who alone gives meaning to the universe. Without man's presence, 'ce spectacle pathétique et sublime de la nature n'est plus qu'une scène triste et muette L'univers se tait; le silence et la nuit s'en emparent.' But with this knowledge one could 'changer la façon commune de penser'. The received body of opinion based on theological constructs could be critically reviewed, the constructs themselves dismantled as phenomena were investigated for their own sake without the intrusion of transcendental assumptions. The detailed inventory of knowledge assembled, affording a measure of control over the world, could lead to action, to an improvement of the human lot as the laws governing nature were better understood. By the broadcasting of knowledge men would become enlightened public opinion would be affected. The *Encyclopédie* was not any more successful than the Enlightenment *philosophes* in general in living up to this high ideal. They too were often bedevilled by unempirical concepts like natural law and human nature; more of their critical thinking than they realised came from their Chris tian background. Yet for the first time in Western Europe a group of intellectuals was seeking in a concerted way to influence public opinion. The new scientific spirit disseminated in the *Encyclopédie* was making an impact upon human attitudes, in education, laws politics, morality, religion and, as we have seen more particu larly, in technology. The *Encyclopédie* saw science as ultimately unified and capable of making a contribution in all fields. All knowledge derived from human experience, instigated by need and the search for happiness. By affirming this unity the Encyclo paedic group opened the way, as René Hubert says,[44] to sociol ogy as an intellectual discipline.

To conclude, let us return to the humbler level of the technical articles. They had an early, perceptible effect in stimulating new studies with the same aim as the *Encyclopédie*, to open up the secrets of manufacture and make them common knowledge From 1761 the Académie des Sciences at last began to publish its own long-meditated *Descriptions des arts et métiers*, often calling on Encyclopaedists' help. Official action moved in the same direc tion of encouraging industry and liberating it from restrictions.[4] In 1783 the Government set up the *École des Mines* for training mining engineers. Two years later the great Schneider foundry near Le Creusot was established with royal support, a modern plant on English lines, using coke rather than charcoal, the first blast furnace to do so in France (the process dated back to 1709 in England). The *Encyclopédie* did not cause all these developments, but it facilitated them by preparing the public for them. Though it did not foresee the Industrial Revolution, it would surely have welcomed the establishment of technocracy as a force for human progress. This great dictionary reflects, focuses and transmits the large changes taking place in social attitudes by the 1750s in France.

NOTES

1. Those without access to a copy of the *Encyclopédie* plates might find considerable consolation in C. C. Gillispie's edition of *A Diderot Pictorial Encyclopedia of Trades and Industry*, (New York: Dover, 1959), 2 vols., which selects nearly 500 plates, usefully classifies them by trades and reproduces them with excellent fidelity, generally to facsimile size. Most of the plates referred to here can be found in this edition. Another modern selection may be found in R. Barthes *et al.*, *L'Univers de l'Encyclopédie* (Paris: Les Libraires Associés, 1964).
2. Vol. IX (that is, of the original edition (Paris, 1762–72), 11 vols.), 'Tapisserie de Haute Lisse des Gobelins', Plate X.
3. Vol. II, 'Cartonnier', Plate I.
4. J. Proust, *Diderot et l'Encyclopédie* (Paris: Colin, 1962), p. 31.
5. J. Proust, *L'Encyclopédie* (Paris: Colin, 1965), p. 175.
6. Proust, *Diderot et l'Encyclopédie*, pp. 50, 54–5. See also J. Proust, 'La Documentation technique de Diderot dans "l'Encyclopédie"', *RHL*, 57 (1957), pp. 335–52.
7. The article 'Soie', probably by Diderot, draws on at least eight different technical sources (see J. Proust, 'La Documentation technique', p. 340).
8. Vol. VI, 'Minéralogie, Ardoiserie de la Meuse', Plate IV.
9. Proust, *Diderot et l'Encyclopédie*, pp. 49–56.
10. The *Descriptions des arts et métiers* based on his work was published in successive volumes, 1761–88. The allegation of plagiarism, raised first in 1759 against the *Encyclopédie* in this respect, has been much debated. J. Lough gives a measured answer, generally but not completely exonerating the Encyclopaedists: *The Encyclopédie* (Longman, 1971), pp. 86–90.
11. Proust, *L'Encyclopédie*, pp. 37–40.
12. Proust, *L'Encyclopédie*, pp. 44–5.
13. 'The Enlightenment view of "homo faber"', *Studs. Volt.*, 25 (1963), pp. 837–59.
14. Proust, *Diderot et l'Encyclopédie*, p. 218.

15. Proust, *Diderot et l'Encyclopédie*, p. 213. See the whole of this excellent section, 'Problèmes littéraires de la technologie', pp. 205–20.
16. Vol. X, 'Verrerie en Bois', Plates XIX, XX, XXII.
17. Hampson, *A Social History*, p. 19.
18. G. V. Taylor, 'Types of Capitalism in Eighteenth-Century France', *English Historical Review*, 79 (1964), pp. 493–4.
19. *Diderot et l'Encyclopédie*, p. 168.
20. *Diderot et l'Encyclopédie*, pp. 166–7.
21. A fascinating article on how to 'read' the plates has been written by J Proust, 'L'Image du peuple au travail dans les planches de l' "Encyclopédie"', *Images du peuple au dix-huitième siècle* (Colloque d'Aix-en-Provence 25 et 26 octobre 1969) (Paris: Colin, 1973), pp. 65–85.
22. 'Encyclopédistes et académiciens', *Livre et société dans la France du XVIII siècle*, Vol II, (Paris/The Hague: Mouton, 1970), p. 82.
23. Proust, *Diderot et l'Encyclopédie*, pp. 23–6. For a detailed account of the social background of all the collaborators in the *Encyclopédie*, see Proust, *Diderot e l'Encyclopédie*, Chapter I.
24. *L'Encyclopédie*, pp. 92–3. Lough is sceptical about the value of treating the contributors on a sociological basis (see *The Encyclopédie*, pp. 56–7).
25. R. N. Schwab and W. E. Rex, *Inventory of Diderot's* 'Encyclopédie, Vol. VI *Studs. Volt.*, 93 (1972), pp. 9–237.
26. M. Tourneux, *Diderot et Catherine II* (Paris: Calmann-Lévy, 1899), p. 431 cited in Proust, *Diderot et l'Encyclopédie*, p. 20.
27. In this regard see the interesting article by A. M. Wilson, 'The Philosophe in the light of the present-day theories of modernisation', *Studs. Volt.*, 58 (1967), pp. 1893–913.
28. One should not however oversimplify what is a highly complex picture. D Roche ('Encyclopédistes et académiciens', pp. 79–80) has drawn attention to the fact that the nobility who contributed to the *Encyclopédie* did not as a rule abandon any of their own particular privileges or activities.
29. *L'Idée de nature en France dans la première moitié du XVIIIᵉ siècle*, Vol. II (Paris Service d'Edition et de Vente des Publications de l'Education Nationale [hereafter S.E.V.P.E.N.], 1963), p. 740.
30. See G. V. Taylor, 'Types of Capitalism', pp. 479–87.
31. See E. M. Strenski, 'Diderot, for and against the physiocrats', *Studs. Volt.* 57 (1967), pp. 1435–55.
32. Lough, *The Encyclopédie*, p. 59.
33. A Lyons silk worker and his wife, for example, could expect to earn together not much more than 600 *livres* in a year (Proust, *Diderot et l'Encyclopédie*, p 61).
34. J. Lough, 'The Contemporary influence of the *Encyclopédie*', *Studs. Volt.*, 26 (1963), pp. 1072–3.
35. Proust, *Diderot et l'Encyclopédie*, p. 58.
36. Proust, *Diderot et l'Encyclopédie*, pp. 46–7.
37. One of the *Encyclopédie*'s most ardent supporters throughout had been Madame de Pompadour, and her influence here over the King must have been of importance. La Tour's famous portrait of her (1755) shows Volume IV of the work on the table beside her, along with Voltaire's *La Henriade* and Volume III of Montesquieu's *De l'esprit des lois*.

38. Proust, *L'Encyclopédie*, pp. 180–3.
39. Lough, *The Encyclopédie*, pp. 107–9.
40. See above, pp. 45–6 and below, 128ff.
41. Lough, *The Encyclopédie*, pp. 101–4, 111, 130.
42. *L'Encyclopédie*, pp. 184–5.
43. On the general implications of the *Encyclopédie*, Herbert Dieckmann has written a penetrating article, 'The Concept of Knowledge in the *Encyclopédie*', in *Essays in Comparative Literature*, edited by Dieckmann *et al.* (St Louis: Washington University Studies, 1961), pp. 73–107.
44. *Les Sciences sociales dans l'Encyclopédie* (Paris: Alcan, 1923).
45. *Diderot et l'Encyclopédie*, pp. 224–5.

6 Genevan Theatre and the Middle Classes: Jean-Jacques Rousseau (1712–78)

Lettre à d'Alembert (1758)

Most of the chapters in this section concentrate on life in Paris. The provinces, by contrast, tended to languish and cultural activity there lacked the brilliance and density of the capital, even though the provincial Academies went some way toward redressing the balance. A similar study on literature and society in eighteenth-century England might profitably look in some detail at a town like Bath; such profit is likely to be worthless when one considers France, unless the study is of a specialist nature. As Alexis de Tocqueville made clear (perhaps to the point of exaggeration),[1] Paris overwhelmed and devoured the provinces during the eighteenth century. So if one wishes to look at French cultural life outside Paris at this period, it is best to leave France altogether. The closest approach to autonomy is to be seen in the city and independent republic of Geneva. Even there, as we shall see, the social influences emanating from the French capital were strong.

In August 1756 d'Alembert visited Voltaire at his Genevan home *Les Délices* and had the pleasure of meeting many of the city's leading figures. The literary fruits of his stay were seen a year later in the article 'Genève' which he composed for the *Encyclopédie* and which appeared in Volume VII of that work in late 1757. In this article the author made two assertions about Geneva, both of them laden with consequences. A brief section devoted to the Genevan pastors claimed that they were often pure Socinians, believing in neither the divinity of Christ nor the eternity of Hell, and holders of a faith based on reason rather than revelation. The uproar heard from the Genevan church was considerable; it was one of the most important elements in the growing scandal over the *Encyclopédie* that was to lead to d'Alembert's withdrawal from the enterprise and to its condemnation in 1759; the eighth and subsequent volumes eventually appeared, but only after six years' delay.

The other section of d'Alembert's article to give offence was briefer still. The author expressed his regret that regular theatre was forbidden in Geneva. The inhabitants fear it, he says, not in itself but because it may infect the young with a taste for luxury and debauch. But surely this can be avoided by strict laws? Then the city would reap only benefits – an improvement in taste, 'une finesse de tact, une délicatesse de sentiment' such as one can scarcely learn elsewhere. If actors have such a bad reputation the reason is mainly to be sought in the public's contempt for them. Geneva, however, could begin from scratch, both respecting its actors and keeping them firmly within the law, and so acquire that rare phenomenon, 'une troupe de comédiens estimables', whose influence would gradually improve the status of their fellows everywhere else. D'Alembert sees a way by which Geneva can be the key to better theatrical conditions in France.

At first the controversy centred on the religious aspects of the notorious article, the pastors banding together to issue a statement in February rejecting its inflammatory statements on that subject. The remarks on the theatre, by contrast, led to one isolated reply, that of a friend of Rousseau, J.-F. Deluc, dated 26 April 1758, and appearing for the first time in the *Journal helvétique* in May. Deluc politely but firmly rejected d'Alembert's claims, both about actors and about Geneva. The city had no particular strengths which made it especially immune to vice, and the introduction of theatre was likely to 'ouvrir la bergerie au loup, pour qu'il abandonne avec les brebis sa férocité naturelle'.[2] The acting profession is prey to too many temptations, and the actors will seduce the good citizenry of Geneva, possessing as they do 'le malheureux talent de rendre le vice aimable' (p. 193). The matter is different in large cities, where theatrical performances are on balance an advantage; but in Geneva the moral harm would outweigh the cultural assets.

Deluc's reply is short and unremarkable, though it uses some of the same arguments as Rousseau. The latter's own *Lettre à M.*

d'Alembert sur les spectacles was, in fact, already complete by 9 March, when he offered it to the publisher Marc-Michel Rey.[3] If we are to believe Rousseau's *Confessions*, he composed the whole essay within three weeks, in a state of considerable emotion: 'En l'écrivant, que je versai de délicieuses larmes!'[4] Diderot had told him the previous December that the *Encyclopédie* article had been 'concerté avec des Genevois du haut étage', and Rousseau had been 'indigné de tout ce manège de séduction dans ma patrie'.[5] Already two subjective factors of key importance are apparent. Rousseau found distasteful the manipulation of Genevan affairs by French intellectuals for their own interests, assisted by upper-class Genevans betraying, as he saw it, their country's future welfare. As he was to reveal later,[6] it was also clear to him that Voltaire himself had had a considerable share in the article 'Genève', a further source of irritation.[7]

For several months Rousseau kept his work a close secret. It was sent to Rey in Amsterdam on 14 May (Leigh 645) and Rey dispatched printed copies to Paris on 21 August (Leigh 682). Rousseau had broken his silence by informing d'Alembert of the work's existence on 25 June (Leigh 659). D'Alembert, whatever his private feelings, immediately replied with courtesy, undertaking to act as censor for the work so that it might be approved for publication in France (Leigh 660); by mid-September Rousseau is writing that 'beaucoup de gens ont lu mon ouvrage' in Paris (Leigh 691).

After a brief section defending the Genevan pastors against the charge of heresy, Rousseau comes to the main burden of his letter. The argument, despite its somewhat casual composition, falls into two broad sections, the first and shorter dealing with moral, psychological and aesthetic questions, the second with social problems. From the outset it is clear that for Rousseau theatre-going is *ipso facto* a matter for censure. The very need indicates a lack of inner resources; ill at ease with himself, the spectator, in true Pascalian fashion, has to seek *divertissement* elsewhere. The experience, far from fulfilling the need, leaves the playgoer as dissatisfied as ever: 'L'on croit s'assembler au spectacle, et c'est là que chacun s'isole' (p. 21). But these are only the initial broadsides. Rousseau's main battle here is with those who hold that the theatre improves morality. This it cannot do, he claims, since it never directs taste but merely follows it. Even when our pity is aroused the emotion is flabby because disinterested, arising out of those natural instincts for sympathy of which Rousseau had already written in works like the *Discours sur l'inégalité* (1755); it has nothing at all to do with true virtue, which implies triumph after a struggle. As we walk out of the theatre we merely readjust to everyday life as our self-interested motives come into play. For this reason, tragedy has no morally cathartic effect. Reason alone can purge the passions, and reason does not operate in the theatre. Only laws, public opinion or the pleasure principle can influence morality; none of these is relevant to an audience at a play. Even tragedy has its dubious side, for it often encourages us to feel sympathy for the worst crimes; at best its effect is neutral: 'quelques affections passagères, stériles et sans effet' (p. 34).

But it is with comedy that the stage's capacity for demoralising its audience is seen to full effect. Rousseau selects Molière as the target for his criticism, because he is 'le plus parfait auteur comique dont les ouvrages nous soient connus' (p. 45); and by particular reference to *Le Misanthrope* he seeks to show how the playwright debases his portrait of Alceste, a basically noble character, in order to appeal to the taste of his audience. Comedy shows no respect for the family or old age. Its main defect, however, is that it focuses on romantic interest. The consequences of portraying love on the stage are always dangerous, Rousseau claims, even when the love affair is itself perfectly legitimate. Passions are aroused which in the outside world may be employed in more dubious pursuits:

> Qu'on nous peigne l'amour comme on voudra: il séduit, ou ce n'est pas lui ... Une si douce image amollit insensiblement le cœur: on prend de la passion ce qui mène au plaisir, on en laisse ce qui tourmente. Personne ne se croit obligé d'être un héros, et c'est ainsi qu'admirant l'amour honnête on se livre à l'amour criminel (p.74).

Nor is tragedy free of this same effect, regardless of its ostensible message: 'l'effet d'une tragédie est tout à fait indépendant de celui du dénouement' (p. 73).

What emerges clearly from this discussion is Rousseau's fatalistic view of the effect of passions when witnessed on the stage. He seems to overlook the possibility that drama may affect audiences for the better by broadening their understanding of human nature, whether sympathy or ridicule is involved. On the other hand he sees all too readily the anarchic possibilities inherent in either romance or satire on the stage. He exhibits a strong distrust of human nature, as being ever ready to give in to its worst inclinations under the influence of unhealthy social institutions. Whatever the limitations of this view, Rousseau has seized upon one element which concerns many playgoers today who would not subscribe to his other arguments: the highly artificial convention of orthodox theatre whereby one group (the audience) watches another group (the actors), who must somehow play to the audience while yet ignoring its existence. Rousseau's own unease at this split between audience and stage is manifest (though in his case the concern is felt more on moral than aesthetic grounds), and in the second part he will suggest remedies. It worries him that actors are not fully at one with what they are saying, that they are coldly calculating their effects on the audience, that their art is, as he puts it later, 'de se passionner de sang-froid' (p. 106). (The central argument of Diderot's *Paradoxe sur le comédien* (1773–78), that the successful actor is one who subdues his sensibility, is here already adumbrated.) It equally troubles Rousseau that the audience, like the actors, is not fully involved and not obliged to limit its imagination to what is going on before its eyes. Jean Starobinski considers that the most cogent arguments of the *Lettre* are to be found where Rousseau denounces 'la division des consciences, le "chacun pour soi" d'un plaisir privatisé, aliéné, où les forces comprimantes de l'amour-propre font échec aux forces expansives de la sympathie'.[8] For Rousseau, any moral enhancement that theatre might provide is nullified by the voyeuristic conditions under which it takes place.

The larger part of the *Lettre* is, however, reserved for describing the pernicious social consequences of introducing the theatre into Geneva. Rousseau, like Deluc, distinguishes between large and small towns. The former are already so corrupted by inequality, luxury, vain ostentation and *amour-propre* that theatre may even perform a service in keeping idle people from boredom and vice for a few hours. But in Geneva no such need is apparent. The people work hard, are self-sufficient, enjoy their home-made culture; time does not hang heavy on their hands. The result of bringing in a theatre would be a decrease in work, an increase in private and public expenditure, a growth in luxury; many will be forced to leave, there will be economic decline and disaster. This is but the most impersonal aspect of the matter, for Rousseau has not yet dwelt on the situation and influence of the actors. As we have observed, he sees acting as a mercenary and meretricious business, a kind of prostitution that inevitably degrades those who participate in it. Worse yet, it involves women as well as men, and for Rousseau, who believes that woman's place is in the home ('leur partage doit être une vie domestique et retirée', p. 117) and that biology commands her to be modest and sought after, the effect upon any decent woman must be to destroy her morally.

Geneva is in any case too small to support a theatre. The financial problems are insurmountable, the more so when one adds that people have to work hard simply to maintain a decent standard of living. Introducing theatre, furthermore, will upset or destroy many of the townspeople's present pursuits. What will happen to the Genevan's love of the countryside and hunting? Will not the *cercles*, those small clubs of a dozen or so members, come to an end? These societies where men can meet and discuss politics are virile institutions, unlike the modern way of life in polite society, based on salons run by women, a constrained and effeminate invention of Paris. Better a little drunkenness in the *cercles* ('Mais enfin, le goût du vin n'est pas un crime, il en fait rarement commettre, il rend l'homme stupide et non pas méchant': p. 146), even perhaps the occasional brawl, than 'le désordre des femmes' (p. 147)! For the one is frank and open, while the other places too much stress on the clever innuendo, the mental reservation.

Rousseau allows however for certain kinds of theatre. The *théâtres de la foire*, for instance, are acceptable, being temporary and, if coarse, at least openly and honestly so: 'il vaudrait mieux qu'une jeune fille vît cent parades qu'une seule représentation de l'Oracle' (p. 166). But this is merely a way of coming to terms with human vulgarity. Rousseau has a higher expectation of what can be achieved by general entertainments and he concludes his essay with some account of them. Above all he pleads for open-air amateur spectacles where all are actors and all are audiences, coming together in unfeigned delight, no one feeling discontent at another's social superiority. Similarly, in winter he advocates that dances be held, though only for engaged couples while their parents look proudly on. In such ways the Genevans will feel that patriotic spirit which will later, in Rousseau's

Contrat social (1762), be the essential basis for founding the General Will. Rousseau nostalgically recalls an evening from his childhood when the soldiers resting after their supper in the Place Saint-Gervais suddenly began dancing together; the spontaneous gaiety drew people from all around, families were united, everyone caught up in the general rejoicing. His father uses this moment of epiphany to impress a lesson upon him: 'Jean-Jacques, me disait-il, aime ton pays. Vois-tu ces bons Genevois; ils sont tous amis, ils sont tous frères ... tu ne trouveras jamais leur pareil' (p. 182,n).

It is perhaps of little significance for our present concerns that both d'Alembert and Rousseau are arguing a limited case, since neither deigns to consider the much more realistic possibility of a visiting company who will remain only for limited periods. However, by taking their stand on the issue: Theatre or no theatre? they raise the argument above the level of practical expediency. Rousseau's strictures are in the line of an anti-theatre tradition of great antiquity, at least as old as the time when early Christianity conquered paganism. In France no actor could receive the sacraments or be buried in consecrated ground. Voltaire had pointed the contrast in his *Lettres philosophiques* (1734) between the English actress Mrs Oldfield, buried with honour in Westminster Abbey in 1730, and Adrienne Lecouvreur who died in the same year and whose body was 'jeté à la voirie'.[9] His various interventions on behalf of actors of the Comédie Française, especially between 1730 and 1734, may have helped to change the psychological climate, but the effects were not immediately apparent.[10] In 1738 the Paris Parlement included actors in the ranks of 'hommes diffamés dont le crime est aussi public que la profession qu'ils exercent est solennellement défendue'.[11] Although the obstacles raised were so draconian that certain dioceses like that of Rennes apparently did not invoke them,[12] it is clear that actors' lives were governed by discrimination and insecurity, the more bitterly ironic because the members of the Comédie Française enjoyed success and official recognition. Plays at the Comédie Française, as at the other royal theatres (the Comédie Italienne, the Opéra and the Opéra Comique), were organised by the Government through the *Intendants des menus*, who were *gentilshommes de la chambre du roi*, and the players had to put up with a highly authoritarian system. Their appointment, remuneration and conduct were subject to strict control, as was the choice of plays to be performed; in return the Comédie Française received an annual subsidy.[13] Infractions of the rules were punished by imprisonment at Fort-l'Evêque, kept specially for actors. In the circumstances, being treated as outlaws they not surprisingly behaved like them, provoking regular scandals. F. C. Green found that the police inspectors' reports for 1739–49 contained on almost every page an allusion to the love affairs of some actress or other.[14]

In the Introduction to his edition of the *Lettre* Fuchs traces the development of the quarrel in France about theatre from the time of Bossuet's intervention against it in 1694. Bossuet's *Maximes et Réflexions sur la Comédie* had stated the principal objections to the *genre*: it ridicules virtue and countenances corruption, it excites the passions and excuses love as a weakness; furthermore, it is so much more dangerous than a book because it is presented as a living phenomenon and takes place in a collective atmosphere where emotion can be easily stirred up. Opposition to the theatre was not lacking in the years between 1694 and 1758.[15] One of the most successful of these attacks, Desprez de Boissy's *Lettres sur les spectacles* (1756), went through seven editions in 24 years. Boissy anticipates Rousseau in noting with pleasure that no theatre exists in Geneva and condemning the presentation of emotion on the stage as blunting our capacity for genuine feeling. Arrayed against such views were many *philosophes* and most notably Voltaire. In *Le Monde comme il va* (1748) Voltaire had his hero attend two collective celebrations. The first, where 'un mage' holds forth in boring and useless banalities, is a church, the second, where the naïve hero thinks he hears 'les prédicateurs de l'empire', so edifying and beautiful are the sentiments expressed, is a playhouse. The provocative juxtaposition is not purely anti-clerical but a plea for the human dignity and cultural value of the theatre.

Yet the Paris theatre had its unsavoury side too, as Voltaire would be well aware. There were first of all the *théâtres de la foire* with their vulgar knockabout farces, and the *théâtres des boulevards* which were emerging at the time of Rousseau's *Lettre*. Writers like Mercier and Pixérécourt, themselves dramatists and committed to the cause of theatre, nevertheless deplored the moral corruption revealed by this popular element, which Bachaumont in his *Mémoires secrets* labelled as 'l'école de tous les vices'.[16] In order to prevent public disorder at the Comédie Française there was a permanent detachment of guards on duty.[17] On occasion the numbers were augmented, sometimes to a considerable degree, if Beaumarchais's figure of 184 soldiers for each performance of *Le Barbier de Séville* (1775) is anything to go by.[18] The Comédie Française incurred the charges of bad taste, frivolity, inconstancy and rowdyism, while some of the customs of theatregoers suggest that the play was not the thing for which primarily they went. Until 1759 the usage prevailed of putting seats on the stage, long after it had become a painful frustration because of the growing need for spectacle and movement in eighteenth-century theatre. The stage, in the form of a semi-ellipse, was 9.4 metres broad at the front at its widest part; but the spectators restricted the actors to only 4.6 metres in front and 3.4 metres at the back.[19] These seats generally attracted rich male aristocrats, often princes of the blood who paid dearly for the privilege of being so conspicuously seen (a financial consideration that immediately explains why the custom survived so long). Both Voltaire, in the 'Dissertation sur la tragédie' which acts as a Preface to *Sémiramis* (1749), and Diderot in his *Entretiens sur le Fils naturel* (1757), objected to the practice as inimical to dramatic action. Eventually it was abolished, but only because the comte de Lauraguais paid a considerable sum to the actors in lieu of lost revenues. Only when the custom had disappeared could one say that, in Barbier's words, 'L'action des acteurs est libre et l'illusion est bien mieux conservée'.[20] Even so, the improvement was only partially successful.[21]

But at the time one bad practice was disappearing another was just beginning. From about mid-century (the earliest mention would seem to occur in abbé de La Porte's *Spectacles de Paris* in 1757, where it is referred to as an innovation), the Comédie Française had been hiring out private boxes (*petites loges*) on the lucrative basis of 500 *livres* per annum. Possessing grilled fronts, so that they guaranteed privacy for the occupants while the latter surveyed all else, the boxes were to become very popular and go on increasing throughout the years up to 1789, at the expense of the other places in the theatre. In each box 'règne en beauté une reine tyrannique, qui n'est venue au spectacle que pour être courtisée; l'ouverture sur la scène compte moins que la porte sur le couloir', comments Starobinski, who goes on to cite the famous remark from Mercier's *Tableau de Paris* (1783–89): 'Il faut donc, quand on est femme, avoir dans une *petite loge* son épagneul, son coussin, sa chaufferette; mais surtout un petit fat à lorg-

nettes...'[22] Here, it would seem, the activities on the stage were
a mere excuse for the real drama taking place in the individual
boxes, which had become, in Green's phrase, 'véritables bou-
doirs'.[23] The occupants were so noisy that it was hard for the rest
of the audience to follow the play.[24] This development of the
petites loges is of course mainly posterior to the composition of
Rousseau's *Lettre*, but it merely accentuates the trend of aristocratic theatregoing,[25] which revolved around love intrigues and
social gossip rather than the play, as numerous references in
eighteenth-century novels make clear. Here we are at the opposite extreme from Rousseau's ideal of total and universal involvement, and one perceives very clearly the attitude, based on idle,
sophisticated self-indulgence and luxury, against which he
inveighed so forcefully in his work.

But what of the situation in Geneva? Here the struggle over establishing a theatre had been going on ever since 1617, when its
prohibition had come within the domain of the sumptuary laws.
A fairly clear-cut social distinction developed between the
opponents of theatre, mainly drawn from the less privileged
classes, and its supporters, who were especially to be found
among the aristocratic sections of the community. This latter
group looked towards Paris for its culture and was eager to
import the *mores* of French polite society; so eighteenth-century
Geneva witnessed repeated instances of plays brought in by visiting troupes or put on by Genevans being repressed each time by
the authorities, with the *Consistoire* (the body of Genevan pastors)
actively hostile to any such innovations. As Michel Launay
makes clear,[26] the cause of theatre became central to the whole
Genevan policy towards France. The aristocrats were only too
happy to avail themselves of the protection offered by France
through its *Résident* at Geneva, who was himself active in promoting the introduction of a dramatic troupe. In 1737 Jean du Pan,
then *Procureur Général*, defended the value of such a policy,
arguing that theatre 'châtie et corrige en badinant les mauvaises
habitudes et les ridicules, avec beaucoup plus de succès que les
Prédications les plus austères'; it would give entertainment and
have the decided political advantage of diverting the people from
criticising the government.[27] That same year French influence
secured the entry of a troupe of players, but they went bankrupt
and a year later withdrew ignominiously. Against all blandish-
ments in favour of staging plays the *Consistoire* stood firm. In

1748, for instance, it raised strong objection to a performance of Corneille's *Polyeucte* in a private house (even though the tragedy was played, as the *Consistoire* admitted, with perfect decorum and no mingling of sexes, as all the rôles were taken by girls), on the grounds that it was 'une chose défendue' and could set a bad example.[28] The very innocence of the way the play was put on demonstrates the *Consistoire*'s alertness and total intransigence on the theatre issue. But the opposition was not only religious, as Launay demonstrates by quoting from the work of François Delachanas. The latter, a shopkeeper and artisan, in his *Portrait raccourci de Genève enjouée* (begun in 1697) links up an attack on the theatre with a general fulmination against the importing of libertine and effeminate French ways. He affirms the need to maintain the good old simple customs against the foreigner, and amongst others he blames the pastors for acting as the lackeys of the aristocracy.[29] It becomes clear, therefore, that the picture is more complex than it has been represented heretofore, even by Fuchs in his generally reliable edition.

Voltaire's arrival in Geneva in 1755 added a further complication for the natives. Here was the exemplar of Parisian culture in their midst, and although aristocrats like his doctor Théodore Tronchin and some of the more intellectual pastors welcomed his arrival, he was quickly to incur the wrath of the authorities by performing plays at *Les Délices* before guests. The article 'Genève' by d'Alembert therefore appears as a key element in the mounting struggle over the place of sophisticated culture in Genevan life, a struggle in which, as Peter Gay says, Voltaire and Rousseau acquire symbolic rôles.[30]

Rousseau's picture of Genevan society in the *Lettre* represents it less as it was then as it should be. Grimm said as much in his *Correspondance littéraire* when reviewing the work,[31] and he was not alone. Théodore Tronchin, for instance, pointed out that the city's morality was far from emulating the purity of Sparta, to which Rousseau had admiringly referred (Leigh 734). He claimed that the *cercles* which Rousseau had praised so much were in reality a source of idleness and dissipation. Fathers, spending too much time away from home, were ceasing to exercise parental responsibility and children were running wild; the problem was exacerbated in those families where the mother also went off to her own *cercle*. Rousseau's reply was an acknowledgement that such abuses existed; but, he claimed, worse ones would occur if the clubs ceased to function (Leigh 743). The pastor Jacob Vernet, while pointing out that there was less drunkenness than Rousseau supposed, thought that the clubs did not perform a useful political function and that those for the young were morally corrupt (Leigh 742). In 1745, at least, the *cercles* (of which at that time about 50 existed) had given the ruling authorities cause for concern because of the troubles arising from over-indulgence in wine; these abuses had apparently first made their appearance about 30 years before and gone on increasing ever since. No action was taken however by the *Petit Conseil*, the main legislative body before whom the complaint was heard (Leigh appendix 196); and judging from the above letters of Tronchin and Vernet, the disorderliness had continued unabated after that.

Was Rousseau merely being perverse or blind, in arguing the claims of these clubs, considering their notorious fondness for alcohol? His reply to Tronchin suggests otherwise. In developing his argument, Rousseau refuses to accept Tronchin's pessimistic evaluation of Genevan society. Our artisans, he says, are not like those in other countries: 'Un horloger de Genève est un homme à présenter partout; un horloger de Paris n'est bon qu'à parler de montres'. He goes on to claim that in this respect he knows, better than his correspondent, whereof he speaks: 'Cet état des artisans est le mien, celui dans lequel je suis né, dans lequel j'aurais dû vivre, et que je n'ai quitté que pour mon malheur'. The trouble in Geneva lies rather with the whole social order. Corruption spreads from the rich downwards and there is no proper education to inculcate a true sense of values in the ordinary people.

Rousseau's unequivocal position colours his whole approach to the theatre question in the *Lettre*. The clubs were, as he makes clear, places of political discussion; as he well knew, they provided an effective means of organising opposition to the established government.[32] We have already noticed the passage, coming as a sort of climax in the work, where the author recalls with joyful pride that evening in the Place Saint-Gervais. Jean-Louis Du Pau, a Genevan aristocrat, interpreted the incident quite differently: it was clearly a sordid debauch where the most abject women of Geneva had left their beds to join drunken soldiers emerging from the tavern. If Rousseau's father had given him any useful advice, it must have been never to open his mouth about such a shameful spectacle outside of Geneva for fear of shaming all his fellow-citizens.[33] The contrast is dramatic and it is impossible now to decide which portrait is nearer the actual truth. One may more fruitfully consider instead the relationship of Rousseau the boy who watched such scenes to Rousseau the author of the *Lettre*. Launay carefully delineates the tradition of political involvement in Rousseau's family.[34] His grandfather had been one of the ringleaders of the popular revolt in 1707 and was closely associated with the uprising in 1718. His father Isaac was obliged to flee from the city definitively in 1722, for reasons connected with politics, when Rousseau was only ten years old. Although a *Citoyen*, and therefore technically of the highest class in Geneva, Isaac clearly belonged to the 'gens du bas', and the result of an altercation with 'un homme du haut', a landed proprietor and French army officer who technically belonged to a lower order, was permanent exile.

It is this complicated social status that helps to explain Rousseau's views on Geneva at this time. The social order was divided into five classes, namely, in descending order, the *Citoyens, Bourgeois, Natifs, Habitants*, and *Sujets*.[35] In practice the *Sujets* were virtually devoid of rights, and in the period that concerns us the *Citoyens* and *Bourgeois* made common cause, enjoying a variety of economic and political privileges. When Rousseau therefore entitles his *Lettre*: 'J.-J. Rousseau, Citoyen de Genève', it is essential not to read this as pure egalitarianism but as a proud assertion of the rights to which he was born. Were that all, however, he would be simply an aristocrat, defending his ancient privileges and in all probability arguing for the introduction of theatre to the city. The reality of his social setting is quite different. He acquired from his family a tradition of independent thinking and reading, on his mother's side he could pretend to more elevated origins; but he grew up in humble circumstances, and Rousseau as a child witnessed the crucial moment of social *déclassement* at the age of five when the family literally ceased to be 'gens du haut', moving from the *haute ville* to the popular quarter.[36] His father's flight five years later and his own subsequent apprenticeship engraved on him a sense of social injustice which never thereafter left him through all his painful experiences as lackey, tutor, secretary, musician, in a life filled with humiliation and poverty. By 1750 and the publication of his *Discours sur les sciences et les arts* he had become resigned to failure and was bitter about the poisonous atmosphere of Parisian culture against which he could do nothing. For a while, especially when finding an agreeable inter-lude in Lyons in the early 1740s, he was tempted to see luxury and inequality with a complacent eye, as the *Epître à Monsieur Parisot* (1742) shows; but, like Voltaire in 1726, he moved on from security and comfort to define himself more clearly.[37] Fargher points out that by accepting the patronage of rich men and the *philosophe* party Rousseau could have amassed a fortune at least as easily as the less talented Marmontel, who by his fifties pos-sessed a comfortable capital of 130,000 *livres* securely invested.[38] But, characteristically, Rousseau's works are not concerned with money; and for the *Lettre à d'Alembert* he received only 720 *livres*.[39] This work springs from a strong sense of injustice. Nothing in his life fitted him for sympathising with the rich and sophisticated of Geneva; nor on the other hand did he have any particular interest in the rootless servility of the lower classes. The true life-blood of its society, in his view, came from the middle class, the skilled art-isans, who reflected a way of life based on austerity, hard work, Biblical culture and republicanism.

In political terms the aspirations of this section of the com-munity were clear-cut. In theory the *Conseil Général* (formed of *Citoyens* and *Bourgeois*) was sovereign; but in practice real power had since the middle of the sixteenth century come to be dele-gated to the *Grand Conseil* (of 200 members) and above all to the *Petit Conseil* (of 25 members). It was the aim of the various upris-ings in the eighteenth century to win back these lost rights; in 1758 the rebels were as far from success as ever. So Rousseau had, in the words of his contemporary Formey, turned his gaze towards Geneva but had really seen a utopia.[40] Yet Venturi is surely right to insist that 'one of the springs of Rousseau's politi-cal thought lay in this very contrast between reality and vision, in this desire to see the ideal republic in the survival of the archaic Genevan constitution'.[41]

According to Grimm there were at least 300 replies to Rouss-eau's *Lettre* in the year after its publication.[42] Unfortunately for the author his only support came from the religious party. Others like Théodore Tronchin or d'Alembert were polite, even compli-mentary, but kept their distance. It became a commonplace to point out, as La Porte did in his long review for *L'Observateur lit-téraire* (20 October 1758), the discrepancy between this work and Rousseau's earlier writings for the theatre.[43] Voltaire maintained that in reality Geneva was wildly enthusiastic for plays: 'la comédie ... devient le troisième sacrement de Genève'.[44] As was to occur later with the *Contrat social*, Rousseau's ideas were attacked by his enemies and not defended by those in Geneva for whom he had written, and eventually in 1763, after mounting disillusionment, he renounced his citizenship of the city. Another break was already upon him in 1758. The *Lettre à d'Alembert* marked the definitive parting of the ways with the *philosophes*, at a time when they were already on the defensive over Helvétius's *De l'esprit*. Voltaire found this desertion at such a critical moment unforgivable. Henceforth Rousseau was a man in virtual isolation, drawing both pleasures and pains from that.

On the immediate issue however he triumphed. His *Lettre* ensured that no theatre would be established in Geneva for a long while. A further attempt made by the French in 1766 was defeated and the institution was confirmed as a symbol of foreign interference. Not till 1782 did the local aristocrats finally win their point.[45] Thus, after Rousseau's intervention, the theatre in Geneva became a clear demarcation of the classes;[46] to defend it one had to justify the existence and increase of oligarchic rule and social injustice. For over twenty years no one was to succeed in overcoming Rousseau's eloquent denunciation of alien customs and support for Genevan independence against the constant threats from France and Savoy. Never, perhaps, has drama as a *genre* been more politicised.

At one stage near the end of his *Lettre*, Rousseau envisages the possibility, as in ancient Greece, of patriotic and popular tragedy, though he is not very enthusiastic about its capacity for success (pp. 160–2). What would he have thought of the collective demonstrations of patriotism under the Revolution, mounting to the great massacres of 1793–94? It is another aspect of the old question as to whether Rousseau is a totalitarian. Given what we know of his fundamental need for liberty, it is hard to believe that he would have been anything but horrified. Nonetheless, some of the seeds of those communal events may be discerned in the *Lettre*, notably the demand for transparent hearts and feelings which can so easily lead, if unchecked, to an intolerant opposition of those with more complex attitudes of mind. More truly liberal are Rousseau's fierce denunciations of the ways an oligarchy conserves and builds on its instruments of inequality. In the *Encyclopédie* we witnessed a staunch defence of the artisan; but the artisan is himself silent, object not subject. With Rousseau the true voice of a class as yet foreign to literature is at last heard, even if ironically the audience for whom he wrote failed to recognise the importance of the new phenomenon.

NOTES

1. Alexis de Tocqueville, *L'Ancien Régime et la Revolution* (1856).
2. *Lettre à M. d'Alembert sur les spectacles*, edited by M. Fuchs (Lille/Genève: Giard/Droz, 1948), Appendice III, p. 192. All references to Rousseau's *Lettre* will be taken from this edition.
3. *Correspondance complète de Jean-Jacques Rousseau*, edited by R. A. Leigh (Geneva, Banbury and Oxford, 1965–?), Vol. V, no. 626. References to the Rousseau Correspondence will hereafter be cited as Leigh and the appropriate number.
4. *Oeuvres complètes*, edited by B. Gagnebin and M. Raymond (Paris: NRF, Pléiade), Vol. I (1964), p. 496.
5. *Oeuvres complètes*, pp. 494–5.
6. 'Je n'ignorais pas que l'article Genève était en partie de M. de Voltaire; quoique j'aie eu la discrétion de n'en rien dire, il vous sera aisé de voir par la lecture de l'ouvrage que je savais en l'écrivant à quoi m'en tenir', Rousseau to Vernes, 22 October 1758 (Leigh 715).
7. Voltaire's part in the article is generally agreed by modern scholars; see, for example, R. Pomeau, *La Religion de Voltaire*, 2nd edition (Paris: Nizet, 1969), p. 304; R. Naves, *Voltaire et l'Encyclopédie* (Paris: Presses Modernes, 1938), pp. 38–45.
8. *L'Invention de la liberté, 1700–1789*, p. 100. See also Starobinski, *Jean-Jacques Rousseau: La transparence et l'obstacle* (Paris: Gallimard, 1971), pp. 116–9.
9. Lanson edition, Vol. II, p. 159.
10. P. M. Conlon, *Voltaire's literary career from 1728 to 1750*, pp. 116–20.
11. Cited in the Fuchs edition, p. x, note 1.
12. Fuchs edition, p. x, note 2. Sometimes too the rules were winked at; for instance, an actor would resign for 24 hours in order to get married, with the connivance of the priest.
13. F. C. Green, *The Ancien Régime*, pp. 47–8.
14. In *La Peinture des mœurs de la bonne société dans le roman français de 1715 à 1761* (Paris: P.U.F., 1924), p. 194.
15. See the Fuchs edition, Bibliography, pp. 197–204; M.M. Moffat, *Rousseau et la querelle du théâtre au XVIII* siècle* (Paris, 1930).
16. J. Lough, *Paris Theatre Audiences in the Seventeenth and Eighteenth Centuries*, p. 209.
17. H. Lagrave, *Le Théâtre et le public à Paris de 1715 à 1750*, pp. 55–8.
18. C. Alasseur, *La Comédie Francaise au 18* siècle*, p.31.

19. Conlon, *Voltaire's literary career*, pp. 95–6; Lagrave, *Le Théâtre et le public*, p. 77 and figure 3.
20. *Journal d'un bourgeois*, April 1759, edited by Bernard, p. 282. Barbier had previously made the obvious point: 'Il n'était pas même vraisemblable qu'un roi parlant à son confident, ou tenant un conseil d'Etat, ou un prince avec sa maîtresse parlant en secret, fussent entourés de plus de deux cents personnes'.
21. Lagrave, *Le Théâtre et le public*, pp. 112–13.
22. *L'Invention de la liberté*, p. 100.
23. *La Peinture des mœurs*, p. 201.
24. Alasseur, *La Comédie Française*, p. 28.
25. Boxes had existed before: the innovation of the *petites loges* was to confer a long-term hire, thereby making them into a much more personal property of the occupants.
26. *Jean-Jacques Rousseau: écrivain politique, 1712–1762* (Cannes/Grenoble: Coopérative d'Enseignement Laïc/A.C.E.R., 1971), p. 49. See also H. Lüthy, *La Banque protestante en France de la Révocation de l'Edit de Nantes à la Révolution* (Paris, S.E.V.P.E.N., 1959–61), 2 vols., Vol. II, pp. 54–5.
27. Launay, *Jean-Jacques Rousseau*, p. 50.
28. Leigh, *Correspondance complète*, Vol. V, app. 197.
29. Launay, *Jean-Jacques Rousseau*, pp. 46–8.
30. *The Party of Humanity* (Weidenfeld and Nicolson, 1964), pp. 71–2.
31. 1 February 1759, edited by M. Tourneux (Paris: Garnier, 1877–82), 16 vols., Vol. IV, pp. 75–8.
32. Launay, *Jean-Jacques Rousseau*, p. 20; Leigh, *Correspondance complète*, Vol. V, p. 213, note *c*.
33. Launay, *Jean-Jacques Rousseau*, p. 21.
34. *Jean-Jacques Rousseau*, pp. 15–26.
35. A detailed description is given by Launay, *Jean-Jacques Rousseau*, pp. 34–43. See also P. Gay, *Voltaire's Politics: The Poet as Realist* (New York: Vintage, 1965), Chapter IV; Gay, *The Party of Humanity*, pp. 65–71.
36. Launay, *Jean-Jacques Rousseau*, pp. 14–15.
37. For a useful brief account of these early years, see G. R. Havens, 'The road to Rousseau's *Discours sur l'inégalité*', *Yale French Studies* 40 (1968), pp. 18–25. All was not adversity, however; Rousseau received over 5,000 *livres* for *Le Devin du village* (1752): Lough, *An Introduction to Eighteenth Century France*, pp. 242–3.
38. *Life and Letters*, p. 109. See Lough, *Writer and Public*, pp. 233–4.
39. Lough, *Writer and Public*, p. 210. Only *Emile* (1762) of his later works brought him much money; for it he received 6000 *livres*. Towards the end of his life he had amassed an annuity of 1600 *livres*, mainly by selling the rights to an edition of his complete works.
40. F. Venturi, *Utopia and Reform in the Enlightenment*, p. 77.
41. *Utopia and Reform in the Enlightenment*, p. 77.
42. J. Guéhenno, *Jean-Jacques* (Paris: Gallimard, 1962), 2 vols., Vol. II, p. 17. See also R. Trousson, *Rousseau et sa fortune littéraire* (Saint-Médard-en-Jalles: Ducros, 1971), pp. 17–21.
43. 'On le lira avec plaisir, et on ira de là au *Devin de village*'; cited by Leigh, Vol. V, p. 190.

44. That is, after the only two sacraments permitted by the Calvinist faith, baptism and communion: letter to d'Alembert, 2 September 1758, Best. D 7842.
45. Fuchs edition, pp. xxxix–xli.
46. See P. Chaponnière, *Voltaire chez les calvinistes* (Paris: Perrin, 1936), pp. 161–2.

7 Commerce, Class-distinction and Realist Drama: Sedaine (1719–97)

Le Philosophe sans le savoir (1765)

Like Rousseau, Michel-Jean Sedaine was an artisan; like Rousseau's, Sedaine's life became harder in childhood, when at the age of thirteen he witnessed the financial ruin of his father. Both found themselves in exile at an early age; for Sedaine, the change in family fortunes meant leaving home in Paris and settling in the Berry. But there the likenesses stop: a useful reminder of the pitfalls which beset those who try to explain writers purely by social and family origins. Sedaine's artisan status was as important in determining a career as Rousseau's had been; but the specific nature of the results is very different.

Sedaine came back to learn his trade as a mason in Paris, was fortunate to find a patron in the architect Baron, who recognised his literary talent, and from 1752 he enjoyed success as a writer. In 1756 his first play was performed, a comic opera entitled *Le Diable à quatre*, performed at one of the *théâtres de la foire*. This was to be his most characteristic type of production; of some 40 plays which he composed 33 can be called comic operas,[1] put on at either one of the fairgrounds or the Théâtre-Italien after it merged with the Opéra-Comique in 1762. His apparently effortless skill in constructing simple, fluent plays drew a gracious tribute from Vigny in 'La Veillée de Vincennes' (1834). Not surprisingly, critics have traced this talent to the apprenticeship Sedaine served in the fairground theatres, under conditions where complex intellectual devices would simply have gone unrecognised and even unheard by the audience. Be that as it may, it was in 1765 that he produced his best-known play, *Le Philosophe sans le savoir,* exceptionally at the Comédie Française; unlike most of his dramatic works, little in it is comic and nothing operatic.

The play seems to have its origins in a complicated set of circumstances going back five years. In 1760 Palissot, a writer of the anti-Encyclopaedist party, had given the Comédie Française a play called *Les Philosophes* which enjoyed for a time a *succès de scandale* on account of its audacious satire upon writers like Helvétius, Duclos, Diderot and Rousseau.[2] The *philosophes* are portrayed as dangerous scoundrels, tearing the social fabric to pieces by their doctrine of cynical self-interest, which clearly refers to the main thesis of Helvétius's materialist essay, *De l'esprit* (1758). Smarting under the recent troubles which they had encountered when the *Encyclopédie* was obliged to cease publication, the victims were keen to hit back. Diderot was particularly irritated by his appearance in the play as the ignoble Dortidius. And though by this time, as we have seen, Rousseau was no longer a member of the group, the manner in which he was treated seemed especially scurrilous. Thinly disguised, he appears near the end of the play on all fours, proclaiming as he does:

> En nous civilisant, nous avons tout perdu,
> La santé, le bonheur, et même la vertu.
> Je me renferme donc dans la vie animale;
> Vous voyez ma cuisine, elle est simple et frugale
> (Il tire une laitue de sa poche). (III, 9)

Such defamations clearly deserved a riposte. Various expressions of indignation found their way into print and onto the stage, among them Voltaire's play *L'Ecossaise* (1760) which, less than two months after *Les Philosophes,* was to enjoy even greater success;[3] but a feeling persisted that the retort was not yet enough. (Diderot himself was to brood over Palissot for some years and execute his revenge in *Le Neveu de Rameau,* though that did not appear publicly till the nineteenth century.) So Sedaine was drawn in, eventually producing his own particular defence of the *philosophes,* which was first played at the end of 1765. It was due for its *première* on 21 October under the title *Le Duel,* but the censor argued that as it stood the play was an apology for the forbidden custom of duelling and Sedaine was reluctantly obliged to make some changes in order to have it passed by the censorship and the police. Only after a judicial committee had seen the play performed in its modified form could it be approved for the public, making its delayed appearance on 2 December.[4]

Le Philosophe sans le savoir draws a well-nigh idyllic portrait of the hero, Vanderk *père*, who on the day of his daughter's wedding discovers that his son has become involved in a duel. With almost superhuman courage he keeps the news from his wife and daughter and goes ahead with the marriage ceremonies as normal, while striving to help his son. Even when he believes, falsely as it turns out, that the latter has been killed he still maintains silence, and goes on at his moment of greatest despair to give financial aid to the father of the other duellist. The credibility of this characterisation may leave something to be desired; for the moment, however, let us look at the social context in which the hero operates.

Vanderk *père* is a *négociant* (or *commerçant*: the words are used interchangeably) and apparently quite wealthy. Like Jacques in *Candide*, he knows how to combine right thinking and living with sound business principles. On the eve of the wedding he gives his loyal servant Antoine 25 *louis* (that is, 600 *livres*) for expenses on the morrow (I, 4);[5] this sum was large enough to comprise the annual salary of, for instance, a famous dancer at the Opéra during the same period.[6] A little later he hands his daughter an even larger sum of 30 *louis* for her use next day (I, 6). The totals reflect the depredations any 'father of the bride' undergoes and they serve to remind us of Vanderk's generosity (each servant, for example, will receive twelve *livres* as a gift); even so, only a rich man could afford to be so open-handed. We know little about the appurtenances of wealth in the household, and what we learn of Vanderk suggests that he will never squander his wealth, yet we discover that his wife has her own *carrosse* (III, 2) and that his daughter is liberally adorned with diamonds for the wedding (I, 3). The display of wealth is solidly backed up by cash reserves, as one might expect of a good bourgeois. When d'Esparville comes with an urgent request for money he is able to cash a *lettre de change* without delay for 2400 *livres*, and then transform that large sum into gold *louis* when d'Esparville makes this further request (V, 4).

From these indications, it is clear that Vanderk belongs to the socially powerful group of *négociants* that flourished in the eighteenth century, mainly in large ports like Nantes or Marseilles.

The play is set in 'une grande ville de France', therefore presumably not Paris; this would fit in with the pattern that the *négociants* were generally found in the provinces.[7] One is tempted to guess that it is a northern port not too far trom the capital (there are no indications of regional dialect amongst the servants and the atmosphere of the play is quasi-Parisian, especially in contrast with the ridiculously provincial aunt), somewhere like Rouen, which would have been a natural place for the Dutchman who trained Vanderk in commerce to settle down (II, 4). D'Esparville carries a *lettre de change* from Cadiz (V, 4), Sophie's *billet à ordre* originated in Holland (I, 5); we know that Rouen was in direct trading contact with Spain and Holland as well as many other countries.[8] From the help Vanderk affords d'Esparville it is evident that he also provides banking services, as was general among the *négociants* in the absence of any comprehensive banking system in the eighteenth century.[9] D'Esparville's difficulties in getting his letter of exchange cashed would have had a firm basis in reality.

Vanderk is, as we have already seen, a model of his kind. Not only does he help out d'Esparville even though in a personal crisis himself, he refuses to take any commission, despite the fact that d'Esparville, totally ignorant of such matters, would have willingly paid almost any price to obtain the cash (V, 4). While one would not expect the hero in such an edifying play even to consider exploiting his client's ingenuousness, it is something out of the ordinary for Vanderk to forgo a reasonable charge for his services. Sedaine is clearly bent on the staunchest possible defence of the *commerçant*. He is far from the first to do so; Voltaire had done the same thing 30 years earlier in the *Lettres philosophiques*, and the attitude was itself hackneyed by this time. Yet the case was clearly far from won. Vanderk's son is, after all, fighting the duel precisely because of the derogatory words about merchants which he had heard uttered by d'Esparville *fils*: 'Oui, tous ces négociants, tous ces commerçants sont des fripons, sont des misérables' (III, 8). The defence of commerce by Vanderk (II, 4) is so blatantly didactic that the playwright evidently thought it still to be necessary. It is reminiscent of similar professions in English drama by Steele, Defoe, Gay and Lillo in the 1720s and 1730s[10] and bears obvious traces of Lillo's remarks in *The London Merchant* (1731), which had been translated into French in 1748 and enjoyed considerable success in both capitals.

Commerce, in short, had not yet achieved the status which its apologists had sought for it.[11] The surest criticism of this failure lies in the attitude shown by the nobility towards trade. Ever since 1642 successive royal edicts and declarations had made patently clear the French government's policy of consistently encouraging aristocratic interest in wholesale and maritime trade by removing from it the stigma of derogation; but the response from the nobility was consistently lukewarm.[12] Changes in law could not avail against the influence of custom, which continued to require a noble to refrain from trade. In the 1750s the issue seemed to come to a head in the quarrel that occurred around the abbé Coyer's *La Noblesse commerçante* (1756), a work that acquired enough notoriety to run through four editions in a year. Coyer followed in the steps of earlier apologists by pleading for a commercial nobility engaged in trade, though he sharpened the argument in certain respects; the case he made on behalf of the impoverished aristocrats of the provinces, cut off from the only viable livelihood open to them, was particularly eloquent, and made in direct opposition to the *grands seigneurs* who wished only to preserve their prerogatives. Furthermore, Coyer had the audacity to demand that nobility engaged even in retail trade should also avoid derogation.

Coyer's work provoked a lively reaction, particularly over the next three years, though the quarrel was to go on fitfully until 1789.[13] While it had no practical effect in altering attitudes towards trade, it had the merit of simplifying the issue because it looked at trade globally, without the traditional distinction between wholesale and retail. Coyer saw too that the debate involved a moral question, the notion of honour. Montesquieu had already in *De l'esprit des lois* (1748) argued that in a monarchy a *noblesse commerçante* was a contradiction in terms. Honour is the basic principle of a monarchy, its nature is to seek out distinctions and privileges. Trade would destroy that principle: 'Il est contre l'esprit du commerce, que la noblesse le fasse dans une monarchie'.[14] Coyer's answer to this problem is to suggest a redefinition of 'honour', so that it no longer has an exclusively aristocratic connotation. Why should honour not be based on industry and integrity? Did it necessarily have to be consonant with military service? Could it not be practised in times of peace?

But Coyer's proposals were ultimately too narrow to be useful.

He wanted new privileges for the nobility, while yet they retained all their existing prerogatives. Had his wishes been implemented the aristocracy would have been granted with impunity a vast range of new advantages over the bourgeoisie, with possibly shattering consequences for the social order. Nor does Coyer appear to understand the implications of his redefinition of 'honour', which thus defined could undermine the whole hierarchical structure of the Ancien Régime. But at least he had the merit of highlighting moral assumptions underlying the social problem.

The government, failing to involve the nobility in trade, also tried the converse approach: it sought to ennoble merchants. The beneficiaries in all were few – only 24 have been traced in Brittany, nineteen in Bordeaux, twelve in Rouen, to name the three main areas.[15] Here too the results obtained were meagre. While some amongst the highest nobility became increasingly involved in commercial or industrial activities, directly or indirectly, 'les anoblis fuient très vite le négoce pour immobiliser leur fortune en terres, titres et offices'.[16] To prevent this, it had been envisaged as early as 1701 by the *Conseil de commerce* that only a progressive nobility should be granted to merchants, not becoming fully operative until the fourth generation.[17] Nothing came of the idea, and the reappearance of virtually the same proposal in Dudevant's *L'Apologie du commerce* as late as 1777[18] seems to indicate how hard it was to keep the new nobleman permanently in the business which had been responsible for his promotion.

Between the Scylla of a noble *commerçant* and the Charybdis of a *commerçant anobli*, Sedaine plots an interesting course for his exemplary merchant. For Vanderk is a nobleman already, of excellent pedigree. If therefore he makes outward profession of being a commoner, it is with the inward knowledge that his status is impeccable. More to the point, it is Sedaine rather than his hero who seems to feel the need to boost his confidence in this perfect merchant. His hero is a trading nobleman of a sort, but not at all the kind Coyer had in mind. Forced out of his comfortable station by the circumstances of a precipitate flight from France as the result of a duel, he has indeed embraced commerce. But his way of life is bourgeois, he has not sought to retain the prerogatives of the aristocracy as Coyer would have wished to do. The advantages deriving from this noble background seem wholly moral ones.[19]

Vanderk's clandestine nobility is not, however, an eccentric oddity in the play but is related to other aristocratic values. It has often been pointed out that for all his praise of commerce, the merchant admits that two professions may be superior to it: 'Le magistrat, qui fait parler les lois, et le guerrier, qui défend la patrie' (II, 4): representatives respectively of the *noblesse de robe* and the *noblesse d'épée*. Nor have his bourgeois appearances prevented him from attaining that most difficult of all links with the nobility: intermarriage. His daughter is being married to a *président*, one assumes of a provincial *Parlement* such as that of Rouen.[20] As such he belongs to a high social grade ('une des premières places dans la robe' – II, 4), certainly no lower than Class 6 of the 22 which Louis XIV had (differentiating by wealth rather than rank) distinguished for the country as a whole, paupers excluded, when levying the capitation tax in 1695. According to this scale, which one contemporary scholar has found the most useful social index available for eighteenth-century nobility,[21] the son-in-law would outrank the majority of marquesses, counts, viscounts and barons of France. Madame Vanderk might well exclaim with justified pride: 'toute cette famille est si respectable, si honnête! la bonne robe est sage comme les lois' (IV, 12).

Further aristocratic tone is lent by Vanderk *fils*, who is a naval officer. Here some ambiguity enters in. Since his uniform is 'bleu' with 'parements rouges' (I, 1) he is clearly not a member of the administrative class, the despised *plumitifs* who generally came from the bourgeoisie, as the latter's uniform was iron-grey.[22] He belongs to the status-conscious military side. But he is also not yet fully qualified and is not even attending a naval officer's school such as existed at Brest, Toulon and Rochefort; he will begin military duties only when 'par ses services, il aura mérité la faveur de la cour' (II, 9). His aunt wonders whether he has a *régiment* (II, 9), which makes him sound like an army officer, but this is doubtless only part of her general lack of perspicacity and snobbish desire to give him the highest possible prestige. In practice Sedaine's choice of a naval commission, but of the worthier kind, neatly fits the general picture. Naval officers did not usually come from the highest nobility, duties at sea were unfashionable as they kept aristocrats away from the boudoir obligations of Versailles.[23] But while naval commission did not normally attain to the summit of prestige, they were in all other ways eminently respectable. Vanderk *fils* could only gain in status from holding such an office. Indeed, one wonders how his father, posing as a mere bourgeois, could have obtained his son's entry. Perhaps for the latter's present status the production of a noble title might not have been necessary, but what of the future? Is the honest Vanderk disposed, on an essential occasion like this, to use his aristocratic background to seek his son's preferment? The question, clearly unanswerable and probably never occurring explicitly to Sedaine, serves to highlight the general confusion about the family's exact situation *vis-à-vis* the nobility.

One interesting aspect of the social hierarchy emerges. Aristocratic notions prevail, yet there is apparently no distinction in prestige between the *noblesse d'épée* and the *noblesse de robe*. Vanderk's actual name and pedigree are imposing: 'chevalier . . . ancien baron de Salvières, de Clavières, de . . . etc', and he is related to most noble families; he clearly comes from the military aristocracy, since his father had commanded a regiment while still quite young (II, 4). Yet there is no hint that marrying into the *noblesse de robe* will be in any way a derogation and indeed the evidence afforded by the play suggests the contrary, for at this point Vanderk's sister becomes of significant concern to us. This ridiculous snob, the only character in the play who might have stepped out of Molière, voices all the foolish prejudices that the audience is expected to scorn, such as that 'le commerce rétrécit l'âme' or that her brother has lost 'toute idée de noblesse, de grandeur' by indulging in trade (IV, 5). This sort of comment is obviously meant for satire, fitting in with the foolish notions of a woman who lives a blinkered existence 'dans le fond du Berry' (II, 6); Sedaine, condemned to spend part of his younger days in that same province, is clearly taking his revenge! Certain of the aunt's comments are however more broadly significant. She, unlike everyone else, holds on to the old distinction between *noblesse d'épée* and *noblesse de robe*. Vanderk tells his son in advance of her arrival that for her 'Quiconque n'est pas militaire n'est rien' (II, 6); she amply bears this out by her cool attitude to the bridegroom (II, 9), as contrasted with the enthusiasm she displays for Vanderk *fils* who is in uniform (another nice aristocratic touch in a bourgeois play!). These postures are as ridiculous as her concern with armorial bearings and the fief near her home which was taken from the family in 1574 and never returned (IV, 4), or the extravagant dress and manners of her servants. Surely this, for Paris in 1765, is 'la vieille France'. F. L. Ford's res-

earches bear out this conclusion. After the failure of the old nobility to run the country under the Regency the *noblesse de robe*, it
power firmly based on the provinces, took over the leadership o
the aristocracy, and by 1750 the distinction between the two
types of aristocrat in Paris and provincial centres was blurred
The marquise who is Vanderk's sister, cloistered in the quie
world of 'le fond du Berry', is simply living in the past.

The reasons for Sedaine's concentration upon the nobility are
not far to seek. The audience reaction was largely dominated by
the aristocratic element, which had probably not declined at al
in the past hundred years[24] and through simple patronage had a
determining effect upon the choice of plays presented and there
fore on public taste. As Rousseau argues in *La Nouvelle Héloïse*
Parisian spectators did not care to watch the activities of the
lower classes.[25] Nobles, as we have seen,[26] uniquely held status
they were the norm and commoners were deviants.

Given these assumptions, it was difficult for a writer to create a
noble character who was not of noble birth. In Diderot's *Le Père
de famille* (1758) the aristocratic hero is concerned at the way a
girl, suspected of being a commoner, has captivated his son. Bur
the 'père de famille' comes to recognise that his son's beloved has
fine qualities too: 'vous paraissez bien née', he tells her (II, 4)
The reason is eventually made clear; she happily turns out to be
socially 'bien née' like her lover. Voltaire's *Nanine* (1749) is
scarcely more daring. Although the heroine, virtuous but o
humble birth, eventually marries a nobleman, she is merely
acquiescing in her aristocratic companions' right to dispose o
her fate.[27] Later, in *Le Droit du seigneur* (1762), Voltaire avoids a
similar dénouement by having the apparent *roturière* Acanthe
turn out to be socially equal to her lover the marquis. Compared
with these Marivaux had been a good deal more audacious in his
Iles plays.

There seems to be no unambivalent theatrical defence of the
bourgeois position before 1765. In that year however was staged
Belloy's *Le Siège de Calais*, with bourgeois heroes. Was this to be a
breakthrough? For in this version of the famous story about
Edward III and Calais, the bourgeois Mayor and his five
kinsmen offer themselves up for sacrifice, to such effect that
Edward III is moved by their heroism to relent. But on closer investigation it turns out that the burghers have but one function,
to sacrifice themselves. Far from being a radical play, this is a

patriotic fable about the Middle Ages in which they have duties, not rights. The world portrayed is a strictly hierarchical one in which everyone knew his place.[28]

These instances help to explain how Sedaine came to write a *drame bourgeois* about an aristocrat. In addition, it must be remembered that although the *philosophes* were in the ascendant, he was entering a contentious area by making propaganda for them on the stage; as we have noted, the play was put on only after resistance by authority had been overcome. Hence, in all probability, the choice of a *philosophe* as merchant. If *philosophes* were still considered subversive intellectuals in some quarters, what better than to embody *philosophie* in a man who is manifestly neither? Politically Vanderk is loyal to his country, while seeking to promote international harmony through trade; religiously he is free of all free-thinking; socially he is above suspicion. All his philosophy is devoted to conspicuously useful ends.

So the play, apparently about the middle class, probably tells us more about the structure of the nobility at the time. There still remains something to be said in favour of its claims as a *drame bourgeois*. We cannot deny the dramatic importance of knowing that Vanderk is an aristocrat; but we should not forget that he has kept this a secret from the outside world and even from members of his family and that by affirming daily the virtues of a merchant's life he is doing great good for the cause. It is dangerous to try to draw firm distinctions between aristocratic and bourgeois morality. If, however, one takes a contemporary's view of the latter's code of honour, one can see how fully Vanderk carries it out: 'one must know how to live frugally and have no debts; one must do no harm of any kind to anyone; nor do harm to oneself, either by neglecting one's affairs and letting them fall apart, or by any excess ruinous to health'.[29] If not exactly frugal Vanderk is prudent with his money, hard-headed, industrious and punctual (he apologises to d'Esparville for being exactly sixteen minutes late – (V, 4); one feels that only a major upheaval could have induced such an error). Unlike the intellectual *philosophes*, he exhibits not a trace of cultural interest. No one in his household goes to the theatre, no one has heard of the *Encyclopédie* or *Candide*, still less of Helvétius and his insidious doctrines of self-interest in *De l'esprit*. One would not expect to meet Vanderk in a provincial Academy, and this too seems to be in keeping with contemporary reality, for the *grands négociants* of a city like Bordeaux were not found in its Academy unless exceptional reasons prevailed.[30]

But though not a *philosophe* himself he represents a valid mode of social conduct for the middle class. He sees his situation as a force for peace, since he has links with merchants in other lands and serves all nations; he is 'l'homme de l'univers' (II, 4).[31] Unlike the false concept of honour held by the marquise his high sense of integrity is relevant to the needs of his time. He is naturally tolerant to Protestants like d'Esparville (unlike some other merchants who have turned d'Esparville down flat because of his religion – V, 4): with him, as on the London Stock Exchange depicted by Voltaire in the *Lettres philosophiques*, religion is irrelevant to business. He treats his servants kindly but firmly, his children too; Antoine is more than a servant, he is 'mon vieux camarade', with whom Vanderk lapses into *tutoiement* at particularly emotional moments (IV, 9). Though one who believes in obeying the law, he is critical of a society that is still barbarous and vain enough to condone duelling, a custom that the audience would automatically associate with aristocratic codes of honour.[32] He is socially responsible, personally honest, professionally successful, an exemplary modernist of the sort the Encyclopaedists were looking to for creating an enlightened new world.

Even so, as we have seen, Sedaine's most obvious intentions are undercut by complications arising out of the nature of eighteenth-century society. Mandrou sums up the situation in the light of the best recent research: 'l'essor de la bourgeoisie n'a pas détruit le fondement social de base qu'est le rapport seigneurial hérité du Moyen Age'.[33] Sedaine's personal position aptly symbolises the problem. Unlike his fellow-artisan Rousseau, who opted out of polite society, Sedaine seems to have adopted it with ease. Treading the usual path to fame followed by the author of successful plays, he obtained official patronage shortly after the production of *Le Philosophe sans le savoir* by being appointed secretary of the *Académie royale d'architecture* with a modest salary but 'un beau logement au Louvre';[34] in 1786 he obtained the supreme accolade of election to the *Académie Française*. Being, in Diderot's words, 'immobile et froid',[35] he does not seem to have felt the excruciating embarrassments which Rousseau underwent in mingling with high society. Indeed, an anecdote in Bachaumont's *Mémoires secrets* shows him standing up to a court official in a way that would have been accounted crude insolence at the time of Voltaire's exile to England 60 years earlier; John Lough uses it as an illustration of how far things had changed by the time the incident occurred in 1786.[36] But just as Rousseau's social unease had the priceless benefit of safeguarding his intellectual independence, Sedaine paid a price for his comfortable position. There is nothing particularly radical about his espousal of the merchant's cause within the terms he establishes. Even the polemic of his reply to Palissot must be seen as conducted from sheltered ground. If by box-office standards *Le Philosophe sans le savoir* was one of the most successful plays of the period,[37] the reason must partly be sought in its timeliness. By 1765, though he needed to walk warily, Sedaine was on the winning side. The Encyclopaedist group was gaining dominance within the world of Parisian culture; the final ten volumes of text of the *Encyclopédie* were ready to be distributed to the subscribers; Jean Calas had been rehabilitated, thanks to Voltaire's crusade; the Jesuits had been expelled from France. Sedaine's play, positive in its attitude but never too advanced to upset public opinion, proved a stepping-stone, not a millstone, for its author.

Finally, it should be noted that even the justly praised social realism of the play reveals that limitation which we noted earlier in discussing *Manon Lescaut*. Although Sedaine gives us a real sense of money affairs and introduces a technical vocabulary which marks a step forward, he too declines to show us money actually being made (even specifically preventing Vanderk from taking a commission, as we have seen). Vanderk twice sends servants to the cash-desk to get money, but the desk remains resolutely off-stage. There is no sign of the counting-house with its tables, stools and ledgers which would presumably be the environment in which Vanderk's daily working life is spent. Here too Sedaine takes care not to offend against the conventions of his day. His attitude bears out Rousseau's caustic remark in *La Nouvelle Héloïse*: 'Les auteurs d'aujourd'hui ... se croiraient déshonorés s'ils savaient ce qui se passe au comptoir d'un marchand ou dans la boutique d'un ouvrier....'[38] This literary purism also works to preserve the ideal picture of the hero. Sedaine allows no harm to befall Vanderk through identification with the financiers who were so often detested in his day, and no problems arise as to the business in which Vanderk is engaged. Yet he could, for instance, very easily be active in the slave trade, for all we know to the contrary.

After Law's crash the Comédie Française showed a steep drop in receipts in 1721–22, from over 400,000 *livres* the previous year to not much more than 160,000. There was a slump in theatregoing at the Comédie Française until the 1740s, and it was 1749–50 before the total annual figure once more climbed above 300,000 *livres*,[39] never to descend below it again during the Ancien Régime. Why this recession? Claude Alasseur considers that the reasons might be economic, social (competition from other theatres and entertainments) or literary (mediocrity of the plays or the productions or both). She indicates a certain amount of correlation with the price of corn (a fundamental index of the economy in the eighteenth century), though adding that other phenomena have clearly had an influence as well. One of the most interesting features of this setback in the fortunes of the Comédie Française is that certain plays, particularly new ones, did very well during the period 1720–50: Voltaire's *Hérode et Mariamne* (1725) and *Zaïre* (1732), for instance, but above all La Motte's *Inès de Castro*, first played in 1723, which had a phenomenal run of 41 performances and was seen by nearly 34,000 spectators. No other play matched these figures before Beaumarchais's *Le Mariage de Figaro* in 1784 (even his *Le Barbier de Séville*, performed in 1775, fell far short). Yet the season in which *Inès de Castro* appeared was one of the worst of the 30 lean years! The receipts from this play alone represented well over a third of that year's takings. The plays which drew particularly poor audiences were mainly revivals, Molière (despite remaining popular with certain favourites like *Le Bourgeois Gentilhomme* and *Le Malade imaginaire*) often being seen by very few people.[40] In 1746 the great comic dramatist's popularity had fallen so low that the duc d'Aumont, at that time the *gentilhomme de la chambre* responsible for the Comédie Française, forbade the revival until further notice of Molière's five-act plays.[41]

It is possible to talk of a crisis in the Comédie Française during these years, so far as the established repertoire was concerned; and one wonders whether it may not have had its part in determining the rise of the *drame bourgeois*. The theories of critics like Diderot may be in part a direct reaction to this fallow period, seeking to interpret a felt malaise for which we now have some statistical support. Not only Molière but also Regnard and Voltaire, all of them representatives of classical comedy or tragedy,

were often unsuccessful.[42] By contrast, the crowds flocked to the
sentimental tragedy *Inès de Castro* or the *comédies larmoyantes* of
Nivelle de La Chaussée, who between 1735 and 1744 put on three
of the seven most successful plays at the Comédie Française.[43]

Here is not the place to chart the development of the new trend
towards sentimental drama that overtook the French theatre in
the early eighteenth century.[44] We have however already seen
that Rousseau, in his diatribe against the Genevan theatre, is
expressing many comments which Diderot later shared;[45] both
writers felt that classical comedy and tragedy had nothing more
to offer. The conclusions Rousseau drew were generally negative
for the legitimate theatre. He saw no salvation in the virtuous
play, upon which Diderot placed so much stress. In Rousseau's
view edifying theatre was merely boring. Diderot by contrast
expended much energy upon attempting to demonstrate the
moral effect of art. He cast a wide net for his examples, drawing
them from the ancient Roman theatre of Terence or even going
outside literature altogether, as in his famous encomiums upon
the painters Greuze and Chardin. However, the prescription for
what he sought on the stage is essentially contained, not in observations upon a dramatist, but in what he has to say about the
English novelist Richardson:

> Cet auteur ne fait point couler le sang le long des lambris; il ne vous
> transporte point dans des contrées éloignées; il ne vous expose point à
> être dévoré par des sauvages; il ne se renferme point dans des lieux
> clandestins de débauche; il ne se perd jamais dans les régions de la
> féerie. Le monde où nous vivons est le lieu de la scène; le fond de son
> drame est vrai; ses personnages ont toute la réalité possible; ses carac-
> tères sont pris du milieu de la société; ses incidents sont dans les
> mœurs de toutes les nations policées; les passions qu'il peint sont
> telles que je les éprouve en moi: ce sont les mêmes objets qui les émeu-
> vent, elles ont l'énergie que je leur connais; les traverses et les afflic-
> tions de ses personnages sont de la nature de celles qui me menacent
> sans cesse; il me montre le cours général des choses qui m'environ-
> nent.[46]

Here is the aesthetic for a sentimental realism, as applicable to
the stage as to the novel or the art gallery. The ideal artist com-
poses for Everyman, from the raw material which Everyman
finds around him. He imitates ordinary reality, avoiding the fan-
tastic or the gothic, uncovers the dynamism in day-to-day exist-

ence, and moves his audience by the intensity of his revelations. These principles lie behind Diderot's prescriptions for the contemporary theatre as set forth in the *Entretiens sur Le Fils naturel* (1757) and the *Discours de la poésie dramatique* (1758) and exemplified with less success in the two *drames* to which these treatises are linked, *Le Fils naturel* (1757) and *Le Père de famille* (1758). Diderot advocates the *drame bourgeois* as the theatrical *genre* which his age needs, a combination of the comic and tragic that avoids the extremes of both modes and portrays ordinary human beings (that is, bourgeois) in ordinary situations, such as at home in the family. The emphasis has swung from the individual to the social context; one must represent not characters, but *conditions*, by which Diderot means a man's job and also his situation in society. It is this more abstract element which should now become paramount: 'C'est la condition, ses devoirs, ses avantages, ses embarras, qui doivent servir de base à l'ouvrage. Il me semble que cette source est plus féconde, plus étendue et plus utile que celle des caractères.'[47] Whereas a spectator might refuse to identify himself with a particular character, he cannot deny the truth of the situation being played out before him. In order to press home this point the whole theatrical technique must be as realistic as possible: speech, dress, *décor*, setting, movement, gesture. The truthfulness of detail will be moving, and the audience, being moved, will respond the more readily to the moral lessons which the author wishes to teach. Diderot is outlining a kind of theatre many of whose elements are still prominent in much of contemporary drama: one in which the director dominates all, where the visual effects of the staging are a central element, where there is a strong didactic purpose.

It follows naturally then that Diderot should have greeted Sedaine's play with delight; only professional jealousy could have prevented him and Diderot was much too generous for that. He told Grimm the next day that he had cried out in the theatre, in admiration at Sedaine's apparent simplicity and in despair at his own failure to do the same: 'cet homme me coupe l'herbe sous les pieds'.[48] A few weeks later he explained to Sophie Volland that Sedaine had achieved the fusion of modes he himself had called for: 'Ce sont les terreurs de la tragédie produites avec les moyens de l'opéra-comique'.[49] His enthusiasm knew no limits when he eventually unearthed Sedaine to congratulate him; to which the phlegmatic playwright merely returned: 'Ah!

Monsieur Diderot, que vous êtes beau!'[50]

Not all the critics, however, agree that Sedaine obtained much from Diderot. Daniel Mornet claims that the play is a 'drame à peu près sans le savoir'.[51] While accepting that Sedaine, in his direct unscholarly way, went about his play without constant reference to Diderot's theories, it is hard to see the validity of Mornet's paradox which, in any case, flies in the face of the historical evidence that Diderot himself was well content with the manner in which his arguments had been exploited. *Le Philosophe sans le savoir* represents the bourgeois in a serious and honourable way. The merchant's problems are set in context, as are the crises arising from being a *père de famille*. Sedaine displays the essential element of sensibility and the play seeks to move the audience; some scenes (V, 6–7) were in fact accounted so harrowing that they were excised from the production. The play is unambiguously moral in tone. With the exception of the foolish aunt everyone is virtuously inclined, and where tragic possibilities arise it is because, though human nature is good, social institutions are often bad. (The logical inconsistency in this position is not permitted to disturb the audience.) As if the picture were not itself edifying enough, the playwright does not hesitate to moralise on occasion so that no advantage to be derived from didacticism shall remain unexploited. The use of *décor*, too, though perhaps less striking than Diderot had envisaged, is in accordance with his suggestions; striking tableaux are to be found (as at the end of III, 11), inarticulate pantomime is made to act as eloquently as speech, as in the confrontation scene between father and son when Vanderk learns the brutal truth (III, 8) or in Vanderk's grief on hearing the false news of his son's death (V, 5). The author throughout uses a simple, quite banal situation, with appropriately informal dialogue, to create a work of high pathos, exactly as Diderot wished. If ever a theory predicted a work of art, surely it is here.

The success of Sedaine's play fits into a wider European movement that we can do no more than mention here, a movement that flows from England, with plays like Lillo's *The London Merchant*, novels like Richardson's, philosophical defences of the passions like Shaftesbury's, and into Germany, where from the 1750s Lessing was beginning to attack French classical tragedy and declaring its inferiority to Shakespeare. Whereas for Lessing Shakespeare was a genius who, though untutored, conveyed the

sense of life and nature with powerful realism, French tragedy
was remote and desiccated. Lessing had already written his first
middle-class tragedy, *Miss Sara Sampson* (1755), before Diderot.
After Sedaine came Beaumarchais with his *Essai sur le genre dramatique sérieux* (1767) and such *drames* as *Eugénie* (which ac-
companied the *Essai*) and *Les Deux Amis* (1770). In 1773
Sébastien Mercier's *Du théâtre* went further than Diderot had
done in demanding that the *drame* should simply usurp the traditional comedy and tragedy. Corneille, Racine, Voltaire, even
Molière, he claimed, gave no help in conveying the character of
the people and the times, 'une idée juste de la forme de notre
législation, de la trempe de notre esprit, du tour de notre imagination, de la manière enfin dont nous [envisageons] le trône et la
cour ... le tableau de nos mœurs actuelles, l'intérieur de nos
maisons'.[52] The *drame*, he argued, is committed literature, as
befits a nation that is growing daily in political and social awareness.

For all these manifestos, the *drame bourgeois* never caught on
completely in Paris, enjoying more success in the provincial
centres.[53] Sedaine himself, despite the popularity of *Le Philosophe
sans le savoir* at the Comédie Française, had most of his later plays
performed elsewhere, usually at the Comédie Italienne.
Although Condorcet later became a leading Revolutionary figure
he objected strongly to Falbaire's *drame Le Fabricant de Londres*
(1771), writing to Turgot: 'Les mœurs insipides de la petite bourgeoisie y étaient peintes avec une vérité dégoûtante'.[54] The reaction is characteristic of the Paris playgoer under the Ancien
Régime.

The history of the *drame* in the eighteenth century is therefore
one of hesitations and half-successes at best. Sedaine's play is acknowledged by most critics as pre-eminent amongst its kind, but
it was hardly epochal in the sense of transforming the *genre* and
broadening its horizons. Perhaps there were no horizons to
broaden. In studying the *drame bourgeois* one is constantly dogged
by the suspicion that it could never have been a first-class form of
literature. David Williams points out that a basic conflict lay at
its heart, since the *drame* was supposed to be a realistic imitation
of nature but also to have an idealistic approach, showing the
characters in a favourable light for purposes of social propaganda.[55] This difficulty is obvious in *Le Philosophe sans le savoir*:
Vanderk is such an exemplary character that he ceases to be an

autonomous one. Sedaine centres the dramatic tension on the hero's concept of honour, which involves him in a paradoxical situation that causes deep distress: the custom of duelling is barbarous, yet 'quand on a pris un engagement vis-à-vis du public, on doit le tenir, quoi qu'il en coûte à la raison, et même à la nature' (III, 8). He is, in brief, the prisoner of a convention.[56] But the notion of self-discovery through suffering which we associate with the tragedies of ancient Greece or Louis XIV's France or Shakespeare is relevant here only to the minor figure of the son, who merely learns not to be so impetuous in future. There is none of the sense which high tragedy communicates to us, that at the bottom of human experience there lies some awful, primeval disaster, whether one calls it Original Sin, or the anger of the gods, or physical determinism or some other general name. The universe of *Le Philosophe sans le savoir* merely needs a little tinkering with in order to be wholly satisfactory: a change in public opinion that would truly prohibit duels would be enough. If this play still deserves respect and attention (and a modern production might well be worth attempting), it is because Sedaine is above all a fine craftsman, managing the technical elements of theatre – dialogue, plot, setting – with much skill. What is lacking to give it greatness is that sense of the dramatic which sensibility alone will not provide.

For George Steiner middle-class tragedy is a private, interior tragedy, where the audience is no longer an organic community linked by shared concepts like grace and damnation. Being private, it is not suited to the stage but to the individual reader; the novelist takes over as the new tragedian.[57] This distinction was not appreciated by Diderot, who felt that the lessons taught by Richardson were also applicable outside the novel: 'il n'y a point de bon drame dont on ne puisse faire un excellent roman'.[58] The questions raised by Steiner about 'the death of tragedy' are highly relevant here. The solution proposed by the eighteenth century was not wholly successful, and after the Revolution the Romantics attempted another formula, which many felt to be even less seminal for future developments. It is arguable, indeed, that the French theatre had been so dominated by the three great figures of the seventeenth century that no real emancipation was possible until quite recently, when at last two foreigners, Ionesco and Beckett, found a wholly new approach to serious theatre.

Clearly such speculations are beyond our brief here. Let us

rather stress in conclusion the central place of drama in eighteenth-century French culture. The great passion among the Parisian élite of the time was not science or technology or politics, still less religion; it was theatre.[59] The playhouse spectacle was direct and the experience collective – Diderot speaks of 2000 people in the audience for Sedaine's *première*.[60] The radical effect of plays, themselves intrinsically moderate, could therefore be considerable, and Sedaine's contribution helped to set the seal upon the triumph of *philosophique* ideals. But above all it is the class consciousness revealed here, a good twenty years before the Revolution, which is interesting to the modern reader. The ambiguities of eighteenth-century society are mirrored, often unconsciously. Aristocratic values act as the basis for exploration, even in a work that sets out deliberately to justify bourgeois ways. Let us, however, hold in balance both sides of the paradox. Despite the idealisation of Vanderk's character, despite the overt aims of propaganda that reduce the hero's dramatic autonomy, Sedaine takes an important step forward in defining workable middle-class criteria for living, albeit by reference to the ubiquitous values of the Second Estate.[61]

NOTES

1. Sedaine, *La Gageure imprévue*, edited by R. Niklaus (University of Exeter, 1970), pp. vi–vii.
2. See H. H. Freud, *Palissot and 'Les Philosophes'*, Diderot Studies, IX (1967), which gives a full account of the work and its consequences, except that she surprisingly omits all reference to Sedaine.
3. With 21 performances and over 17,000 spectators, compared with thirteen and just over 12,000 respeccively for Palissot: C. Alasseur, *La Comédie Française au 18ᵉ siècle*, p. 141.
4. Ira Wade argues that the duel issue was merely an excuse for the authorities to intervene and reduce the *philosophique* import of the play: 'The Title of Sedaine's *Le Philosophe sans le savoir*', *Publications of the Modern Language Association of America*, XLIII (1928), pp. 1026–38.
5. All textual references are to the Classiques Larousse edition, edited by E. Feuillatre, 1936.
6. V. Fournel, *Curiosités théâtrales* (Paris, 1859), p. 132; cited in Alasseur, *La Comédie Française* p. 130.
7. The anonymous *Le Négociant patriote* (Amsterdam, 1784) represents Paris as

'cette grande ville pleine de *marchands* et vide de *négociants*' (p. 225); cited in R. Mauzi, *L'Idée du bonheur*, p. 288, note 3. See also N. Perry, 'French and English Merchants in the Eighteenth Century: Voltaire Revisited', *Studies in Eighteenth-Century Literature presented to Professor Robert Niklaus* (University of Exeter, 1975), pp. 193–213.

8. R. Mandrou, *La France aux XVIIe et XVIIIe siècles*, p. 84.

9. See above, p. 21.

10. Perry, 'French and English Merchants in the Eighteenth Century'.

11. See above. p. 22.

12. A lucid general survey of this complex topic has been provided by G. Richard, *Noblesse d'affaires au XVIIIe siècle* (Paris: Colin, 1974).

13. Richard, *Noblesse d'affaires*, pp. 53–70. See also J. Q. C. Mackrell, *The Attack on 'Feudalism' in Eighteenth-Century France* (Routledge, 1973), pp. 77–103; L. Adams, 'Coyer and the Enlightenment', *Studs. Volt.*, 123 (1974); F. C. Green, 'L'Abbé Coyer–A Society in Transition', in *Eighteenth-Century France* (Dent, 1929), especially pp. 93–110; J. N. Pappas, 'Les Philosophes contre l'honneur', *Studs. Volt.* 205 (to appear) Saint-Lambert's *Encyclopédie* article 'Honneur' is of interest also, so far as contemporary definitions of honour are concerned.

14. Book XX, chapter XXI, *Oeuvres complètes*, edited by R. Caillois (Paris: Gallimard, 1949–51), Vol. II, p. 598.

15. Richard, *Noblesse d'affaires*, p. 67.

16. Richard, *Noblesse d'affaires*, p. 119.

17. Richard, *Noblesse d'affaires*, p. 51.

18. E. G. Barber, *The Bourgeoisie in Eighteenth-Century France*, pp. 61–2.

19. To my knowledge, Professor Lough was the first to point out this anomaly and generalise the point by wide reference to many other contemporary dramas which claim to support the bourgeoisie yet make their heroes aristocratic (see *Paris Theatre Audiences*, pp. 248–68).

20. There were twelve *Parlements* at this time: Paris, Rouen, Toulouse, Grenoble, Bordeaux, Dijon, Aix-en-Provence, Rennes, Pau, Metz, Besançon and Douai (Nancy was added in 1775).

21. F. L. Ford, *Robe and Sword*, pp. 32–3.

22. M. Loir, *La Marine royale en 1789* (Paris: Colin, 1892), p. 113; F. Bluche, *La Vie quotidienne de la noblesse française au XVIIIe siècle* (Paris: Hachette, 1973), pp. 159–65. Bluche gives a full description of the trainee officer's uniform (p. 161).

23. See Bluche, *La Vie quotidienne de la noblesse française*, p. 159; Loir, *La Marine royale*, pp. 19–21.

24. Lough makes the point that there was probably no larger a proportion of bourgeois at the *première* of *Le Philosophe sans le savoir* than of *Le Misanthrope* a century earlier (*Paris Theatre Audiences*, pp. 185–6).

25. Edited by H. Coulet and B. Guyon (Paris: Pléiade, 1964), p. 252.

26. See above, p. 19.

27. This is well perceived by J. Truchet in his edition of *Théâtre du XVIIIe siècle* (Paris: Pléiade, 1972), Vol. I, pp. 1444–5.

28. See R. Fargher, *Life and Letters*, pp. 118–27.

29. Grosley, *Vie de M. Grosley* (1787); cited in E. G. Barber, *The Bourgeoisie*, pp. 38–9.

30. D. Roche, *Le Siècle des lumières en province*, Vol. I, pp. 249–55, II, p. 96.

31. Le négociant est présent partout; il dispose de véritables 'réseaux' de facteurs et de correspondants. J.-B. Bruny a des comptoirs et des agents dans les Echelles, à Anvers et à Amsterdam, à Gênes et à Livourne, à Cadiz il étend ses relations dans toute la France. Aux Antilles, les correspondants des grands commerçants de Marseille sont, eux-mêmes, des marchands notables; nombreux à Saint-Pierre de la Martinique, ils deviennent indispensables.

   P. Léon, 'Les Nouvelles Elites' in E. Labrousse *et al.*, *Histoire économique et sociale de la France*, Vol. II, *1660–1789* (Paris: P.U.F., 1970), pp. 613–14.

32. The confusion between custom and law which Sedaine brings out in this play had already been outlined by Montesquieu when discussing duelling in the *Lettres persanes* (Lett. XC); the similarity is close enough to suggest that Sedaine derived his idea from this source.

33. *La France aux XVIIe et XVIIIe siècles*, p. 72.

34. Grimm, *Correspondance littéraire*, VIII, p. 132; cited in Lough, *Writer and Public*, p. 231.

35. *Paradoxe sur le comédien*, in *Oeuvres esthétiques*, edited by P. Vernière (Paris: Garnier, 1965), p. 330.

36. *Writer and Public*, pp. 239–40.

37. Lough, *Paris Theatre Audiences*, p. 181; Alasseur, *La Comédie Française*, p. 141: 27 performances and over 20,000 spectators.

38. Edited by Coulet and Guyon, p. 252.

39. Alasseur, *La Comédie Française*, pp. 48–56, 136.

40. Alasseur, *La Comédie Française*, pp. 63–4; Lagrave, *Le Théâtre et le public*, pp. 327–8.

41. M. Descotes, *Molière et sa fortune littéraire* (Saint-Médard-en-Jalles: Ducros, 1970), p. 48; Lagrave, *Le Théâtre et le public*, pp. 328–9. The edict appears however to have been frequently relaxed.

42. Alasseur, *La Comédie Française*, p. 62.

43. Alasseur, *La Comédie Française*, p. 140. One must not forget, however, that some of Voltaire's tragedies did even better than Nivelle de La Chaussée's plays (See Lough, *Paris Theatre Audiences*, pp. 178–9).

44. The classic study remains G. Lanson, *Nivelle de La Chaussée et la comédie larmoyante* (Paris: Hachette, 1887). Also useful is F. Gaiffe, *Le Drame en France au XVIIIe siècle* (Paris: Colin, 1910).

45. See R. Niklaus, 'Diderot et Rousseau: Pour et contre le théâtre', *Diderot Studies*, 4 (1963), pp. 153–89.

46. *Eloge de Richardson* (1762), in *Oeuvres esthétiques*, edited by Vernière, pp. 30–1.

47. *Entretiens sur le Fils naturel*, in *Oeuvres esthétiques*, edited by Vernière, p. 153.

48. Letter to Grimm [3 December 1765]. *Correspondance*, edited by G. Roth and J. Varloot (Paris: Editions de Minuit, 1955–70), 16 vols.,Vol. V, p. 206.

49. [20 December 1765], *Correspondance*, edited by Roth and Varloot, Vol. V, p. 230.

50. *Paradoxe sur le comédien*, in *Oeuvres esthétiques*, edited by Vernière, p. 330.

51. In J. Bédier and P. Hazard, *Littérature française* (Paris: Larousse, 1948–49), 2 vols., Vol. II, p. 139.

52. (Amsterdam, 1773), p. 103.

53. Lough, *Paris Theatre Audiences*, pp. 265–8.
54. Cited in Lough, *Paris Theatre Audiences*, p. 262.
55. *Voltaire: Literary Critic, Studs. Volt.*, 48 (1966), p. 271.
56. It was this section which the censorship obliged Sedaine to change. In the modified version Vanderk refuses his son leave to depart for the duel and sends him to his room. Since the son has to arrive at the duel somehow for the play to proceed, Sedaine has him slip out unobserved. The hard-headed, liberal father thereby becomes both a tyrant and a fool, the son, otherwise a model of filial piety, a furtive rebel; the characterisation of both is ruined. Little wonder that Sedaine obeyed the censor with much reluctance and only after protest had been of no avail!
57. *The Death of Tragedy* (Faber, 1961), pp. 194–7.
58. *De la poésie dramatique*, in *Oeuvres esthétiques*, edited by Vernière, p. 215.
59. J.-L. and M. Flandrin, 'La Circulation du livre dans la société du 18ᵉ siècle', *Livre et société dans la France du XVIIIᵉ siècle*, Vol. II, pp. 39–72. Jean Starobinski asserts that 'pour la plupart des grands esprits du XVIIIᵉ siècle, l'expérience du théâtre [a] été décisive', *L'Invention de la liberté*, p. 106.
60. *Correspondance*, Vol. V, p. 229.
61. I am indebted to the Editor of *French Studies* for kindly allowing me to reproduce sections of my article, '*Le Philosophe sans le savoir*: An Aristocratic *Drame Bourgeois?*', *French Studies*, 30 (1976), pp. 405–18; in that article some of the considerations touched on in this chapter have been treated at somewhat greater length.

Another reading of *Le Philosophe sans le savoir* is provided by E. Guibert, *Voies idéologiques de la Révolution française* (Paris: Editions Sociales, 1976), pp. 92–121. I have made some observations upon an earlier version of this chapter in my *French Studies* article.

8 Crime and Punishment: Voltaire (1694–1778)

Commentaire sur le livre des délits et des peines (1766)

As one advances through the eighteenth century, the impact of works written during the century itself becomes of increasing importance. In Italy as in France reformers were appearing; one group in Milan, called *L'Accademia dei Pugni* and heavily influenced by the writings of the French *philosophes*, came together in the early 1760s. Amongst them was the young aristocrat Cesare Beccaria, who credited Montesquieu's *Lettres persanes* with being the decisive factor in his 'conversion to philosophy', which had wiped out, he said, the unfortunate effects of the 'fanatical' Jesuit education he had received.[1] Beccaria belongs to the last of the three generations which Peter Gay discerns in the Enlightenment,[2] drawing heavily upon the first (in Montesquieu) and second (Hume, Rousseau, Diderot, Helvétius and d'Alembert); but such is the chronological overlap that he himself will influence, in Voltaire, one who had helped, like Montesquieu, to set the stage for the Enlightenment and then survived to participate actively in its fullest flowering.

Beccaria began writing his treatise on crime and punishment (*Dei delitti e delle pene*) early in 1763. It was published the following year and immediately proved a success, going through six editions in Italian during the next eighteen months. But it was only when translated into French by the *philosophe* Morellet late in 1765 that the essay achieved its full measure of fame. Praise for it was well-nigh universal amongst reform-minded thinkers; indeed, the spontaneous coincidence of so many voices indicates in practical form just what sort of changes in the social structure were now regarded as desirable by the *philosophes* generally. Helvétius, d'Alembert, Buffon, d'Holbach, Grimm and Turgot found themselves in agreement with many outside France; Fre derick the Great in Prussia, Hume and Bentham in England, Catherine in Russia, even Maria Theresa in Austria and the Grand Duke Leopold of Tuscany greeted it with enthusiasm.[3] Its fame soon penetrated to the American colonies, where it was published three times before 1800 (even Montesquieu's *De l'esprit des lois* was not published there till 1802);[4] John Adams used an eloquent passage from it with memorable effect in defending British soldiers in Boston in 1770.[5] Morellet invited Beccaria to Paris in 1766, where he was received with adulation, too much so for his rather reserved temperament. He fled home after a few weeks and thereafter did not leave Italy, occupying himself with academic and public offices till his death in 1794. His book, however, recognized no frontiers. It was destined to remain one of the Enlightenment classics throughout the Western world.

The reasons for this success are not hard to seek. Beccaria had attempted to establish a rational approach to penology, based on fixed principles. It was part of the new science of man and society which had been developing throughout the course of the century; to the burgeoning studies of psychology, economics, technology was now added a handbook for practical use in the field of criminal law. Furthermore, it sought to establish liberty through law and a moderate scale of punishments where hitherto had prevailed arbitrariness, privilege and arcane obscurity. It pleaded for making the laws more accessible, so as to improve men's understanding of the social arrangements under which they lived, to encourage civic-mindedness and improve the human lot. It appealed to man's love of pleasure as the true incentive to doing good, and it based the notion of 'good' upon what was useful to the greatest happiness of the greatest number ('la massima felicità divisa nel maggior numero'), a phrase destined to fame when Bentham copied it as the keystone of his utilitarian code.[6] Montesquieu's moderate liberalism was allied to Helvétius's hedonist and utilitarian views; Rousseau's notion of the General Will as authority for the law was echoed. Beccaria took familiar concepts and applied them usefully to a domain where they could be put to practical effect. All this was couched in language which, if abstract, was also lucid, concise and often passionate. Finally, the essay had the good fortune to appear at the right time. It would be hard to devise a more perfect recipe for a successful Enlightenment work.

Beccaria's position throughout *Dei delitti e delle pene* is that punishment is a necessary evil to be embarked upon only after taking all possible safeguards. It must always be an admission of defeat; better always to prevent crimes than punish them. Hence his campaign to obtain the greatest possible publicity for the laws of the land; but in order to achieve that, the law must be codified and written down, so that men might guide their lives by its firm tenets, which are applicable to all: 'I find no exception to this general axiom, that every citizen should know when he is guilty of crime and when he is innocent . . . Uncertainty regarding their lot has sacrificed more victims to secret tyranny than have ever suffered from public and solemn cruelty' (p. 79). No magistrate must be allowed a personal interpretation of criminal justice; the judge's task is simply to ascertain the facts, and in every case he is 'required to complete a perfect syllogism in which the major premise must be the general law; the minor, the action that conforms or does not conform to the law; and the conclusion, acquittal or punishment' (p. 15). Punishment must fit the crime, in order that, as Montesquieu had already argued in *De l'esprit des lois*, a properly graduated scale of crimes be established, 'parce qu'il est essentiel que l'on évite plutôt un grand crime qu'un moindre, ce qui attaque la société, que ce qui la choque moins' (VI, Chapter 16). Likewise Beccaria, in line with Montesquieu, maintained that the punishment should be as mild as is compatible with proving an effective deterrent (pp. 42–4). It is not the rigour of the penalty which is important but the certainty and promptness of punishment. The law, once invoked, must be humane but inexorable. There must be no room for clemency and pardon, for they merely sap at the system: 'To make men see that crimes can be pardoned or that punishment is not their necessary consequence foments a flattering hope of impunity' (p. 59).

In practical terms Beccaria's proposals are almost impeccably liberal. The accused should be presumed innocent until proved otherwise, and prosecutions should be 'informative' rather than 'offensive' (p. 93). Suicide should escape punishment, being a matter regarding the private individual, not affecting society. With offences like adultery, pederasty and infanticide the legislator should not be content merely to punish but should try to penetrate the fundamental causes. A similar humanity informs the discussion about appropriate penalties for such crimes as robbery, smuggling, bankruptcy, incitement to public disorder.

But the most arresting argument in this respect concerns the abolition of capital punishment. Beccaria's revulsion against violence is seen here at its clearest. No man, he says, has ever alienated to others the right to kill him. The death penalty is 'the war of a nation against a citizen' (p. 45), a barbarous institution, the usurpation by men of a prerogative which should be left to 'necessity alone which, with its sceptre of iron, rules the universe' (p. 50). It is not merely odious but ineffective; much more impressive is the threat of lengthy imprisonment, not just a moment of suffering but a continuous and enduring deprivation of that liberty which is part of the human condition (pp. 46–7). Beccaria does not however advocate unconditional abolition. In exceptional circumstances the death sentence may be necessary, if the murderer 'still has connections and power such as endanger the security of the nation' or if his execution is 'the only way of restraining others from committing crimes' (p. 46). But normally, when law is supreme and order prevails, there should be no need for recourse to this form of legalised killing.

Perhaps Beccaria's single most effective protest, however, was against a usage even more hateful, that of torture. He is revolted by the absurd and horrible notion that pain, as he puts it concisely, 'be made the crucible of truth, as if its criterion lay in the muscles and sinews of a miserable wretch' (p. 31). Quite apart from its loathsome cruelty, the principle behind torture is also repellent; for in racking the limbs of a suspect it immediately presumes his guilt. This leads to an awful paradox: the innocent man *must* lose ('Either he confesses the crime and is condemned, or he is declared innocent and has suffered a punishment he did not deserve' : p. 33); whereas the guilty man, if strong-minded enough, may get off with impunity. Yet military law manages perfectly well without torture and so do a few countries like England and Prussia,[7] proving that this abomination is no longer necessary.

Behind these various proposals one theme gradually emerges, albeit hedged round with necessary circumspections. The law as Beccaria envisages it is a secular instrument, free from the transcendental encumbrances of Church and Divine Right monarchy. Clemency and pardon are royal prerogatives, still perhaps necessary, Beccaria concedes, for the sake of appearances, but to be 'excluded from perfect legislation' (p. 58). The same general objection may be raised to places of asylum; they too are a state within the State, subverting the due authority of the legal process. 'To multiply asylums is to create a multitude of petty sovereignties' (p. 60). Beccaria carefully distinguishes between sin and crime, as in suicide: 'although it is a fault that God may punish ... it is not a crime in man's eyes' (p. 83). Torture likewise has its origin in 'religious and spiritual ideas' (p. 35), linked to the antique institution of the ordeal as a judgement of God and in a more general sense to the Christian doctrines of shriving body and soul by penance and confession. Public utility has, in brief, replaced God as the sheet-anchor of human justice; men can punish crimes on that basis but sin is a secret matter, depending on the 'inscrutable malice of the heart', and no punitive norm can ever be based on it (p. 66). Franco Venturi sums it up appropriately: 'Beccaria's radical thinking, implicitly but nonetheless definitively, denied every religious conception of evil, every original sin'.[8]

Yet Beccaria was contributing little if anything that was really new. His denunciation of torture, for instance, was but the latest of a long and distinguished line that included amongst others Cicero, St Augustine, Montaigne, La Bruyère and Montesquieu. Augustin Nicolas, Président of the *Parlement* of Dijon, had eloquently condemned the practice nearly a century earlier in 1682.[9] Beccaria was not the first to demand abolition of the death penalty;[10] and the idea that punishment should be a deterrent, not an expiation, goes back at least to Seneca.[11] The main value of *Dei delitti e delle pene* lay in its succinct coverage of a broad field and in its timeliness. In France it was read by men living under a system of criminal law that had changed little in 500 years. The *ordonnance criminelle* of 1670 had to some extent rationalized procedure but done nothing to mitigate the medieval cruelties. No clear distinction between sins and crimes was made. Offences against religion were punished with the utmost severity. The death penalty was common, being applicable to over a hundred crimes. Executions were public, an occasion for entertainment, even (or perhaps the more so) such horrendous spectacles as Damiens's execution in 1757. Amongst the non-capital penalties available to the courts were the galleys, maiming corporal punishment, public exposure in the stocks or on the scaffold branding and the *carcan* (iron collar in the pillory). Imprisonment did not technically exist as a punishment, being in principle used merely as a preventive measure; this meant, as we have earlier

noted,[12] that no limit was attached to periods in gaol and intern-
ment might well be for life. It is hardly necessary to add that
prisons were generally vile, unless one could, like the Chevalier
des Grieux, purchase special consideration. Furthermore, people
were often sent to prison without a trial on a *lettre de cachet*
obtained from the king. Procedure did not favour the accused,
who at an early stage was subjected to the torture of the *question
préparatoire* so that a confession could be wrung from him. He was
generally locked away from all communication with the outside
world, could not properly prepare any sort of defence, was at the
mercy of prosecution witnesses testifying against him in secret
and whom he did not meet until the judge was ready for the
moment of confrontation. Often he did not know the nature of his
offence until that moment. Sentences were arbitrary, depending
(despite the codification of the 1670 *ordonnance*) upon local circumstances of time, place and personality, and open to the widest
discretionary powers of the judges; needless to say, aristocrats
enjoyed many privileges and immunities. It was an inquisitorial
legal system, ferocious, degrading and horrible.[13]

Voltaire, like his fellow-*philosophes* generally, had greeted the
essay by Beccaria with enthusiasm. He noted in a letter to his
friend Damilaville on 16 October 1765 that he had begun reading
the work and already recognised a kindred spirit: 'l'auteur est un
frère' (Best. D 12938). Subsequent letters, such as one the following June to Damilaville (Best. D 13371), reveal that his first enthusiasm had been confirmed; Voltaire later praised Beccaria for
his reason and humanity (Best. D 15044). Damilaville was
informed on 28 July that Voltaire's own *Commentaire sur le livre des
délits et des peines* should appear soon (Best. D 13456) and by 13
September the author had sent a copy to his friends the d'Argen-
tals (Best. D 13551).

Voltaire had read the works of earlier liberal writers on criminal law like Montesquieu but without at that time reacting very
strongly to them. As Peter Gay puts it, 'he learned even more
from experience than he learned from books';[14] between the
reading of *De l'esprit des lois* and the reception of Beccaria's essay
lay the cases, crucial in determining Voltaire's outlook, of Calas,
Sirven and La Barre. In 1762 Jean Calas, a Protestant merchant
in Toulouse, had been found guilty by the *Parlement* of that city of
murdering his son. His case was conducted with almost scrupu-
lous regard for the 1670 Ordinance, which is to say that he was

interrogated privately, hearsay evidence was admitted, he was submitted to both the *question préparatoire* and the *question préalable* (the later torture for criminals once convicted, to secure the names of any accomplices), publicly broken on the wheel and finally strangled by the executioner. All this would be terrible enough for a guilty man; but later investigations were to demonstrate that Calas, as he had maintained throughout his trial and sufferings, was almost certainly innocent and that his son had committed suicide. Voltaire had very quickly begun to have doubts about the merchant's guilt and was soon by his defence of Calas to make the case the most famous in French criminal justice during the century, ending in a complete rehabilitation of Calas's name in 1765.[15] The Sirven story was very similar and also derived from the *Parlement* of Toulouse. Here too, in the same year of 1762, a Protestant father was accused and later convicted of murdering a child (this time a daughter) who had in fact committed suicide; but the great difference was that he was able to flee with his family (his wife and a daughter had also been sentenced to death) to Switzerland, where Voltaire worked on their behalf to secure acquittal and rehabilitation. Perhaps because the Sirven case lacked the pathetic drama of a real martyr (as Voltaire ironically put it, 'il n'y a eu malheureusement personne de roué' – Best. D 12969) it took much longer than for Calas, complete victory not being achieved until 1771.

But the case which had excited Voltaire's real horror was more recent and in a sense even more terrible, as Voltaire was himself to argue (Best. D 15044). Little enough is to be said in mitigation of the Calas sentence, but one may at least concede that the evidence was complicated, that Calas had confused the issue by at first denying that his son had committed suicide (for the perfectly understandable reason that as a suicide his son's body would have been subjected to public humiliation and hanging) and that murder is the gravest of crimes. The La Barre case could not be justified on similar grounds. Everything suggests that he was guilty of the stated offence. No miscarriage of justice confuses the issue; it was the punishment for the crime which was so odious. In February 1766 the nineteen-year-old Chevalier de La Barre was convicted in Abbeville of mutilating a wooden crucifix, failing to remove his hat when a religious procession bearing the Sacrament passed by, and uttering blasphemies. He was condemned to have his tongue and right hand, as the offending parts of the body, cut off, and to be burned at the stake. Despite appeals to the *Parlement* of Paris the verdict was upheld (except that the barbaric sentence was modified to simple decapitation), and on 1 July La Barre, after being tortured at length, died heroically. Voltaire's attitude is made clear in his *Relation de la mort du chevalier de La Barre*, dedicated to Beccaria, which appeared a mere fortnight after the execution, and in which he expresses 'l'attendrissement et l'horreur' that had seized him on hearing the news.[16] The shock was profound and enduring; nor was Voltaire to succeed in rehabilitating La Barre as he had Calas and Sirven. *L'Ingénu* (1767) is coloured by it, many important details relating specifically to the La Barre case.[17] But this was only the cumulative horror in an age-long sequence of such persecutions; for Voltaire the whole Christian era was one of continuous infamy. In August 1766 Voltaire, referring to the Chevalier, wrote: 'Je ne crois pas que depuis quinze siècles il se soit passé une seule année où l'Europe chrétienne n'ait vu de pareilles horreurs et de beaucoup plus abominables, toutes produites par la superstition et par le fanatisme' (Best. D 13512). In such a mood of solemn compassion the *Commentaire* on Beccaria's work was written.

Voltaire's commentary is in effect a free improvisation around a given theme. Sharing Beccaria's humanitarianism, he finds no difficulty in echoing the Italian writer's views, often with explicit acknowledgement. The section on torture repeats the arguments that the innocent suffer and that other lands have abolished it; indeed, Voltaire concludes with the generous comment: 'J'ai honte d'avoir parlé sur ce sujet après ce qu'en a dit l'auteur *Des Délits et des Peines*. Je dois me borner à souhaiter qu'on relise souvent l'ouvrage de cet amateur de l'humanite.'[18] Voltaire follows in the line of Beccaria and Montesquieu in denouncing disproportionate punishments; it is a perilous thing for society, he writes, when 'un petit vol domestique est puni par la mort' (p. 567). Like Beccaria he believes that punishment should be preventive and he objects to the death penalty, to treating suicide as a penal offence and to confiscation of a criminal's goods as falling unjustly upon the innocent dependents. His remark that criminal prosecution is 'une guerre que la justice humaine fait à la méchanceté' (p. 573) is probably an echo of Beccaria's phrase about capital punishment quoted earlier, the same point being made: legal punishment involves aggression, therefore let society be as compassionate about the unavoidable severities as possible.

But a thoroughgoing comparison of the two texts is not our present purpose. It is clear from the most perfunctory reading of both works that Voltaire has benefited greatly from Beccaria and also that he has been inspired to go beyond merely covering the same ground and has produced a characteristically Voltairean work. Beccaria is general and abstract in his argument, Voltaire is detailed and pragmatic: 'he saw the improvement of the jurisprudence as his goal, rather than the transformation of society itself by means of a new code of laws'.[19] The language of the Italian work is neutral in tone, much like that of Montesquieu's *De l'esprit des lois*. When it seeks a rhetorical effect it does so in a somewhat stilted manner. By contrast Voltaire employs all the stratagems of eloquence known to him – immediacy, variety, concision, hyperbole, contrast, dramatic irony. It is interesting to note the difference precisely at a point where Voltaire seems to be following Beccaria closely. Beccaria has an important point to make, but the statement is somewhat long-winded:

> Of two men, equally innocent or equally guilty, the strong and courageous will be acquitted, the weak and timid condemned, by virtue of this rigorous rational argument: 'I, the judge, was supposed to find you guilty of such and such a crime; you, the strong, have been able to resist the pain, and I therefore absolve you; you, the weak, have yielded, and I therefore condemn you. I am aware that a confession wrenched forth by torments ought to be of no weight whatsoever, but I'll torment you again if you don't confirm what you have confessed (pp. 32–3).

Voltaire sees the value of the device which, using an argument that is similar but not identical, he strips down to the minimum:

> Quoi! j'ignore encore si tu es coupable, et il faudra que je te tourmente pour m'éclairer; et si tu es innocent, je n'expierai point envers toi ces mille morts que je t'ai fait souffrir, au lieu d'une seule que je te préparais! Chacun frissonne à cette idée (p. 558).

For Voltaire wishes to write an essay on crimes and punishments for specific use in the Ancien Régime. He is concerned about religious toleration, advocating the view that heresies never do harm unless themselves persecuted: 'Voulez-vous donc empêcher qu'une secte ne bouleverse un Etat, usez de tolérance' (p. 545). Later, when discussing confiscation of a criminal's goods, he clearly has the Huguenots in mind: 'lorsqu'un père de famille aura été condamné aux galères perpétuelles par une sentence arbitraire, soit pour avoir donné retraite chez soi à un prédicant, soit pour avoir écouté son sermon dans quelque caverne ou dans quelque désert' (p. 570); and in a footnote he refers to the edict of 1724 which had promulgated these measures. As for sacrilege, that is essentially a young man's crime and should therefore be judged with mercy. In any case it is an offence against God not man and should be treated accordingly: 'Usez-en avec lui comme Dieu même. S'il fait pénitence, Dieu lui pardonne. Imposez-lui une pénitence forte, et pardonnez-lui ... comme le dit le judicieux auteur *Des Délits et des Peines* ... il est absurde qu'un insecte croie venger l'Etre suprême' (p. 548). Crimes against religion become of importance to the law only when they enter the secular domain. Yet Christian courts have despatched in all more than 100,000 witches. Such widespread legal murder has turned Christendom into 'un vaste échafaud couvert de bourreaux et de victimes, entouré de juges, de sbires, et de spectateurs' (p. 554). One should instead emulate the Romans, who though as pious a people as any let the criterion of public order decide what was permissible in these matters. The same canon law exposes to infamy the body of a suicide, yet surely a man should be allowed as in Rome to dispose of his own life if he wishes.

Criminal justice has become much more severe since the 1670 Ordinance, Voltaire claims. He enumerates the procedural abuses mentioned above: secret hearings of witnesses, the accused kept incommunicado and not allowed to challenge witnesses' depositions until the confrontation (by which time it is too late), the judge's excessively wide powers of discretion in selecting witnesses, the essentially inquisitorial rôle forced on him by the law. Voltaire reserves particular scorn for the *Parlement* of Toulouse, which has refined the casuistry of legal evidence to the point of determining not simply what constitutes half-truths (that happened in other places too) but what can count as a quarter or even one-eighth of a proof; hence eight vague pieces of hearsay testimony can condemn a man – 'et c'est à peu près sur ce principe que Jean Calas fut condamné à la roue' (p. 576).

To sum up: 'De quelque côté qu'on jette les yeux, on trouve la contrariété, la dureté, l' incertitude, l'arbitraire' (p. 577). What is needed throughout France is a regular and uniform code of jurisprudence, one in which civil and ecclesiastical law are clearly separated one from another, where the King reviews and signs all death sentences (as occurs in England, Germany and most Northern countries), where verdicts are not delivered without stated reasons. This is the first full discussion of criminal law that Voltaire has undertaken; by now he 'clearly understands that the criminal system constitutes *in itself* one of the strongholds of obscurantism, prejudice and barbarity'.[20]

Voltaire's own words were not uttered in a void. Between 1760 and 1780 attitudes changed radically. In 1766 the *Avocat Général* to the *Parlement* of Grenoble, Michel Servan, gave a *Discours sur l'administration de la justice criminelle* before the *Parlement*, in which he too demanded the reform of the 1670 Ordinance and the establishment of a clear, precise code. Servan, who admitted his debt to Beccaria in a letter to Morellet, criticized the use of torture, insidious interrogations, detention pending trial, and the theory behind legal proofs.[21] In 1770 another lawyer, Louis Philippon, published a work urging the need to abolish capital punishment; and this liberal movement continued to gain adherents in France up to the Revolution.[22] According to Morellet the new sensibility introduced by Beccaria's work became so widespread that in a decade the French courts had changed radically.[23] In the 1780s the number of those condemned to death by the Paris *Parlement* fell dramatically.[24] In 1784 Breteuil, Minister for the King's Household, reviewed the cases of all prisoners detained by a *lettre de cachet* and liberated many of them; thereafter the powers of the *lettre* were considerably reduced.[25] One of the rare reforms instituted under the Ancien Régime occurred in the field of criminal legislation when the *question préparatoire* was abolished in 1780. In 1788 a new pronouncement by the King brought further amendments, including the abolition of the *question préalable*, the establishment of a single court for registering royal edicts, and the requirement that the judge henceforth justify the sentence he is giving. These changes were never implemented because the Revolution supervened; but the Ordinance of 1670 was abolished by the Revolution and the new code of 1791 drastically reduced the number of penal crimes. This cleared the way for the new Civil and Criminal Codes, eventually promulgated under Napoleon between 1804 and 1810, which at last gave the unified and coherent system of laws of which Voltaire had asked in the *Commentaire* – though the death penalty and various corporal punishments still remained.

The closing years of the century witnessed a similar change of heart throughout most of Europe. Between 1772 and 1789 the use of torture was abolished in the Hapsburg Empire, Sweden, Poland and Tuscany; Russia began restricting it in 1762 and completed the work in 1801. Likewise the death penalty was becoming more and more confined to serious crimes. Yet in France the changes were coming too late to affect mass opinion. In the *Cahiers de doléances* drawn up at the beginning of 1789 the destruction of the Bastille and of the *lettres de cachet* are amongst the most common demands, even though both were by then largely nominal instruments of repression.[26] Venturi points out too that we should not exaggerate this new mood where France was concerned, for penal reform was making slow and uncertain headway against the opposition of the *Parlements* and the growing threat represented by the lower classes.[27] Furthermore, as he goes on to argue, there is some evidence that the *philosophes* distrusted partial reforms and felt that only by a total recasting of society could Beccaria's reforms be made to work. The evidence he presents is, however, brief and fragmentary[28] and the subject requires much more detailed attention before we can see it with complete clarity. One should not forget or belittle the reception accorded Beccaria, who fitted into the direct tradition of the *philosophe* movement seeking to reform abuses in the present system rather than to overturn it in favour of a visionary utopia. Voltaire's position is characteristically pragmatic. Inveighing against torture and capital punishment, he urges hard labour in the colonies in place of the latter. Perhaps this is, as Gay argues, 'a chilly, commercial kind of humanity' typical of bourgeois liberalism in the eighteenth century;[29] it seems, however, fairer to suggest that instead of making passionate but useless pleas for abolition in the abstract Voltaire is performing the more practical function of offering an alternative solution worthy of being taken seriously by government.[30] As Gay himself immediately goes on to add, the practical effect was humane; and that is surely what matters. The *Commentaire sur le livre des délits et des peines* is but one brief shot from the Ferney arsenal; though one of the most interesting of Voltaire's polemical works in the last twenty years of his life, it could be matched in importance by a dozen others equally significant, most of them on quite different abuses in the society of his time, and one, the *Prix de la justice et de l'humanité* (1777), a more thorough discussion of criminal law than the *Commentaire*. But the combined weight of Beccaria and Voltaire forms an integral part of the later decades in the Ancien Régime, as that society moved through ever greater self-questioning towards the final irreducible conflicts.

NOTES

1. P. Gay, *The Enlightenment*, Vol. II, p. 437.
2. *The Enlightenment*, Vol. I, p. 17.
3. Beccaria, *On Crimes and Punishments*, translated and edited by H. Paolucci (Indianapolis/New York: Bobbs-Merrill Company, 1963), p. x. All textual references are to this edition. For an account of the welcome Beccaria's essay received in France, see also *Des délits et des peines*, edited by F. Venturi, translated by M. Chevallier (Geneva: Droz, 1965), pp. xxvi*ff*.
4. P.M. Spurlin, 'Beccaria's Essay on Crimes and Punishments in eighteenth-century America', *Studs. Volt.*, 27 (1963), pp. 1489–90.
5. Paolucci edition, p. xi.
6. For an account of the complicated history of this phrase, originating with the Scottish philosopher Francis Hutcheson in 1725 and moving through French and Italian translations before returning to English, where Bentham found and used it 50 years later, see R. Shackleton, '"The greatest happiness of the greatest number": the history of Bentham's phrase', *Studs. Volt.*, 90 (1972), pp. 1461–82. The phrase occurs in the introductory chapter of Beccaria's work.
7. Torture apparently went out in England in 1640, and in Prussia for all but certain special cases in 1740: J. Heath, *Eighteenth Century Penal Theory* (Oxford University Press, 1963), pp. 48, 55, note 2.
8. *Utopia and Reform in the Enlightenment*, p. 100. The author however continues by adding that Beccaria denies 'all public sanctions of morality', which seems to contradict Beccaria's insistence upon public utility as previously noted.
9. N. Kotta, *L'Homme aux quarante écus* (The Hague/Paris: Mouton, 1966), pp. 116–7; Heath, *Eighteenth Century Penal Theory*, p. 53, note 2; M. T. Maestro, *Voltaire and Beccaria As Reformers of Criminal Law* (Columbia University Press, 1942), pp. 14–27.
10. One thinks of Thomas More's *Utopia*, for instance. For this and other texts, see R. Favre, *La Mort dans la littérature et la pensée françaises au siècle des lumières*, p. 308.
11. Paolucci edition, p. 42n.
12. See above pp. 95, 103, note 19. R. Anchel, *Crimes et châtiments au XVIII*ᵉ *siècle*, devotes a chapter to the various corporal punishments (pp. 109–19).
13. P. Gay, *Voltaire's Politics*, pp. 284–6, 295–9; N. Hampson, *The Enlightenment*,

p. 156; Kotta, *L'Homme aux quarante écus*, pp. 112–16; F. C. Green, *The Ancien Régime*, pp. 28–9; Heath, *Eighteenth Century Penal Theory*, pp. 41–3.

Latterly, Michel Foucault has placed the Beccaria essay within a more general context in brilliantly outlining the change in European and more specifically French methods of criminal justice during the late eighteenth and early nineteenth centuries, away from the horrors of corporal punishment, carried out with intent to expiate the crime, and towards the 'birth' of imprisonment as a deliberate and specific penalty aimed at correcting the criminal's soul: *Surveiller et punir: Naissance de la prison* (Paris: Gallimard, 1975).

14. *Voltaire's Politics*, p. 287. See also Maestro, *Voltaire and Beccaria*, pp. 34–50.

15. Numerous studies have been devoted to the Calas case. Amongst the most useful is D. D. Bien, *The Calas Affair: Persecution, Toleration and Heresy in Eighteenth-Century Toulouse* (Princeton University Press, 1960), which contains a comprehensive bibliography of works on the subject.

16. *Oeuvres complètes*, edited by L. Moland (Paris: Garnier, 1877–85), 52 vols., Vol. XXV, p. 516. Voltaire was directly implicated in the La Barre case because a copy of his *Dictionnaire philosophique* was found among La Barre's possessions; a copy of the work was burned with La Barre's body.

17. See F. Pruner, 'Recherches sur la création romanesque dans *l'Ingénu* de Voltaire', *Archives des lettres modernes*, 30 (1960); H. T. Mason, 'The Unity of Voltaire's *L'Ingénu*', *The Age of Enlightenment*, pp. 93–106.

18. Moland edition, Vol. XXV, p. 558. All references are to this edition.

19. Venturi, *Utopia and Reform in the Enlightenment*, p. 109.

20. Maestro, *Voltaire and Beccaria*, p. 90: author's italics.

21. Maestro, *Voltaire and Beccaria*, p. 110.

22. See Kotta, *L'Homme aux quarante écus*, pp. 138–41; Maestro, *Voltaire and Beccaria*, pp. 125–7; D. Mornet, *Les Origines intellectuelles de la Révolution française*, pp. 249–51; D. Muller, 'Magistrats français et peine de mort au 18ᵉ siècle', *Dix-huitième Siecle*, 4 (1972), pp. 102–7.

23. Green, *The Ancien Régime*, p. 29.

24. Muller, 'Magistrats français', pp. 89–90.

25. Cobban, *A History of Modern France*, Vol. I, p. 107.

26. G. Rudé, *Paris and London*, pp.77–8: The storming of the Bastille in 1789 led to the liberation of precisely seven prisoners: four forgers, two lunatics and a profligate Count committed there by his father (p. 93).

27. Venturi, *Utopia and Reform in the Enlightenment*, pp. 111–12.

28. Venturi, *Utopia and Reform in the Enlightenment*, pp. 109–16.

29. *Voltaire's Politics*, p. 293.

30. Kotta generally takes this line, pp. 133–5. A sympathetic view is also held by Favre, who cites earlier proponents in the century like the economist Melon (*La Mort*, p. 308).

9 The Development of Biological Science: Diderot (1713–84)

Le Rêve de d'Alembert (1769)

'Entre Leibniz et Goethe qui l'écrasent, Diderot est peut-être au dix-huitième siècle notre seul génie encyclopédique.'[1] The statement is provocative, as other names with solid claims to the title immediately spring to mind. Nonetheless, the range and flexibility of Diderot's interests are vast and constantly overflow from one traditional category into another. We have earlier had occasion to look at his dramatic theory; our concern now is with a quite different field, the nature and origins of the physical human being. Yet both relate to that concern for mortal man which is the sheet-anchor of all Diderot's research and writings. To Diderot infinity is a melancholy and sterile subject, because fundamentally outside the human domain. *Le Rêve de d'Alembert* fits perfectly into this context of humanist science.

The work was written in a few weeks during the summer of 1769. As Georges May points out,[2] it was a very different summer from the two respectively ten and twenty years before, 'deux étés de souffrances déchirantes', the first when he was imprisoned at Vincennes, the second when his father died and the *Encyclopédie*, already prohibited from further publication, was ordered to repay the subscribers their deposits – an unenforceable step, but no less unfortunate for that because of the further stresses which it imposed upon the work. But by 1769 he had emerged into the sunlight again. The *Encyclopédie* was at long last complete. On the financial side Diderot's worries had been settled by Catherine the Great, who was emerging as a latter-day Louis XIV in her patronage of the French literary scene.[3] Despite numerous commitments Diderot was ready for the series of masterpieces with which his name is above all associated: after the *Rêve*, he began the *Paradoxe sur le comédien* in 1770, wrote the *Supplément au Voyage de Bougainville* (1772) and *Jacques le fataliste* (1773) and revised *Le Neveu de Rameau* (1774). But with *Le Rêve de d'Alembert* he was completing one of the first of those enigmatic, speculative works, more question than answer, which have made him an endless source of both enrichment and bewilderment for readers ever since. 1769, says May, is the turning-point: 'il est dès lors sur la route qui mène à la sagesse' (p. 154).

Le Rêve de d'Alembert is on a scientific subject; was Diderot however a scientist? The answer depends upon one's definition, in terms appropriate to the eighteenth century, 'when the scientific disciplines were still embryonic in the hands of non-professional, unspecialized amateurs. The professional scientist had not yet become common; scholars, if professional, were not categorized in narrow disciplines, and if amateur, were as yet not subject to the hierarchical organization of the universities, with their degrees and rankings.'[4] Some wealthy gentlemen kept their own laboratories, some few scientists were paid for working in the field full-time; but most of those interested, including Diderot, looked on from the sidelines. Despite the invention of the microscope in the early seventeenth century, scientific development was hampered by the lack of proper method and equipment. The latter was a particularly serious drawback in the life-sciences, more especially so in understanding the arcane processes of human reproduction. One or two details may be enough to highlight the limitations: it was not until 1875, more than a century after Diderot's *Rêve*, that a scientist could observe the insemination of an ovule by a spermatozoon; the existence of the ovule itself in the ovary was not established until 1827.[5] Where information so basic was lacking, how could the whole subject of human fertilisation not be cramped and conjectural in the eighteenth century?

It is another aspect of the same situation that whereas physical science possessed its great theorist in Newton by the beginning of the eighteenth century, biology had to wait for Darwin another 150 years. On a more mundane level medicine, despite notable strides forward, remained primitive. Peter Gay speculates that 'in the eighteenth century a sick man who did not consult a physician had a better chance of surviving than one who did',[6] an apt comment when one recalls the satire on doctors in such works as

Le Sage's *Gil Blas* (1715–35). Given these reservations, one may nevertheless note the same tendency as in the physical sciences towards experimental observation and away from *a priori* conjecture. Roger sees the influence of the English scientist Boyle as outstanding here in urging English science into this new path from about 1660: 'A bien des égards, il fut l'anti-Descartes' (p. 250). By the time Newton was at last accepted in France the ground had been well prepared.

But progress in biology seemed to come to a standstill after 1725 for two decades, and there was even for a time a loss of scientific interest in methods of reproduction.[7] Most of the leading ideas at that date had been definitively established as early as 1680.[8] The basic reason lies in the overwhelming success of one theory, that of the pre-existence of germs, which reigned from around 1705 to 1745 and would not die out completely until the following century. Pre-existence had in its favour the same advantages as the doctrines of Descartes: it was clear and related to simple commonsense. It held that the life in human seed is not produced by the parents but is derived from Adam and Eve at the beginning of the world. Locked up in that primordial couple in the Garden of Eden, like so many boxes one within another, was the whole race of man. Haller calculated that the number of foetuses from the beginning of the world up to the eighteenth century alone amounted to the unit one followed by 30 zeros![9] This kind of observation, however, could not be used to refute the theory, for the latter rested on the Cartesian belief in the infinite divisibility of matter. Furthermore, its philosophical assets of rational lucidity were not its only ones; on theological grounds too it attracted support. For the pre-existence thesis assumed that only God can create a living being, men being merely tenants of the divine will. What however was gained for theology was lost for science.[10] Reproduction fell thereby into the province of metaphysics, there was no further subject for biologists to explore. Besides, species were fixed for all time by this theory and any evolution rendered impossible.[11]

But in spite of the popular impression that this theory conformed to commonsense it fell foul of certain awkward problems, particularly that of monsters. If Nature had no creative power, then, as Jean Ehrard points out, one has to assume that there were 'monstrous' eggs from the very dawn of the world.[12] Monsters were no new problem, since their very existence had always posed difficulties for those wishing to believe in a world of pure divine order; but during the century they became of increasing interest, were paraded about in salons and discussed with illustrations in works like *Les Ecarts de la nature* (1775).[13] The simplest answer was to regard them as freakish developments caused by chance; God was thereby acquitted of responsibility.[14] Others saw in the monster, whose body revealed so much organisation for all its irregularities, merely one more proof of God's admirable ingenuity. The fundamentally religious attitude to human nature which generally prevailed at the time gave such views lasting life, and despite many scientific investigations no further progress was registered on this subject before the 1740s.[15] But with Maupertuis's *Vénus physique* (1745) biology began to move again out of becalmed waters. On the question of monsters, Maupertuis simply refused to accept that they could fit in with the theory of pre-existence of germs. On the wider issue, he resurrected a theory that had long been discredited, the theory of epigenesis.

The epigenetic theory had found a champion in Aristotle and again in modern times in William Harvey (1651). It regarded the formation of a living being as coming from the addition of parts, the production of new elements rather than (as with the pre-existence argument) the mere development of parts already preformed. Maupertuis arrived at this view from a study of the factors affecting biparental heredity. In 1744 he had produced a *Dissertation sur le nègre blanc*, referring to an albino negro child then being shown around Parisian society. The albino condition, Maupertuis decided, must be hereditary and dependent upon both parents. This simple but unorthodox observation was pursued further in *Vénus physique*.[16] The subject of genetics became once more a matter for science and the way was again open for theories of evolution. Despite the unduly mechanistic aspect of a theory which crudely saw the growth of a foetus as a matter of juxtaposing particles, nature was given back an active, autonomous power that it had entirely lost with the apologists of pre-existence.[17] In the *Système de la nature* (1751–54) Maupertuis worked out a theory of heredity, allowing that biological variations might be due to mutations and recombinations in the genes.[18] Thanks to recent scholarship he is now seen as one of the foremost among Darwin's precursors; Glass goes even further and ranks him above all the rest (p. 74).

Meanwhile Buffon was making an impressive contribution in his own way to biological science. Like Maupertuis he was a keen admirer of Newton, but he realised that in moving from the Newtonian fields of astronomy and optics into natural history one could no longer apply the English scientist's methods with the same degree of accuracy. The areas of biological enquiry were 'trop compliqués pour qu'on puisse y appliquer avec avantage le calcul et les mesures';[19] Nature's processes always take place by subtle nuances.[20] Buffon, like Maupertuis, understood the need to move from the principle of certitude to that of probability. One sees here an important psychological shift in approaching the life-sciences, born of the need for continuing study while information was still fragmentary. The danger lay in the notion of probability coming to be so loosely applied that one would drift back into the discredited system-building of philosophers like Descartes, Leibniz and Spinoza, and the eighteenth-century thinkers did not entirely escape this dilemma, arriving unconsciously at new suppositions which went beyond the strict affirmation of the facts.[21] Buffon is himself hesitant about evolution. On the one hand, in his *Histoire naturelle*, a monumental work published in 36 volumes between 1749 and 1789, he looks back over the aeons of geological time and discerns the changes that have taken place whereby what are now mountains were once under the sea. The universe is in constant change: one day, for instance, the sun will probably die. In biology, living beings are formed by spontaneous generation through the action of heat, and organised by some 'moule intérieur' which arranges the organic molecules coherently. Despite the possibly spiritualist implications of the 'moule intérieur', which could so easily seem to be the soul reappearing in a new guise, Buffon's hypothesis was materialistic in conception.

But he stopped short at a theory of evolution. For him, species are well-demarcated, fixed entities, and it is not possible to move from one to the other, as is shown by the infertility that results when one tries to cross-breed and produces hybrids. So results the paradoxical situation that while Buffon does much for the concept of evolution by indicating the modifications that can take place in living beings, he rejects the theory throughout his career because of his firm views on the fixity of basic forms. New varieties are not new species, for the latter are constants in nature. Lovejoy therefore concludes (pp. 111–13) that while Buffon drew attention to the facts of comparative anatomy which warrant a case for evolution, while he did more than any other contemporary to place natural history within a greatly enlarged time-scale, his categorical insistence upon species as real entities, which seemed to explain away mutability as a purely secondary phenomenon, held back the development of the evolutionary notion. His is, as Roger says, 'une pensée solitaire' (p. 582). Buffon remained apart from the Encyclopaedists and went his independent way. Nonetheless, his *Histoire naturelle* was prodigiously successful. The first edition of the first three volumes (1749), printed in 1000 copies, was sold out in six weeks, and two reprintings were necessary. When Mornet carried out his analysis of 500 library catalogues belonging to the second half of the eighteenth century he found that nearly half of them, 220 in all, had copies of the *Histoire naturelle*; no other eighteenth-century work appeared as often.[22]

Buffon and Maupertuis were not the only influential voices commanding Diderot's attention. In 1747 La Mettrie published a work of unremitting materialism, *L'Homme machine*, followed by *L'Homme plante* in 1748 and the *Système d'Epicure* in 1750. As the titles indicate, the author rigorously excludes any particular spiritual category for man. Nature contains an active, sensitive faculty within it, which blindly works to create organic creatures if the accidental circumstances are right: 'ayant fait, sans voir, des yeux qui voient, elle a fait sans penser une machine qui pense'.[23] But La Mettrie, heavily mechanistic in approach, made scarcely any new contribution to biology and none to the concept of evolution; he was essentially following in Lucretius's footsteps, relying upon blind chance at work in a chaotic world, though adding to the Epicurean philosopher's view the argument that matter is inherently dynamic. Yet he will play his part in affecting the creation of Diderot's *Rêve*, particularly by suggesting to him the hypothesis of universal sensitivity in nature.[24]

A far bolder conception was proposed by Maillet in his *Telliamed* (1748), which is generally reckoned to be the first work to provide a genuine concept of transformism. The work is conceived as a fantasy. In it Maillet puts forward the hypothesis that the seas once covered the earth and are receding. The sea acted as the womb for the development of all species, many of which migrated to the land when conditions allowed. Maillet has ima-

ginatively conceived the idea of adaptation to new external circumstances which is at the heart of the evolutionary doctrine.
But with the genuine perceptions go many incredible stories, like
the one about the Dutch cabin-boy who fell overboard at the age
of eight and who, rediscovered twenty years later, was covered in
scales, with hands like fins; he could however still speak Dutch
and had not lost his taste for tobacco! A tale of this kind (and
there are many such) indicates that what we have here is not an
important contribution to biological science but a work of freakish imagination in which some lucky hits have been scored. In
dedicating his work to Cyrano de Bergerac Maillet was honestly
affirming the sources of his inspiration: he displays, as Roger says
(p. 526), a state of mind widespread a hundred years earlier. Yet
the work acquired considerable notoriety and went through four
editions before 1755. La Mettrie and Voltaire both refer to it (the
latter very sarcastically), and it may well have affected Diderot's
thinking.

Finally mention must be made of two discoveries which seized
the educated public's imagination. In 1740 Abraham Trembley
discovered that the freshwater polyp could reproduce itself. Cut
up into as many sections as one wished, it immediately developed
that same number of complete polyps. It was soon discovered
that other species, like starfish or certain types of worms, possessed the same faculty. This new realisation was to trouble
many thinkers, among them Bonnet, Réaumur, Maupertuis, La
Mettrie and Diderot. How could an animal divided in two
become two animals? Vast new perspectives were opened up.
Did this confirm, as Maupertuis thought, that the animal soul
was clearly material? Was La Mettrie right in concluding that
this demonstrated the organising faculty which matter contained within itself?[25] At the least the phenomenon showed
that nature was not passive as the exponents of pre-existence
had imagined.

The other 'discovery' turned out to be a red herring, but not
before exciting similar curiosity. In 1745 John Needham, an
English priest, stated that in examining through the microscope
an ear of blighted corn he had noticed collections of fibres, which
when watered took on a life of their own, wriggling like tiny eels.
How had the water reactivated apparently inanimate matter?
Similarly, meat broth placed in corked bottles was found a few
days later to be swarming with life. What at first seemed to be

spontaneous generation turned out, in experiments under more controlled conditions by Spallanzani twenty years later, to be merely bacteria.[26] Nonetheless, the experiments aroused considerable speculation, and in *Le Rêve* Diderot rejected Voltaire's usual scepticism in these matters: 'Le Voltaire en plaisantera tant qu'il voudra, mais l'Anguillard [that is, Needham] a raison' (p. 299). Always ready to welcome a new idea that seemed, after empirical observation, to enrich his concept of the world, Diderot was delighted with the possibilities unfolded to his imagination. This time however it was Voltaire who turned out to be right; despite that, the narrow rationalism which the latter applied to new scientific developments from the 1740s onwards makes him a less interesting figure in this domain than Diderot.

Diderot's great attention to biological problems, which puts him into a class of his own among the *philosophes*, can be traced back at least to 1744 when he translated Robert James' *Medicinal Dictionary* into French. Though mathematics had hitherto figured prominently amongst his studies, he was later to display indifference in this direction, feeling, as he expressed in it *De l'interprétation de la nature* (1753), that 'les mathématiques ... ne conduisent à rien de précis sans l'expérience ... c'est une espèce de métaphysique générale', and later on predicting its imminent end: 'Cette science s'arrêtera tout court...'.[27] The future lay with natural history, where probability, not certitude, held sway, allowing for the bold use of the imagination in devising hypothetical analogies. Scientific research must proceed by a combination of experiment, observation and reflexion, with a place for intuition in any original discovery. Already in 1753, in this his first serious encounter with physiology, Diderot was wondering whether one could make a categorical distinction between inert and living matter. The relationship of sensitivity and organisation to substance was still unclear to him, but he had evidently been influenced by Buffon, Maupertuis and La Mettrie,[28] and the work was informed by the sense of organic change and an apprehension of the dynamic quality of nature. Furthermore, the deism of his early *Pensées philosophiques* (1746) had disappeared. The questions put in *De l'interprétation de la nature* have man, not God, as their end. Such knowledge must therefore be popularised: 'Hâtons-nous de rendre la philosophie populaire. Si nous voulons que les philosophes marchent en avant, approchons le peuple du point où en sont les philosophes.'[29] Diderot had learnt the lesson handed on by Fontenelle, Montesquieu and Voltaire; in *Le Rêve de d'Alembert* he put it into effect.

It is not easy to describe a work which swarms with ideas in such profusion. One feels that *Le Rêve* is like the cosmos it describes: anything may occur at any time. Reducing it to its main arguments is robbing it of its essential aesthetic qualities. The dream-like mood allows for those audacious imaginings which had always delighted Diderot, just as it fits in closely with his views on the plasticity of things.[30] The dialogues, first between d'Alembert and Diderot, then between d'Alembert, his mistress Julie de Lespinasse and Doctor Bordeu, centre on the rôle of sensibility in the creation of life. Universal sensibility is the one constant in an endless flux. D'Alembert's first speech puts the paradox squarely: 'il faut que la pierre sente' (p. 258); it is a provocative statement of the extreme position, useful for clarifying one's mind at the outset. If movement, whether latent or actual, is always inherent in matter, then a transformist vision of nature immediately becomes possible. The old conundrum as to whether chicken or egg came first ceases to matter, for it presupposes 'que les animaux ont été originairement ce qu'ils sont à présent. Quelle folie!' (p. 267). Movement creates heat and heat turns the egg into life, memory, consciousness, passions, thought. But the fermentation, like Needham's grain, may produce an elephant just as easily as an eel. Both are equally miraculous, though not in any religious sense of the term: 'Le prodige, c'est la vie, c'est la sensibilité; et ce prodige n'en est plus un' (p. 30). The vision of immanent energy is well-nigh terrifying:

> Tout change, tout passe, il n'y a que le tout qui reste. Le monde commence et finit sans cesse; il est à chaque instant à son commencement et à sa fin... Dans cet immense océan de matière, pas une molécule qui ressemble à une molécule, pas une molécule qui se ressemble à elle-même un instant (pp. 299–300).

How then in this bubbling cauldron does one avoid the generation of senseless fragments? What gives unity, particularly to a single human being? Diderot is careful to point out that all such entities are purely provisional, that there is no such thing as individuals, since a being is only 'La somme d'un certain nombre de tendances' (p. 312). Even so, a certain unity is possible, and it comes from the organisation of the nervous system, with its headquarters in the cerebral cortex. Such an organisation has come about epigenetically, just as bees swarm together so that at last they form one single ball. Contiguity becomes eventually continuity; Trembley's polyp has already shown that some animals at least can suffer division without being destroyed (pp. 294–5), revealing thereby the fluid nature of each individual entity. Just as the bees admirably illustrate Diderot's argument here, so does, on a more mundane level, the metaphor of the spider's web later on for exemplifying how internal organisation is imposed. In simple mechanical terms the author explains hallucinations, inertia, loss of memory, seemingly incredible tolerance of pain and torture, even the apparently 'spiritual' faculty of imagination. Sensibility is related to the diaphragm; and the great man must learn to rule the emotions from his head, so that, as Sedaine had once revealed to Diderot,[31] he will always remain cool and lucid, whatever passions rage within him: 'Les êtres sensibles ou les fous sont en scène, il est au parterre' (p. 357). Everything depends on the capacity of the 'faisceau' to dominate all the 'filets du réseau' (p. 346). Yet there is no such thing as freewill; will is only the reaction to some motive or impression or other.

What room is left for an ethical code? Not, it would seem, a great deal. In the closing section, the 'Suite de l'Entretien', Bordeu takes an uncompromisingly descriptive view of nature: 'Tout ce qui est ne peut être ni contre nature ni hors de nature' (p. 380). Still, if ethical norms are impossible to establish, one may at least construct a social morality based on the utilitarian principle. Voluntary celibacy may not be a crime against nature but it is certainly a crime against society (presumably in assisting depopulation, an argument we have already seen used by Montesquieu).[32] Vice and virtue are meaningless, for one cannot affect one's own nature: 'On est heureusement ou malheureusement né' (p. 364). But society can encourage useful inclinations by the judicious invocation of rewards and punishments. For man is still an 'être modifiable' (p. 365). Diderot's whole argument seems however to leave some small part of autonomy to each person. The exercise of will is subject to prior circumstances, but most of those mentioned are subjective: 'quelque motif intérieur ... quelque impression présente ... quelque réminiscence du passé ... quelque passion ... quelque projet dans l'avenir' (p. 363). Since these impressions themselves must relate to earlier circumstances, one may at the very least speak of 'la prodigieuse variété de nos actions', as Diderot had done in his

famous letter to Landois in 1756.[33] In certain circumstances will
may even effect a victory over passion. It can happen with great
men but is not necessarily confined to them. Bordeu relates the
case of the woman whose hysterical condition threatened to
destroy her lover's affections: 'alors elle résolut de guérir ou de
périr' (p. 348). The result of the 'guerre civile' which raged
within her for six months was a victory for the will. While this is
far from a doctrine of liberty, it would seem that men are not
wholly determined; human beings have some power to modify
the effects of experience. It is sometimes claimed that Diderot is
totally deterministic in this work, unlike other writings where he
is more concerned with social propaganda and eager to stress
man's capacity for virtuousness. While admittedly some discrepancy remains, there is no simple antithesis; the ability of each
person to affect his own life, even in face of dire handicaps, is
noted in *Le Rêve*, albeit in somewhat muted form.

Many of the themes we have been pursuing earlier find their
echo here. The problems of spontaneous generation, epigenesis
and pre-existence of germs, the organism of the 'individual' man,
sensibility in human nature, monsters, are all present. From
Bordeu himself and the other doctors with whose articles Diderot
became acquainted in the *Encyclopédie* he developed an account of
the relationship between the nervous 'filets' and the central organisation in the brain, as too the rôle of the diaphragm in the
emotional make-up. Certain details can be traced to specific
sources; the swarm of bees, for instance, was taken from Maupertuis and Bordeu, though Diderot makes a colourful and fertile
elaboration of it. In the fifteen years since his previous biological
work he had kept in close touch with scientific developments
through the *Encyclopédie*, through d'Holbach and his salon,
through Grimm and his *Correspondance littéraire*. *Le Rêve de d'Alembert* is therefore a magnificent *summa* of the complex state of biological knowledge in 1769. It brilliantly anticipates the
chromosome theory through the discussion of the way diversified
organs emanate from 'chacun des brins du faisceau de fils'
(p. 320); following on from Maupertuis it touches on the concept
of recessive genes as an explanation of monsters (p. 327). Most
commentators have pointed out the suggestive phrase by Bordeu,
'les organes produisent les besoins, et réciproquement les besoins
produisent les organes' (p. 308), in which the second phrase
expresses a transformist idea, much as Maillet's *Telliamed* had

done (see pp. 308–9,n).

Yet the *Rêve* is equally significant for what it omits. Its imaginative sweeps do not constitute a genetic theory of heredity and there is no reference to the selective action of external conditions which, according to Lester Crocker, Julian Huxley 'has termed the quintessence of Darwinism'. Crocker continues: 'The history of species is accounted for entirely on the grounds of internal dynamism and viability'.[34] In assuming so much Diderot fails to discriminate. His cosmos is one where any separate, discrete existence is immensely precarious. Sexual distinctions too are uncertain; men are perhaps only female monsters and *vice versa* (p. 328). 'Tout animal est plus ou moins homme, tout minéral est plus ou moins plante, toute plante est plus ou moins animal' (p. 311). There are apparently no rules; monsters are everywhere. In reacting against the fallacious appearance of stability in nature, Diderot seems to have approached close to Sartre's nightmare vision of the absurd in *La Nausée*. Roger claims[35] that Diderot saw each species as having a birth, development and death all of its own; he did not conceive of progress from one form to another more complex. Like his cosmos, Diderot's *Rêve* pulsates with energy while excluding all transcendental factors, but it is an arbitrary mass of circumstances, lacking an overall theory; it is a striking illustration of the moment in scientific development to which it belongs, when the orthodox Christian explanation of life seems no longer compatible with empirical observation but the Darwinian order is still in the future.[36]

Yet we must remember that, in systematising the deliberately unsystematic, an injustice is being done to what is essentially a comedy of ideas, lively and humorous, with the dialogue form ideally suited to Diderot's exploratory and undogmatic approach. Bordeu remarks that 'du train dont nous y allons on effleure tout, et l'on n'approfondit rien', to which Mademoiselle de Lespinasse replies: 'Qu'importe? nous ne composons pas, nous causons' (p. 349). As Herbert Dieckmann perceptively makes clear, the flexibility of points of view within the work blends with 'the dominant principle in the *Rêve* ... metamorphosis...'.[37] The author proceeds throughout by a process of poetic analogy, of which we have already seen examples in the swarm of bees and the spider's web.

Some of the questions we have considered elsewhere concerning the reception and social impact of a work would be irrelevant here. *Le Rêve de d'Alembert* was a private composition, not intended for publication in Diderot's lifetime and known only to a limited circle of initiates. Yet the moral considerations are no less pressing. C. C. Gillispie sees an alarming evocation of social naturalism in the image of the 'cosmic hive, where the laws of community are laws of nature'.[38] One might reply that Diderot's political philosophy must be seen in the round and not deduced from these imprecise images; yet in the abstract this vision of a world where no rules of conduct apply except those imposed by society must be disturbing. Alone with his thoughts, Diderot has taken them to their extreme conclusions; it is not the moment for setting up philosophical safeguards. Yet the *Rêve* demonstrates, on the moral and social plane, the problem of a man-made society acting without reference to transcendental principles. The delightful vivacity does not conceal the tone of earnest enquiry; for the answers, if any, we must look elsewhere.

NOTES

1. Diderot: *Le Rêve de d'Alembert*, edited by P. Vernière (Paris: Didier, 1951), p. xxxv. M. Vernière's edition has aided considerably in the preparation of this section. Textual references, however, will be made to Vernière's edition of Diderot's *Oeuvres philosophiques* (Paris: Garnier, 1964), as being perhaps more easily available. See also the useful edition by J. Varloot (Paris: Editions Sociales, 1962).
2. 'Diderot et l'été 1769: Comment fut écrite la trilogie du *Rêve de d'Alembert*', *Quatre visages de Denis Diderot* (Paris: Boivin, 1951), pp. 101–2.
3. See above, p. 49.
4. H. Brown, 'Maupertuis *philosophe*: Enlightenment and the Berlin academy', *Studs. Volt.*, 24 (1963), p. 260.
5. J. Roger, *Les Sciences de la vie dans la pensée française du XVIIIᵉ siècle*, 2nd edition (Paris: Colin, 1971), p. 457. M. Roger's book had been of inestimable aid for preparing this chapter. J. Mayer, *Diderot, homme de science* (Rennes: Imprimerie Bretonne, 1959), is also authoritative for the present topic.
6. *The Enlightenment*, Vol. II, p. 19. Gusdorf also stresses the mediocrity of French medicine in the eighteenth century, in *Dieu, la nature, l'homme au siècle des lumières* (Paris: Payot, 1972), pp. 424 ff.
7. Roger, *Les Sciences de la vie*, pp. 322–3.
8. Roger, *Les Sciences de la vie*, p. 442.
9. R. Mousnier, *Progrès scientifique et technique au XVIIIᵉ siècle* (Paris: Plon, 1958), p. 370.
10. Roger, *Les Sciences de la vie*, pp. 383–4.

11. Since the terms 'transformism' and 'evolution' are frequently used in the following pages, it may be as well to explain the difference between them as I understand it. Transformism implies the change within a species over a period of time; evolution is an explanation of that change, fully developed only when Darwin's *Origin of Species*, with its central emphasis placed upon natural selection as a response to external conditions, appears in 1859. In brief, eighteenth-century thought is, at best, transformist, foreshadowing only certain elements of the evolutionary theory.

12. *L'Idée de nature en France dans la première moitié du XVIIIe siècle*, (Paris: S.E.V.P.E.N., 1963), 2 vols., Vol I, p. 213.

13. G. N. Laidlaw, 'Diderot's Teratology', *Diderot Studies*, 4 (1963), pp. 116–17; see also E. B. Hill, 'The Rôle of "le monstre" in Diderot's thought', *Studs. Volt.*, 97 (1972), pp. 147–261.

14. Roger, *Les Sciences de la vie*, pp. 397–9.

15. Roger, *Les Sciences de la vie*, pp. 417–18.

16. For fuller details, see B. Glass, 'Maupertuis, pioneer of genetics and evolution', in *Forerunners of Darwin: 1745–1859*, edited by B. Glass *et al.* (Baltimore: Johns Hopkins Press, 1959), pp. 62–7.

17. Roger, *Les Sciences de la vie*, p. 487.

18. L. G. Crocker, 'Diderot and eighteenth-century French transformism', in Glass *et al.* editors *Forerunners of Darwin*, pp. 125–6.

19. *De la manière d'étudier et de traiter l'Histoire Naturelle* (1749), in *Oeuvres philosophiques*, edited by J. Piveteau (1954), p. 26; cited in Gusdorf, *Les Principes de la pensée*, p. 188.

20. *Histoire naturelle*, Vol. I (1749), p. 20; cited in A. O. Lovejoy, 'Buffon and the Problem of Species', Glass *et al.* editors *Forerunners of Darwin*, p. 89.

21. See Gusdorf's excellent chapter on the subject, in *Les Principes de la pensée*, pp. 257–80.

22. D. Mornet, 'Les Enseignements des bibliothèques privées, 1750–1780', *RHL*, 17 (1910), p. 460.

23. *Système d'Epicure*, Section XXVII; cited in Roger, *Les Sciences de la vie*, p. 493.

24. See Ehrard, *L'Idée de nature*, Vol. I, p. 237–8.

25. Roger, *Les Sciences de la vie*, pp. 394–5; Crocker, 'Diderot and eighteenth-century French transformism', pp. 116–117.

26. Roger, *Les Sciences de la vie*, pp. 496, 727–9; B. Glass, 'Heredity and variation in the eighteenth century concept of the species', in Glass *et al.* editors, *Forerunners of Darwin*, p. 170.

27. *Oeuvres philosophiques*, edited by Vernière, pp. 179–80.

28. Crocker, 'Diderot and eighteenth-century French transformism', pp. 132–3.

29. *Oeuvres philosophiques*, p. 216.

30. See A. Vartanian, 'Diderot and the phenomenology of the dream', *Diderot Studies*, 8 (1966), pp. 217–53; and the richly suggestive article by G. Daniel, 'Autour du *Rêve de d'Alembert*: réflexions sur l'esthétique de Diderot', *Diderot Studies*, 12 (1969), pp. 13–73.

31. See above, p. 161.

32. See above, p. 66.

33. 29 June 1756, *Correspondance*, edited by Roth and Varloot, Vol. I, p. 214. It must be added, however, that the observation is used on this occasion solely

to support the determinist argument. In this highly polemical letter Diderot adopts a more rigid position than in the *Rêve*.

34. 'Diderot and eighteenth-century French transformism', p. 131.

35. '*Les Sciences de la vie*', p. 666.

36. *Le Rêve de d'Alembert* would therefore lend considerable support to Michel Foucault's thesis that no sense of evolutionism can enter into eighteenth-century thought, 'car le temps n'est jamais conçu comme principe de développement pour les êtres vivants dans leur organisation interne' (*Les Mots et les choses*, p. 163). The specific point in relation to *Le Rêve* seems undeniable; but the general conclusions to which it leads may occasion some reservations (see below. p. 245, note 7).

37. 'The Metaphoric Structure of the *Rêve de d'Alembert*', *Diderot Studies*, 17 (1973), p. 21.

38. In 'Lamarck and Darwin in the History of Science', Glass *et al.* editors, *Forerunners of Darwin*, p. 281.

10   A Red Herring?
Laclos (1741–1803)

Les Liaisons dangereuses (1782)

At first sight Laclos's *Les Liaisons dangereuses* appears to have much to recommend it as a testimony of the years leading up to the French Revolution. When it appeared in March 1782 it clearly touched a popular chord, for 2000 copies were sold in under two months, there were several reprintings before the end of the year, and fifteen editions of the novel in all saw the light of day during the seven years remaining before the Revolution. The book was much commented upon in salon and press; one is tempted to believe that the public read in these pages the prophetic doom of privileged society, the emptiness of a world which had rights but no obligations.

Les Liaisons dangereuses presents us, in heightened form, with a problem that affects all our reading of eighteenth-century French literature before 1789. We can never dismiss from our minds that the Revolution happened; and it is hard not to see events, historical and literary, as infallibly leading up to it, much as though we were in the middle acts of a well-ordered play awaiting the *dénouement*. The closer to 1789 the greater the problem, especially where the content of a literary work incorporates social criticism in any way. The society Laclos depicts, we may argue, is rotten at the core; like all things rotten, it disintegrated; hence the work is truly pre-revolutionary: *post hoc ergo propter hoc*. Let us then look at Laclos's novel to see precisely what he has to say about this society.

We may usefully begin by exploiting the acuity of Baudelaire, who first noted a social distinction between the Présidente de Tourvel, the single outstanding figure of probity, and the other main characters ('Seule, appartenant à la bourgeoisie. Observation importante').[1] In addition Laclos himself, we know, had good cause to resent the prerogatives of the upper aristocracy. Possessing only three quarters of nobility in his lineage, whereas he needed four to become an officer in the more fashionable branches of the army, he had to content himself with a commission in the artillery. By the spring of 1782, at the age of 40, he had attained only the modest rank of *capitaine-commandant*. His career had been spent in the drab garrisons of provincial towns like Toul, Valence, Besançon. In brief, extrinsic reasons exist for claiming the novel to be a revolutionary document, coming from an exemplary casualty of the Ancien Régime whose talents had been set at naught by the social discrimination of which he was victim.

But one misunderstanding must be cleared up right away. Madame de Tourvel is not a bourgeoise but a member of the *noblesse de robe*. Roger Vailland recognises this distinction in his stimulating if heterodox study of Laclos, but only to blur it immediately: 'Présidente, femme de magistrat, noblesse de robe, *c'est-à-dire* bourgeoise'.[2] This simply will not do. As we have seen, the *noblesse de robe*, far from representing a bourgeois class beneath the aristocratic *noblesse d'épée*, was virtually indistinguishable from the latter by 1782 in terms of social prestige, having indeed assumed the leadership of the nobility during the century. From their ranks came the *parlementaires*, whose power grew under Louis XVI, when he submitted as a new king to their authority in 1774 and reinstated the Paris *Parlement*. Madame de Tourvel's husband is a *président*, like Vanderk *père's* future son-in-law in *Le Philosophe sans le savoir*. As such, Monsieur de Tourvel would outrank a large number of the French nobility, just like Sedaine's bridegroom.

Only one character in the novel ever comments on the social distinction perceived by Baudelaire and Vailland. That is Azolan, Valmont's *chasseur*, who pleads with his master not to humiliate him by ordering him into the service of Madame de Tourvel, where he would have to wear 'une livrée de Robe' (*Lettre* 107). But the exception proves the rule. Azolan's view reflects the exaggerated snobbery of a 'gentleman's gentleman', clinging as does his tribe to subtleties of hierarchy long since forgotten by the world at large. One might compare this case of arrested development with that of the ridiculous aunt in Sedaine's play. The playwright had surely detected an attribute of 'la vieille France'; and doubtless Laclos was equally as aware of the anachronism when he came to ascribe it to Azolan over a decade later.

As has often been pointed out, in terms of firm social documentation Laclos offers very little; this is in striking contrast to, say, Prévost's *Manon Lescaut*, where the protagonists move in a world of clear objects and circumstances. *Les Liaisons dangereuses* places its characters in a time dimension which, if not wholly abstract, is certainly vague. Not a single detail pins it down to the late eighteenth century (apart from literary references to works like Rousseau's *La Nouvelle Héloïse* (1761) and Belloy's *Le Siège de Calais* (1765)).[3] The world of Turgot, Maupeou, Beccaria, the scientific discussions of Buffon, Maupertuis, La Mettrie might just as well not exist.[4]

Madame de Volanges, the Marquise de Merteuil, the Vicomte de Valmont, all belong to the highest strata of Parisian society. After Merteuil's adventure with Prévan, 'la Ville et la Cour' come to her house to offer condolences (*Lettre* 87). Money is no object; Cécile, for instance, has 60,000 *livres* of income settled on her (*Lettre* 2). By comparison, one might note that the total earnings Laclos made on his very successful novel came to 3200 *livres*;[5] and even Catherine the Great's *beau geste* in buying Diderot's extensive library from him in 1765 cost her only 15,000 *livres*.[6] Even in the high society of *Les Liaisons dangereuses* fortunes, it is true, are subject to catastrophe, since Merteuil loses all when her lawsuit goes against her and she leaves 50,000 *livres* of debts in her wake when she flees Paris (*Lettre* 175); but this happens only on the final page of the novel and is not essentially part of the plot structure. Apart from one earlier reference by Merteuil to the fact that her whole fortune is at risk – though she clearly regards it as no more than a theoretical danger (*Lettre* 113), money problems do not enter in. Valmont has 'un beau nom, une grande fortune' (*Lettre* 32) and is thus well set up for playing the game of aristocratic libertinage. Freed of material worries and of responsibilities alike, these people are available for all the pleasures, and all the problems, of idleness. Theatre-going plays a prominent part in their lives, particularly the Opéra, to which we find Valmont repairing immediately on his arrival in town (*Lettre* 47), or later when he flees from the Présidente's arms (*Lettre* 138); for Merteuil too it is a place to visit regularly (*Lettres* 29, 39, 74). But the productions put on there are not even mentioned. The Opéra serves solely as a club, the quickest way to rejoin the social circuit as Valmont's visits indicate, and a convenient meeting-place for starting an intrigue such as Merteuil's with Prévan. It provides a good chance to talk in the privacy of one's *loge*, which is where Merteuil begins her 'sentimental education' of Cécile. As the latter puts it: 'elle [Merteuil] m'a dit que nous y serions toutes seules, et nous causerons tout le temps, sans craindre qu'on nous entende: j'aime bien mieux cela que l'Opéra' (*Lettre* 29). Cécile's naïve comment indicates how irrelevant were the events on stage! The Théâtre-Français and the Théâtre-Italien fulfil similar functions; Prévan develops his attack on Merteuil in his own *loge* at the former (*Lettre* 85), while it is at the latter that she suffers her final humiliation and he his revenge (*Lettre* 173). A typical day for these people might end with an after-theatre supper, itself quite often the occasion for beginning or continuing a love-intrigue. It would be the culmination of a round filled with little more than social visits, gossip, promenades, correspondence. Little wonder that boredom was never far from the surface, especially for a mind as active as Merteuil's; beneath her witticism one detects the melancholy: 'L'automne ne laisse à Paris presque point d'hommes qui aient figure humaine: aussi je suis, depuis un mois, d'une sagesse à périr...' (*Lettre* 38).

Since this is a way of life based upon and feeding off personalities, what less surprising than that eroticism should be the prime motor? It provides physical pleasure, it offers the thrill of the chase, it allows one to observe and calculate human conduct, it permits of a Pascalian *divertissement*; both mind and body are catered for and only the heart gets short shrift. With Cécile Laclos affords us the spectacle of a normal girl, possessing an average mixture of qualities and defects, entering this society a ready-made victim. Kept in the seclusion of the convent until of marriageable age, she knows nothing of social manners, even mistaking the shoemaker for her future husband (*Lettre* 1). Her total credulity in this respect is not without some justification, however, for she already knows that she is likely to be married off to a complete stranger. Her destined *futur*, the Comte de Gercourt, a wealthy member of the *noblesse d'épée* and colonel of a regiment, is in his late thirties (*Lettre* 39), hence more than twenty years her senior. But though, having fallen in love with Danceny, she hates the thought of this arranged match, she knows that to refuse is to risk being sent back to the convent (*Lettre* 39); indeed, her mother explicitly threatens this a few days later (*Lettre* 62).

Marriage is intended for financial security and social standing. Happiness must lie in extra-marital pursuits, and Cécile quickly realises that the society around her condones this: 'car j'ai entendu Maman elle-même dire que Madame D...aimait M. M... et elle n'en parlait pas comme d'une chose qui serait si mal...'. Why then should she be the exception to the rule?: 'je ne vois pas pourquoi je serais la seule à m'en empêcher; ou bien est-ce que ce n'est un mal que pour les demoiselles?' (*Lettre* 27). So it is that, under the careful coaching of Merteuil and Valmont, she comes to welcome marriage: 'Je le désire même, puisque j'aurai plus de liberté; et j'espère qu'alors je pourrai m'arranger de façon à ne plus songer qu'à Danceny' (*Lettre* 109). As it turns out, of course, the diabolical engineering of her life by her two mentors destroys all hopes of this compromise and she returns to the convent as an escape from the odiousness of social reality.

As for *Maman*, Madame de Volanges, here is the exemplar of this society, more contemptible than Valmont and Merteuil because more mediocre. She does not question the values by which she lives, she merely conforms. In her youth 'la bonne Dame a eu ses petites faiblesses comme une autre...' (*Lettre* 106). Now, however, she professes to be horrified at such actions. Even so, she has not the courage of her convictions. While totally condemning Valmont behind his back ('jamais il n'eut un projet qui ne fût malhonnête ou criminel' – *Lettre* 9), she will not close her door to him. Is it for fear of his ridiculing her, as she claims (*Lettre* 32)? Or does she, like all others, succumb to his charm? Whatever the motives, she is no help to her daughter, who consequently seeks out Merteuil as a substitute mother: 'car le peu que je sais, c'est elle qui me l'a appris...' (*Lettre* 39). She is for a long time blind to Cécile's affair with Danceny, as she is blind to Merteuil's wickedness and indeed to the whole conspiracy going on about her; so it is poetic justice that she is punished at the end by being denied the full truth about her daughter. In a word, she lacks both principles and resolution.[7] Her one enlightened impulse to abandon Gercourt for Danceny as a future son-in-law is easily overruled by Merteuil. Danceny is unacceptable because, as Merteuil reminds her, he has no money, despite coming from an equally aristocratic family. By playing on Madame de Volanges's prejudices, the Marquise quickly suppresses the nascent goodwill of mother toward daughter.

By contrast the Présidente de Tourvel, though also from Paris and knowing its society well (she is able to recognise Emilie at once as a notorious prostitute), seems more at home in the country. Madame de Rosemonde's château is only ten leagues, or about 40 kilometres, from Paris (*Lettre* 80), but it is set in a wholly different world. The Présidente, one surmises, does not go to the Opéra. At any event, her life is ruled by her deep religious piety, and it was in this connection that she had come to Merteuil's attention 'ce jour où elle quêtait à Saint-Roch...' (*Lettre* 5). Her stay in the country is punctuated, at least till her feelings are aroused, by devotions, charitable works and the minimum of entertainment: 'Une messe chaque jour, quelques visites aux Pauvres du canton, des prières du matin et du soir, des promenades solitaires, de pieux entretiens avec ma vieille tante [Madame de Rosemonde], et quelquefois un triste Wisk, devaient être ses seules distractions' (*Lettre* 4); tapestry-weaving is added to this domesticated list a little later (*Lettre* 23). Yet she is still quite young, just 22, and has been married for less than two years (*Lettre* 5). Her husband is in Dijon (*Lettre* 34), involved in a 'grand procès' (*Lettre* 4). He never appears on the scene, even at the height of the crisis; so we may surmise that Madame de Volanges is characteristically imperceptive in claiming that 'elle était adorée' (*Lettre* 165). Certainly, her remark in the same sentence that the Présidente loved her husband requires serious qualification, when one recalls the Présidente's ardent confession to Madame de Rosemonde of her passion for Valmont: 'j'aime, oui, j'aime éperdûment ... ce mot que j'écris pour la première fois...' (*Lettre* 102). But whatever the precise relationship, for Madame de Tourvel adultery is nothing less than a mortal sin; hence the true nature of her suffering and the greatness of her sacrifice once she has yielded. She commits herself totally; unlike the others, she experiences defeat in the eyes not merely of society but of God as well, which is the extra element that gives particular savour to this intrigue for Valmont.

However, Madame de Tourvel's virtue has no necessary connection with her class, and any links one makes must be in the most general of terms. It is well known that Jansenist attitudes were common in the ranks of the *parlementaires* in the eighteenth century (albeit manifested more in political than in religious manner). So the creation of a devout *présidente* would carry no special significance in 1782. Indeed, had Laclos wished to pay particular emphasis upon the social distinction between

Madame de Tourvel and the other main characters, it would surely have been more effective to make her, as Beaumarchais was making the eponymous hero of *Le Mariage de Figaro* at just this time, a member of the bourgeoisie plain and simple.

What then are we to make of this society? Are the characters caught in a trap? Is Valmont, for instance, a prisoner of his caste, doomed to idleness? The aristocracy, it is true, had been limited ever since Louis XIV's time to frivolous games at Court. But despite the lack of glamorous foreign wars under Louis XVI, many young aristocrats (like, pre-eminently, Lafayette) fought in the American War of Independence – and returned to reap rewards in feminine hearts![8] A Valmont was not constricted to dull garrison life, as was a Laclos, by insufficiently noble birth. There was great support for the American revolutionaries among many leading members of the nobility on the eve of the French Revolution.[9] Outlets existed too for energetic aristocrats in commerce and industry. Chateaubriand's father was a shipowner; ironworks and textiles were amongst the enterprises in which the nobility were actively involved.[10] This was the more modern element in the nobility; no sign of it appears in *Les Liaisons dangereuses*. Valmont may conceivably have his money invested in industry, but if he does it is assuredly as irrelevant to him as any other aspect of commercial, military or political activity.

More pity is often felt by readers for Madame de Merteuil who as a woman, it is claimed, is less in control of her destiny than Valmont. While this is true, it should not blind us into thinking that she has no recourse as an intelligent woman but to use her wits in this destructive fashion. Just as Valmont might have gone to America, so she might have set up and run a salon. It is even possible to imagine that in different circumstances he might have been the intellectual luminary of that house. Countless salons existed in the second half of the century, run by ladies of intelligence: Madame du Deffand, Julie de Lespinasse, Madame d'Epinay, Madame Necker, to name but a few; perhaps most impressive of them all was Helvétius's widow who continued to receive in their house at Auteuil after her husband's death in 1771 until her own in 1800, her salon becoming a centre not only for the Encyclopaedists but also for the nascent *Idéologue* movement.[11] These possibilities were equally open to Merteuil, and the knowledge of them must be remembered when one attempts to evaluate her social situation.

Neither Valmont nor Merteuil, then, may be accounted wholly representative of aristocratic life in 1782. At most they may be placed in the 'traditional' wing of the high nobility, impervious to the currents of change and reform. It is precisely this traditional quality that helps to give *Les Liaisons dangereuses* a timeless atmosphere. Far from telling us anything precise about the years before the Revolution, its events could belong anywhere in the eighteenth century up to 1789, or even earlier. The basic structure of intrigues and seductions in high society goes back at least to Louis XIV's reign. If one takes, not the diabolical variety represented by Valmont but the more conventional version of a *grand roué* that is Prévan, one is strongly reminded of that erotic busybody the vidame de Chartres in *La Princesse de Clèves* (1678), or the seducer Versac in Crébillon's *Les Egarements du cœur et de l'esprit* (1736–38). Prévan's adventures, like the vidame's, provide the same sort of background to the main plot, serving to remind us that the protagonists' intrigues arise naturally out of their *milieu*. The vidame is however a minor character, whereas in Crébillon's novel Versac plays a key role. Versac is, like Valmont, a cynic who bends society to his will, manipulating people with a control born of his clear-eyed perspicacity in decoding human conduct. Both are in the tradition of the *petit-maître*.[12] One should also mention here Richardson's Lovelace, who forcibly makes Clarissa, now married, his mistress.[13] Even the sadistic element in Valmont's character is not quite as *fin-de-siècle* as is sometimes thought, since it figures in prose fiction at least as early as Challe's *Illustres Françaises* (1713).[14] These narratives provide literary antecedents; for a source in the real world one need look no further than Regency society, whose reputation for cynical licence was second to none. It has been suggested that Laclos may be attempting a general Regency style, to exploit a kind of Belle Epoque myth which the later part of the century felt about that period.[15] Whatever the truth of this thesis, there seem no grounds for believing that *Les Liaisons dangereuses* captures a mood peculiar to the 1780s.[16]

Nor should all this be wondered at if one rereads Laclos's *Avertissement* at the head of his novel. This prefatory note is pervaded by some obvious irony about how the events described must have happened in another time, for in this 'siècle de philosophie' all men have been made honest through enlightenment and all women modest. But at the end Laclos strikes a rather more ambiguous note: 'nous ne voyons point aujourd'hui de Demoiselle, avec soixante mille livres de rente, se faire Religieuse, ni de Présidente, jeune et jolie, mourir de chagrin'. This fictional representation is again stressed in a letter to Madame Riccoboni of April 1782: 'Mme de M... a-t-elle jamais existé? Je l'ignore. Je n'ai point prétendu faire un libelle...'. Laclos goes on to claim that like Molière's Tartuffe, the character is a composite of many depraved and hypocritical women. He adds:

> Mme de M... n'est pas plus une Française qu'une femme de tout autre pays. Partout où il naîtra une femme avec des sens actifs et un cœur incapable d'amour, quelque esprit et une âme vile, qui sera méchante, et dont la méchanceté aura de la profondeur sans énergie, là existera Mme de M..., sous quelque costume qu'elle se présente, et seulement avec des différences locales.[17]

The voluntary association with Molière reveals Laclos's fundamentally classical approach. The novelist is thereby negating the whole evolution towards individualist portraiture during the century, be it in Prévost or Sedaine or Diderot. He is still aiming at the type. Well might he have copied Fielding's words in *Joseph Andrews*: 'I describe not men, but manners; not an individual, but a species' (Book III, Chapter I). For Laclos it is the generalised figure that counts – the Rake, the Debauched Woman, the Innocent, the Ingénue; and it little matters for his purpose whether they move in a setting of 1782, 1732 or any date at all, provided that it is vaguely contemporary.[18]

Two *caveats* must be entered here. The preceding argument in no way implies a denigration of *Les Liaisons dangereuses* but merely seeks to define its nature and in so doing to remove some false conceptions. The literary quality of the novel remains unimpaired if we argue that a knowledge of the contextual society adds few insights to our appreciation of it. A further point to be made is that paradoxically *Les Liaisons dangereuses* can, as we noted earlier, be identified by its literary allusions as belonging to the later eighteenth century. This illuminates a general consideration. Not only is *La Nouvelle Héloïse* referred to on three occasions; more comprehensively, the influence of Rousseau and of sensibility lies heavy on the novel. It is in this line that Laclos's passionate concern for social justice and goodwill makes itself felt, particularly with the women characters. Cécile, Tourvel, Merteuil all in their different ways command sympathy because all are the prisoners of sexual inequality. Erotic activity may be a game, but the results for women are likely to be social humiliation and often, as for the three 'inséparables', even worse than that; one of the three ends her days in a convent, the other two are banished to their estates (*Lettre* 79). Only a woman as extraordinary as Merteuil can dare to attempt her own triumph over the code of conduct, and even she cannot succeed indefinitely. Significantly, the hero of society at the end is Prévan, who had ruined the 'inséparables'. Laclos's feminist treatise, *De l'éducation des femmes*, written just a year after the publication of *Les Liaisons dangereuses*, praises 'la femme naturelle' who is free, powerful and happy and who spontaneously enjoys making love. By contrast, social woman cannot be sexually active 'sans crainte, sans jalousie, sans remords, ou sans l'ennui pénible du devoir ou de l'uniformité' (Chapter VI). *Les Liaisons dangereuses* is the practical demonstration.

This sensibility is not limited to the women. One scene, so precise in its detail as to be unique in the novel, reveals the world outside the aristocratic play. When Valmont, for ulterior motive, visits a family whose goods are distrained because they cannot pay the *taille* and buys their salvation by paying the tax-collector 56 *livres*, 'pour lesquelles on réduisait cinq personnes à la paille et au désespoir' (*Lettre* 21), one senses Laclos's compassion and disgust that for such a small sum (which Cécile, on her income, might have expected to spend three times over every day of the year) so many lives can be ruined. Rousseau himself might have created the vignette.

But women's rights are no new topic in 1782, when feminist works have been appearing for a hundred years in France, and the spectacle of peasant poverty can equally find parallels as far back as the reign of Louis XIV.[19] Here as elsewhere nothing from objective reality dates the work. The underlying problems faced by the two main characters are metaphysical, not social. No reforms of social codes, no revolutionary change in sexual relationships will resolve their lucid but bored disaffection with life: 'Ah! croyez-moi, on n'est heureux que par l'amour', ends Valmont's penultimate letter (*Lettre* 155). As with every expression of sentiment uttered by Valmont, this statement is surrounded by an ironic ambiguity. Nonetheless, from the novel emerges a sense that love is the only avenue to happiness, which Tourvel (the only one of the main characters not totally self-absorbed) alone achieves, however briefly;[20] a sense of futility hangs over the brilliance of Valmont and Merteuil, wasted as it is on the desert air. The mystery of human malice pervades this novel as it does *Othello*. True, in the latter work Iago's evil-doing has no motive, whereas reasons are ascribed for the conspiratorial actions of vicomte and marquise in Laclos's novel; but the reasons are insufficient to explain such destruction of human lives and their capacity for happiness, and merely lead one back at a remove to the same essential question. Crowning glory of the classical novel as it is in so many ways, *Les Liaisons dangereuses* also anticipates the metaphysical defiance by the Romantic hero, the Byronic stance of such as Pechorin, Lermontov's *A Hero of Our Times* (1840). Laclos did not produce a tract for his age. He did something greater, in creating a timeless novel which transcends the limits of purely sociological interest.

NOTES

1. Choderlos de Laclos: *Oeuvres complètes*, edited by M. Allem (Paris: Pléiade, 1951), p. 717. All quotations from Laclos are taken from this text.
2. *Laclos par lui-même* (Paris: Seuil, 1953), p. 8 (my italics).
3. For the sake of complete accuracy one should add the allusion to the 'petite poste' in Paris (*Lettre* 63), which had been functioning since 1760: see *Les Liaisons dangereuses*, edited by Y. Le Hir (Paris: Garnier, 1961), p. 398.
4. Laclos had first situated his correspondence around the late 1770s, and the dates 1778, 1779 and 1780 are to be found respectively on various letters in the manuscript version of the novel: see R. Pomeau, *Laclos* (Paris: Hatier, 1975), p. 91.
5. Pomeau, *Laclos*, p. 168.
6. See above, p. 49.
7. Merteuil describes Cécile correctly as having 'ni caractère ni principes' (*Lettre 38*); there is every reason to believe that if her life had run its normal course she would in time have been the replica of her mother.
8. See L. Versini, *Laclos et la tradition: essai sur les sources et la technique des 'Liaisons dangereuses'* (Paris: Klincksieck, 1968), p. 40.
9. See H. Méthivier, *La Fin de l'ancien régime*, pp. 71–2.
10. P. Goubert, *L'Ancien Régime*, Vol. I, p. 182. G. Chaussinand-Nogaret argues that by this time commercial capitalism in its most modern aspects was in

the hands of the nobility rather than the bourgeoisie: 'Aux origines de la Révolution: noblesse et bourgeoisie', *Annales*, 30 (1975), pp. 265–78.

11. See S. Moravia, *Il tramonto dell'illuminismo: Filosofia e politica nella società francese (1770–1810)* (Bari: Laterza, 1968), pp. 37–45.

12. F. Deloffre traces the lineage of this sub-species in his critical edition of Marivaux's *Le Petit-Maître corrigé* (Geneva: Droz, 1955).

13. Versini sees only superficial resemblances, however, between *Clarissa* and Laclos's novel (pp. 518–19).

14. See 'Histoire de Monsieur Des Frans et de Silvie', *Les Illustres Françoises*, edited by F. Deloffre (Paris: 'Les Belles Lettres', 1967), 2 vols., Vol. II, pp. 281–409.

15. Pomeau, *Laclos*, pp. 115–16.

16. See Versini, *Laclos et la tradition* (p. 49): 'à quelle mode les *Liaisons* se réfèrent-elles? Une mode au moins un peu dépassée ... il faut bien avouer que les ébauches que l'on peut en relever apparaissent bien plutôt chez Crébillon, Duclos ou Dorat que dans les chroniques du temps.' The principal novels of Crébillon and Duclos belong to the period 1736–44; Dorat's appeared in the early 1770s.

17. E. Dard, *Le Général Choderlos de Laclos* (Paris: Perrin, 1936), pp. 484–5.

18. See Versini, *Laclos et la tradition*, who has trenchant comments to make along these lines (pp. 50–2).

19. But doubtless the inability of peasants to pay their taxes became an increasingly common phenomenon during the economic slump of the last decade before the Revolution.

20. Stendhal made the pertinent observation that 'La présidente de Tourvel est plus heureuse que lui [Valmont] tout le long du livre...' (*De l'amour*): cited in Pomeau, *Laclos*, p. 147.

I am indebted to the Editor of *Forum* for kind permission to reprint my article on *Les liaisons dangereuses*, which first appeared in vol. 16 (1978), pp. 35–41.

11 Universal Education: Condorcet (1743–94)

Rapport sur l'instruction publique (1792)

Condorcet's strengths and weaknesses have been well summed up by the editors of his most famous work, the *Esquisse d'un tableau historique* (1794). They feel that he is neglected today largely because his direct, uncomplicated character offers little reward to the modern critic.[1] An unfashionable man in the present Age of Ambiguity, he lacks those self-doubts and contradictions which we prefer to look for. Yet the vigour of a mind firmly possessed of certain principles about human justice and dignity, enunciating them clearly and arguing the practical consequences consistently throughout his life, has much to command the admiration of critics in any age, especially those who concern themselves with the intellectual's commitment in society.

Condorcet's life-history is that of a liberal, and in the end revolutionary, aristocrat. He was himself a marquis and of an unimpeachable background; yet from his adolescence he rejected social privilege and religious affiliation alike. He turned to the study of sciences, won a prize awarded by the Berlin Academy for an essay on comets in his mid-twenties, and at 25 was elected a member of the *Académie des sciences*. By the following year (1770) he had established close enough links with Voltaire to enjoy the honour of a fortnight at Ferney; he had become a firmly committed *philosophe*, moving in the same circles as d'Alembert, Helvétius, Diderot, Turgot, and had contributed articles to the *Encyclopédie*. Thereafter his life was a long series of battles for the liberal cause against State and Church repression. He warmly supported Turgot, an intimate friend, when the latter became *contrôleur général* in 1774, and like many fellow-*philosophes* was downcast at Turgot's dismissal two years later. As the Revolution approached, so his own political philosophy took firmer shape. It became clear in his mind that all his campaigns centred on one basic issue: 'd'accélérer le progrès des lumières'.[2] In this perspective must be seen his ardent defence of black slaves, which led to his becoming founder President of the *Société des Amis des Noirs* in 1788, and his republicanism after the Revolution had begun; and here also we see the philosophical context into which his views on education fitted.

Condorcet's works on behalf of educational reform came as the crowning efforts of the Enlightenment in this field. What passed for schooling did not by any means add up to a national system; and numerous were the plans during the period for improving public education. Rousseau, characteristically, turned his back on such a fashionable enterprise, averring his contempt for 'ces risibles établissements qu'on appelle Collèges',[3] and chose to make his *Emile* (1762), the greatest work of educational theory in the century, turn upon the tutoring of an individual child in isolation. By contrast, d'Alembert's article 'Collège' for the *Encyclopédie* is very much an Enlightenment approach to the problem. D'Alembert attacks a teaching programme from which a young man emerges after ten years 'avec la connaissance très imparfaite d'une langue morte, avec des préceptes de rhétorique et des principes de philosophie qu'il doit tâcher d'oublier'. He wants Latin replaced by French as the main language of study, a reduction of time spent on philosophy and more room for modern languages, history (starting with the contemporary world and working backwards), fine arts, music and sciences. Already in the early 1750s a comprehensive curriculum for the secondary schools has been elaborated. But d'Alembert remains nonetheless lukewarm in his enthusiasm for public education; well aware of its mediocrity, he prefers the advantages of 'une éducation privée, où il est beaucoup plus facile de se procurer les diverses connaissances dont je viens de faire le détail'.

The debate received a considerable impetus from the closing after 1762 of the 124 Jesuit *collèges* in France, which lent the problem of public education a new urgency. Within the next dozen years a whole series of works on the subject appeared.[4] Among these the most famous was La Chalotais's *Essai d'éducation nationale* (1763). The author, a leading figure in the *Parlement* of Rennes and a powerful enemy of the Jesuits, had composed an essentially anti-clerical treatise, seeking to remove education from Church control and have it run by the State. Teachers should be secular, preferably laymen; the instruction in morality should be independent of religion. La Chalotais was not opposed to religion as such, but he felt that it belonged within the churches and the family. Education, on the other hand, was a matter for the State. An important blow had been struck in the struggle for secular education. A decade later Condorcet's friend Turgot, while *contrôleur général*, submitted to the King a memorandum on the organisation of municipalities which included a section on education, mainly notable for advocating the creation of a Council of National Education to coordinate policy – a clear forerunner of a ministerial department. In this way education for all might be provided and everyone could acquire a true civic consciousness, with profound benefit for the country. Turgot's proposals in this domain proved as unavailing as in all the other areas where he held temporary authority, but they were another step on the path to Condorcet's broad scheme of reforms, in which Turgot appears to have had some influence.

At about the same time Diderot conceived his *Plan d'une université* (1775–76) in response to a request from Catherine of Russia. In this system of secondary and higher education he argues the case for a university open to all without distinction, with teachers paid by the State. The administration down to the daily time-table, textbooks, buildings, and qualifications of teachers and students are all to be in the charge of the State; Diderot prefigured in its main outlines the *Université Impériale* that Napoleon established in the next century. As might be expected from the editor of the *Encyclopédie*, sciences hold the chief place, theology, rhetoric and the classical languages being relegated to positions of minor importance.[5]

Talleyrand's report to the Constituent Assembly in 1791 follows the broad lines of Diderot's plan. In both works education is made accessible to all and becomes the business of the State. But when the Constituent Assembly gave way to the Legislative Assembly in September 1791 Condorcet was elected a member of the new body and quickly became President of the *Comité d'Instruction Publique*. His interest in pedagogy was well known. He had already developed his ideas at length in five *Mémoires sur l'instruction publique* (1790–91), and these *Mémoires*, basically unchanged, later formed the basis for his *Rapport et projet de décret sur l'organisation générale de l'instruction publique*.

Although Condorcet's work was in many respects similar to

Talleyrand's report, he and his committee began by setting the latter aside. It was felt better to start from scratch than modify a plan created by a different body. For nearly three months Condorcet and his colleagues deliberated, and by 30 January 1792 he was ready to present his draft report of their labours to them. Discussions ensued throughout February and March, resulting in a substantial acceptance of the original draft; Condorcet, as the leading personality of the Committee, had carried through a project that was essentially his personal creation.[6]

The report was presented by its author to the Legislative Assembly on 20 and 21 April, the reading being interrupted on the first day by a message of a different and more overwhelming kind. Condorcet had not completed one-quarter of the work when Louis XVI arrived to read out a declaration of war upon Austria. In the circumstances, when Condorcet resumed his speech the following day, he must have felt a sense of total anticlimax. The incident is ironically symbolic of the Revolutionary period and of Condorcet's part in it – on the one hand the most noble ideals of human progress, on the other the blight of political reality, the inevitability of war and violence.

The *Rapport* divides public education into five degrees. First, at the primary level, there should be a coeducational school for every village of 400 inhabitants; here will be taught the basic skills: reading, writing, arithmetic, the rudiments of morality. Next come the secondary schools, one for each town of 4000 people and designed for children whose families can dispense with their services for a longer period. The curriculum will include mathematics, natural history, chemistry, commercial training and more advanced elements of morality and social science. The third level of instruction is provided by the institutes, 110 in all, where a wide gamut of disciplines ranging over science, technology and literature will receive attention in depth. As can be seen, Condorcet lays stress on the sciences in line with the pedagogical trends of the time. He also follows the trend in limiting the use of Latin, seeing it as of value for specialists only. Likewise the teaching of ethics is rigorously separated from religious instruction, which is deemed to belong to the church and the home. The fourth grade is the lyceum. The author seems to envisage university education here, for he speaks of sciences being taught in their entirety and of scholars and teachers being prepared in these institutions; there would be nine in all for the whole country. In all these four levels of learning tuition would be completely free. This is essential, Condorcet maintains, if equality of opportunity is to be maintained. By this means the nation will not only exploit its talents more efficiently, the class differences will also become less marked. The brightest children at each level would be supported by national scholarships.

Crowning the whole edifice would be the National Society of Sciences and Arts, established for the purpose of directing the educational structure and for research. Condorcet evidently saw this body as taking over the functions of the various existing Academies. There would be four sections, for mathematics and physical sciences, moral and political sciences, applied science and technology (where the author explicitly recognized the unorthodox nature of his proposals), and finally, almost in an aside, literature and the fine arts – once again, it is clear where Condorcet's enthusiasms lie. Such are the bare bones of this plan, unexciting details until one sees them as part of the new society for which Condorcet looked to the future. Here is the blueprint for a community that has abolished privilege, that has replaced a closed society by a dynamic open one. The author ends, characteristically, on a perspective of limitless hopes and possibilities, looking forward to the day when men would be so enlightened that the need for learned societies would have ceased to exist.[7]

Education is conceived of not simply as a way of improving the national output but as a civic right; the opening phrase of the speech lists Condorcet's order of priorities: needs, welfare, rights and, only lastly, duties: 'Offrir à tous les individus de l'espèce humaine les moyens de pourvoir à leurs besoins, d'assurer leur bien-être, de connaître et d'exercer leurs droits, d'entendre et de remplir leurs devoirs' (p. 36). Education is the means of human emancipation and fulfilment; as such it must therefore be 'un devoir de justice' (p. 37). For Condorcet, one need scarcely add, it must be universal. The optimistic sweep of this vision brings a breath of fresh air after the hesitations or even hostility to the idea of education for all which most of the leading writers on the subject (d'Alembert, Voltaire, La Chalotais, Diderot) had displayed earlier in the century.[8]

Condorcet accepts that men are unequally endowed with natural talents and his programme leads inevitably to a meritocratic élite, but he is anxious to ensure that society will in all other respects be egalitarian and he does not accept that the less talented should be dominated by their better-educated fellows. All should be taught to their full capacities, male and female, young and old alike. Interestingly, the institutions Condorcet describes are expected to offer adult as well as child education. Nor is this education to be used for ideological purposes. Condorcet will have nothing to do with such dangerous ideas as those implicit in the phrase from d'Holbach's *Ethocratie* (1776): 'un bon gouvernement ... doit former des citoyens qui lui ressemblent'.[9] He is at pains to make clear that education must be disinterested and unbiased: 'Jamais un peuple ne jouira d'une liberté constante, assurée, si l'instruction dans les sciences politiques n'est pas générale, si elle n'y est pas indépendante de toutes les institutions sociales, si l'enthousiasme que vous excitez dans l'âme des citoyens n'est pas dirigé par la raison...' (p. 41). Furthermore authority must never suppress new and unwelcome ideas; no place for censorship exists in this grand scheme. All this is intended, in short, to dismantle ancient pomp and elevate man to his true nobility as a simple individual. Condorcet's phrase is eloquently direct; one must 'consentir à n'être qu'un homme et un citoyen' (p. 39). By so doing one builds not a society of subversive intelligences but the truly enlightened democracy which one cherishes with discernment: 'Il faut qu'en aimant les lois, on sache les juger' (p. 40).

Science, as we have seen, is to play an important rôle in this new system. For Condorcet an elementary knowledge of scientific method inculcates judicious thinking, whereas a similar introduction to literature, grammar, history, politics or philosophy will not: 'C'est que, dans les sciences naturelles, les idées sont plus simples, plus rigoureusement circonscrites; c'est que la langue en est plus parfaite, que les mêmes mots y expriment plus exactement les mêmes idées' (p. 39). It is the Cartesian ideal of language as denoting rather than connoting, an ideal which runs right through the prose style of the seventeenth and eighteenth centuries and has often been alleged as the reason for the virtual absence of poetry in the French Enlightenment. Like Descartes Condorcet stresses pure ideas, where words are above all clear signs; the argument is abstract, a kind of geometry of educational reform, which advances from point to point in a well-ordered exposition. Passionate intensity is markedly absent; it would not have fitted with the philosophy of human nature behind the *Rapport* which, as we have seen, maintains that men are to be persuaded by reason, not seduced by emotional demagogy. Indeed, Condorcet explicitly rejects Athenian oratory as dangerous: 'cette même éloquence, nécessaire aux Constitutions anciennes, serait dans la nôtre le germe d'une corruption destructive' (p. 35).

Hence the speech exhibits the minimum of ornament. Clarity and balance are the main features of its style. The opening paragraphs are characteristic. Each of the first pair begins with an infinitive ('Offrir...', 'Assurer...') followed by its predicate, then comes the brief third paragraph: 'Tel doit être le premier but d'une instruction nationale; et...'. There follow two more paragraphs opening with infinitives, and the sixth closes the pattern with: 'Tel doit être l'objet de l'instruction; et...' (pp. 36–7). Nothing could be more rigorously classical. The counterpoise of course helps the listener to follow the thread of the argument, an essential function; but one need only glance at Condorcet's famous *Esquisse*, a work meant for the eye rather than the ear, to find the same sense of a metronome carefully counting out the rhythms.

Are these pages, then, eloquent, as Roland Mortier claims[10]? The elevated belief in humanity and its simple expression go some way to justifying the epithet. There is a nobility about phrases like 'consentir à n'être qu'un homme et un citoyen' (p. 39), 'Le génie veut être libre, toute servitude le flétrit' (p. 38), confirming the view that Revolutionary oratory is the last embodiment of the *style noble*.[11] But some will feel that the speech is too academic in its manner to sustain interest. It was in any case badly read by Condorcet,[12] who was not a skilful speaker; and one may assume that he did not depart from the printed text, as even the more emotional orators like Robespierre read out their speeches, it appears, without improvisation.[13] The formality of style and self-conscious build-up of periods bear witness, paradoxically, to the influence of Latin against which Condorcet so much inveighed and which came distilled through the oratory of the Academies, the Church and the Law.[14]

This style was to change under the pressure of desperate events, as Roger Garaudy notes.[15] After 10 August 1792 and the collapse of the monarchy, as public clamour grew a dramatic form of oratory appeared, appealing to an emotional audience and full of purple passages with high flights of sensibility. A greater contrast could scarcely exist than between Condorcet's

chaste reasonableness and Danton's speech in his own defence on
3 April 1794 when on trial for his life before the Tribunal Révolutionnaire:

> Les lâches qui me calomnient oseraient-ils m'attaquer en face?...
> Qu'ils se montrent, et bientôt je les couvrirai eux-mêmes de l'igno-
> minie, de l'opprobre qui les caractérisent! Je l'ai dit et je le répète :
> mon domicile est bientôt dans le néant et mon nom au Panthéon!...
> Ma tête est là! Elle répond de tout!... La vie m'est à charge; il me
> tarde d'en être délivré! (p. 66)

Here is all the sublimity, even pomp, of a man who knows that in
48 hours he will be dead. Condorcet incarnates the grace of a
world still maintaining the essential civilities; Danton's speech,
by comparison, has the primitive grandeur of a man at bay but
contemptuous of those who will destroy him. Robespierre's
heroic style is different again in nature. Instead of Danton's self-
dramatisation we find an objective nobility that dwells on the
level of principles and Platonic ideas, far above the world of un-
satisfactory mortals. The orotund phrases are much closer to
Condorcet than to Danton's staccato style; yet they deal in un-
abashed personal emotion of a kind that filled Condorcet with
disgust and disdain. Witness this apostrophe from a speech of 7
May 1794 to the Convention:

> O ma Patrie, si le destin m'avait fait naître dans une contrée
> étrangère et lointaine, j'aurais adressé au ciel des vœux continuels
> pour ta prospérité; j'aurais versé des larmes d'attendrissement au
> récit de tes combats et de tes vertus; mon âme attentive aurait suivi
> avec une inquiète ardeur tous les mouvements de ta glorieuse révol-
> ution: j'aurais envié le sort de tes citoyens, j'aurais envié celui de tes
> représentants.... O peuple sublime! reçois le sacrifice de tout mon
> être; heureux celui qui est né au milieu de toi! plus heureux celui qui
> peut mourir pour ton bonheur! (pp. 78–9)

Such prose is totally out of fashion in our more ironic age; even
so, the rhythms are magnificent. One further point should be
mentioned, though almost too obvious to warrant it. In the contrast between Condorcet and Robespierre one sees the passing of
the old literary order. It is no anachronism to think of Condorcet
and Descartes together on the stylistic plane. Robespierre,

imbued with Rousseau's lyricism, anticipates the lyrical nationalism of the nineteenth century, as does the stirring martial music of the Revolutionary period.

Not surprisingly, then, Robespierre poured scorn on Condorcet's report. It was, he felt, both partisan and untimely: 'Le temps où nous sommes est celui des factions; or le temps des factions n'est pas propre à l'établissement d'un système d'instruction publique .... Avant de s'occuper des détails, il faut combiner le plan, et surtout établir les principes.'[16] Reactions generally to Condorcet's work were cool, more than one critic commenting unfavourably on the report's abstract nature;[17] many disliked its élitist quality.[18] In any case, the times were against Condorcet. Other considerations were more pressing, and the Legislative Assembly did not find the time to discuss his project. It bequeathed the work to its successor, the Convention, when the latter came together in September 1792. After some discussion, the Convention adjourned *sine die* any further consideration of the problem.[19] The groundwork was however laid for creating certain scientific and technical establishments, such as the *Muséum d'Histoire naturelle* out of the old *Jardin du Roi*; and the principle of free and compulsory primary education was affirmed. But it was left to the post-Thermidor period to put together some of the elements of the future educational system. Legislation prepared by Lakanal (1794) and Daunou (1795) provided for a national plan of education at three levels, the primary, secondary (*écoles centrales*) and the *Institut national*. The *École polytechnique* is another of the enduring achievements of this period. At long last France had an organised scheme of scientific institutions. Henceforth physics could be taught by a physicist, not a philosopher as had been almost universally the case till the Revolution.[20] The new system survived in its broad outlines until Napoleon in 1802 embarked upon the series of reforms that led to the *Université Impériale*.

Condorcet's own *Rapport* was therefore never implemented; yet its thinking underlay all subsequent reforms, and its optimistic assumptions about the capacity for human nature, if properly enlightened, to seek the path of freedom and happiness remain a crucial challenge to educational philosophy. It is easy to deride Condorcet's visionary picture of human progress, especially as revealed in its most explicit form in the *Esquisse d'un tableau historique*. Even so, much of what he advocated – equal rights and civil liberty for all, religious toleration, State secular education, the crucial position of science, man's capacity to 'affect the historic timetable'–[21] is central to our times. Condorcet stands as a link between the Enlightenment and the post-Revolutionary world: not the profoundest figure of his century but one of the noblest, and a kind of end-point to the period, whom Méthivier can describe without exaggeration as 'le guide et le dépositaire de la pensée du siècle'.[22]

NOTES

1. Condorcet, *Esquisse d'un tableau historique des progrès de l'esprit humain*, edited by M. and F. Hincker (Paris: Editions Sociales, 1966), p. 7.
2. 'De l'influence de la Révolution d'Amérique sur l'Europe' (1786), *Oeuvres complètes* (Paris: Didot, 1847–49), 12 vols., Vol. VIII, p. 30.
3. *Emile*, edited by C. Wirz (Paris: Pléiade, 1969), p. 250.
4. R. Mortier, *Clartés et ombres du siècle des lumières* (Geneva: Droz, 1969), pp. 108–9. In practical terms, however, little seems to have been achieved in the way of reform before 1789: see C. R. Bailey, 'Attempts to institute a "system" of secular secondary education in France, 1762–1789', *Studs. Volt.*, 167 (1977), pp. 105–24.
5. The following have proved useful in preparing this section: Mortier, *Clartés et ombres*, pp. 105–10; Barnard, *Education and the French Revolution*, pp. 18–39; Fontainerie, *French Liberalism and Education in the Eighteenth Century*, pp. 29–310.
6. On this and the discussion of the *Rapport* itself, the most authoritative work remains L. Cahen, *Condorcet et la Révolution française* (Paris: Alcan, 1904): see especially pp. 324–79. A useful presentation of Condorcet's work is also to be found in S. Moravia, *Il tramonto dell' illuminismo*, pp. 327–41; while an important contribution on Condorcet's conception of social science has recently been made by K. M. Baker, *Condorcet: From Natural Philosophy to Social Mathematics* (University of Chicago Press, 1975).
7. *Oeuvres complètes*, Vol. VII, pp. 528–9. (The text of the *Rapport* is to be found at pp. 469–573). It has also been edited by G. Compayré (Paris, 1883). As neither of these editions is easily accessible, all quotations unless otherwise stated have been taken from the extracts in *Les Orateurs de la Révolution française*, edited by R. Garaudy (Paris: Classiques Larousse, n.d.), pp. 36–41; the editor also provides a brief but interesting introduction on the general subject. The *Rapport* is translated unabridged in Fontainerie, pp. 323–78, and abridged in J. H. Stewart, *A Documentary Survey of the French Revolution* (New York: Macmillan, 1951), pp. 346–70.
8. See Mortier, *Clartés et ombres*, pp. 105–11.

9. See p. 22; cited in Mortier, *Clartés et ombres*, p. 113.
10. *Clartés et ombres*, p. 113.
11. See F. Furet, 'La "librairie" du royaume de France au 18ᵉ siècle', *Livre et société dans la France du XVIIIᵉ siècle* (Paris/The Hague: Mouton), Vol. I (1965), p. 20.
12. Cahen, *Condorcet et la Révolution française*, p. 378.
13. J. M. Thompson, *Robespierre and the French Revolution* (English Universities Press, 1952), p. 155.
14. P. Gay, 'Rhetoric and Politics in the French Revolution', *The Party of Humanity*, p. 175; Garaudy (editor), *Les Orateurs*, p. 6.
15. Garaudy (editor), *Les Orateurs*, p. 7.
16. *Lettres à mes Commettans*, no. 2, *Oeuvres*, edited by Laponneraye, Vol. III, pp. 195–6; cited in M. J. Harrison, 'The Conflict of Ideas Between the Gironde and the Montagne As Reflected in the Press: With Particular Reference to February–June 1793', M.A. thesis, unpublished, University of Manchester. I am indebted to Miss Harrison for kindly letting me read her work and allowing me to quote from it.
17. Cahen, *Condorcet et la Révolution française*, p. 378, note 3.
18. R. Hahn, 'Elite scientifique et démocratie politique dans la France révolutionnaire', *Dix-huitième siècle*, I (1969), pp. 233–5.
19. Cahen, *Condorcet et la Révolution française*, pp. 495–6.
20. Gusdorf, *Les Principes de la pensée*, pp. 178–9.
21. F. E. Manuel, *The Prophets of Paris* (New York: Harper, 1962), p. 81.
22. *La Fin de l'ancien régime*, p. 73.

12 Exiles from the Revolution: Sénac de Meilhan (1734–1803)

L'Émigré (1797)

Like all revolutions, the turbulent events of 1789 produced a flood of *émigrés*, rising to a climax with the persecutions of 1793. Many fled immediately after 14 July, among them the King's youngest brother, the Comte d'Artois (the future Charles X). As the *Grande Peur* swept the countryside with peasant uprisings and attacks on châteaux the emigration grew; but this was only the beginning of the exodus. With life becoming more precarious the numbers built up, and by 1791 their size, and especially their presence on the German border, were causing great alarm to the government. Though many came to England, the Rhineland seems to have been the most favoured region. Coblenz became their centre, while at Worms the *Armée des Princes* trained for war and the reconquest of the homeland in the name of the King. Many believed that, with Louis XVI in virtual captivity, their only effective allegiance could be to Artois. Louis for his part feared Artois's ambitions and at first he did not support the *émigré* plans, but after his abortive attempt at escape to join his supporters over the frontier in 1791 his attitude hardened. He encouraged French officers to defect, which they did in such numbers that at the end of 1791 three-quarters of the 8000 were on foreign soil. By August 1792 there were 4000 to 5000 *émigrés* in the Duke of Brunswick's army when it invaded France.[1]

Despite the growing threat to security which the *émigrés* represented, no action was taken against them at first, for it was felt that repressive measures would run counter to the noble ideals incorporated in the Declaration of the Rights of Man (August 1789). This attitude changed only after the royal flight to Varennes in June 1791. In August of that year the first of a long series of decrees against *émigrés* was published, ordering them to return home. A similar edict in November was vetoed by the King, acting constitutionally but imprudently in view of the mounting tension. The following February *émigré* property was declared confiscated unless the owners returned within three months. As the situation at home became more desperate, so the decrees grew more draconian. Coblenz came to be seen as the centre of a vast royal conspiracy. In August 1792 an ordinance provided for the arrest of *émigrés'* relatives. By March 1793 the previous measures were consolidated into a comprehensive law which began with the chilling statements that *émigrés* were banished in perpetuity from French territory and that they were administratively dead.[2]

Long before this last date the *émigrés* had cut their last bridges with their native country. In July 1792 the Duke of Brunswick, as commanding officer of the allied armies at war with France since April, put his signature to a manifesto drawn up by an *émigré*. The Manifesto stated that the aim of the military operation was to liberate the Royal Family and provide for the re-establishment of order in France. The National Guard were called upon to supervise peace and security until the invading armies arrived; they and the other authorities were held responsible for all breaches of law and order. All inhabitants who opposed the allied forces would be punished immediately with due rigour of military law and their houses burned. Paris was threatened with total destruction if the safety and freedom of the Royal Family were not provided for immediately.[3] The effect of such a declaration can easily be guessed at; far from being intimidated, the revolutionaries were stiffened in their resistance. Anger mounted against not only the foreign invaders and their French allies but also the throne, despite Louis XVI's repudiation of the document, and the attack on the Tuileries Palace for which the Manifesto had threatened an 'ever-memorable vengeance' became inevitable. On 10 August the monarchy was overthrown. On 19 August Brunswick's armies crossed into France. The situation was grave and tempers at fever-pitch; it is within this context that one must place the terrible September massacres of prisoners which took place in Paris. But the enemy at the frontier proved less effective than expected, and after the battle of Valmy (20 September) Brunswick began to retreat. The danger to the Revolution from outside was at an end, and although the Revolutionary Calendar was not to be adopted until a year later, it began, suitably enough, on the following day (when the royalty was abolished).

The *émigré* army was disbanded and its soldiers left to their fate. They had never been a very military force from the start, burdened with old men, women and children, short of food, clothing and money.[4] Now they were totally discredited, both helpless and homeless. Some states like Prussia banned them from their territories; others were often inhospitable to these increasingly tedious victims of history. They scattered widely, even as far as Russia. As happens so often among exile groups when despair sets in, internal dissensions grew. After Robespierre's death there was a steady return to the homeland. The French laws against the *émigrés* became more lenient, despite a brief reversal in 1797–99, and in 1802 Napoleon declared an almost total amnesty.[5] But many irreducible monarchists did not return until Louis XVIII was proclaimed King in 1814; and one should not forget those who never went back but became permanent residents of their new country. When the law of indemnity was finally voted for *émigrés* in 1825, two from the Moselle *département*, for instance, were still living in Prague and one each in Luxemburg, the Netherlands, Graz, Nuremberg, Mannheim, New Orleans and Montreal.[6] It is a pattern to which, in our age of mass population movements under pressure of revolution and war, we are well accustomed.

Contrary to popular imagination, this counter-Revolutionary group was not wholly or even mainly aristocratic. It is reckoned that the *émigrés* eventually numbered around 150,000.[7] Of the 97,500 whose status is known, only seventeen per cent were nobility and another 25 per cent were clergy. The majority were Third Estate, with large elements from the working class (fourteen per cent) and peasantry (nineteen per cent), though every class, profession and trade contributed its share. Only about five per cent of the French nobility departed the homeland.[8] The picture of an isolated and privileged aristocracy fleeing out of fear or self-interest does not do justice to the complexity of this movement.

Sénac de Meilhan was one of the most interesting figures among the *émigrés* and, although he suffered no catastrophes, his story is a characteristically melancholy one. Chateaubriand and those of his generation who were coming to maturity in 1789 generally survived, however great their difficulties, and returned to post-Revolutionary France. But Sénac was over 50 when the Bastille fell, a man formed in a henceforth unchangeable mould, with a past of some distinction but no future. Whereas Chateaubriand is a nineteenth-century figure, Sénac belongs to the Ancien Régime, and his main interest for our study lies in the way he reacted to the great historical events that came comparatively late in his life. He was born into the most distinguished reaches of the *noblesse de robe*, his father being chief physician to Louis XV; from his earliest days he moved in the highest social circles. When he was just over twenty he had already fulfilled an invitation from Voltaire to stay in Geneva with him. In 1762 he began his administrative career and four years later became *Intendant* at La Rochelle; this was followed by similar posts at Aix in 1773 and at Valenciennes in 1775. These successes whetted his appetite for even greater things, and in 1783 he made a discreet bid for the post of *contrôleur général*, but despite a two-hour interview with the King he was passed over in favour of Calonne. Sénac published his *Considérations sur les richesses et le luxe* in 1787, further evidence of his competence in fiscal matters, and his later writings resound with a passionate contempt for Necker's policies as being one of the most crucial elements in setting off the Revolution. His own prescription echoed Turgot's ideas, placing the emphasis upon free trade and industry unhampered by monopolies and restrictive practices.

But Sénac was never to be a minister. When the Revolution broke out he played no public part, continued to go along to the Tuileries Palace to pay court to the King, and then, in the middle of 1790, he emigrated to England. Thereafter he led a wandering existence, through Germany, Russia (where he discussed with Catherine the Great a history of Russia that she had commissioned him to write), Poland, and Austria, ending up in Vienna, where he was to die in 1803. As with so many other *émigrés*, what began as a fairly comfortable, worldly situation deteriorated into a lonely, impoverished old age. Despite many difficulties with Catherine over the work he was preparing for her, her pension seems to have kept him in relative ease, but her death in 1796 proved an unhappy landmark in his life, since her successor Paul I terminated both commission and payments.[9] Sénac died virtually forgotten, and his novel *L'Émigré*, by which his name is now best remembered, was virtually unknown until Sainte-Beuve rediscovered it and gave a critical account of it in his *Causeries du lundi* in 1856.[10] It is only in recent years, indeed, that *L'Émigré* has become easily available.[11]

The story, told entirely through letters, is set in the Rhineland in July 1793, where the family of Victorine the Comtesse de Loewenstein comes upon the wounded Marquis de Saint-Alban, who while serving in the Prussian army had fallen into an ambush laid by French troops. The Marquis is a conventional romance hero, young, handsome, courteous and brave. He and the Comtesse soon fall in love with each other, although all avowal on her part must be suppressed as she is married, to a man both older and quite unglamorous. Saint-Alban comes from the highest ranks of the *noblesse d'épée*, had been presented at Court at nineteen years of age (p. 1579), and his family had been extremely wealthy: 'Vingt-six villages dépendaient de la terre de son nom . . . Il avait deux châteaux superbes' (p. 1556), but all this has been lost. He had emigrated to escape arrest and fought in the *Armée des Princes* in 1792, sufficient evidence of his continuing hostility to the French Revolution. For most of the novel his love for the Comtesse appears doomed to be forever unrequited, but at last the Comte conveniently dies from a heart attack and Victorine is free to marry her lover. Alas! at the height of their joy the Marquis, now fully recovered from his wounds, is recalled to join Condé's army. He is captured by the enemy, taken to Paris, tried and convicted, but before the authorities can guillotine him he commits suicide. Victorine, on hearing the tragic news, goes mad and dies of grief.

All this is the most hackneyed of romance plots and Sénac de Meilhan does little to rejuvenate it. Much is owed to Richardson, to Madame de La Fayette's *La Princesse de Clèves* and Rousseau's *La Nouvelle Héloïse* amongst other romances,[12] but Sénac's psychological insight is not profound enough to put his novel in the same class as they. However, the work has much to recommend it. In particular the author provides a realistic account of *émigré* life with all its miseries and privations. The Président de Longueil, a fellow-exile who acts as a kind of father-figure to Saint-Alban, tells of the mass flight which took place from Nice to Turin before the French armies in the autumn of 1792:

Dans peu d'heures le chemin du col de Tende fut couvert de monde, de vieillards, d'enfants, de femmes grosses, d'autres qui portaient sur leurs bras leur enfant qu'elles nourrissaient; des magistrats, des évêques, des moines dispersés sur cette route fuyaient consternés. Un évêque de quatre-vingt-trois ans, entre autres, offrait le spectacle le plus touchant; hors d'état de marcher, il était porté par des prêtres qui se relayaient tour à tour; une femme d'un nom distingué se trouva au milieu du voyage pressée des douleurs de l'enfantement, et accoucha sur le chemin, dénuée de tout secours; pour comble de malheur, des soldats piémontais entendant la nuit un grand bruit sur la route, et ne distinguant rien, se figurèrent qu'un détachement de Patriotes arrivait sur eux, ils tirèrent et blessèrent plusieurs des personnes qui marchaient en avant de notre misérable troupe (pp.1608–9).

The tale of banal despair and courage continues: inundations from the continual rain, confiscation of property by the Piedmontese troops, no lodging once Turin is reached, exorbitant charges for transport and an order to leave the city within a week. Only after they had set out for Venice do they find warm hospitality. (We are told later in the novel that Russia, England, Prussia and Brunswick have also offered a welcome to *émigrés*.) Poverty is the common lot of these people and necessity has urged them into whatever work they can find, teaching for the more fortunate, for the less so jobs like that of apprentice carpenters or liquor salesmen. These experiences would, however, arouse our sympathy more if Sénac did not appear to be at least as concerned about the indignity as the poverty of such occupations. The liquor retailer, we learn from another *émigré*, was 'un des meilleurs gentilshommes de ma province' and now 'je l'ai vu en tablier dans sa baraque' (p. 1614). One views the *émigrés* with less mixed feelings of compassion when this snobbishness is absent, as in the letter from the Marquis about the woman who, when all money and hope were gone, committed suicide with simple courage (p. 1740).

Nevertheless, the contrast between past and present is not entirely a function of Sénac's aristocratic sentiments. He is clearly fascinated by the way people react to this overturning of their lives and advances as a general proposition that 'On y voit souvent l'homme rendu en quelque sorte à son état primitif' (p. 1816). Sometimes this brings out great courage in persons formerly weak and timid, like the lady who had committed suicide and whom, before the Revolution, great wealth had permitted an excessive indulgence in her own delicacy and comforts. Others, however, become totally demoralised and turn into despoilers of one another. But in practice the majority of the individual examples of *émigré* behaviour we witness are of the most noble kind, presumably because Sénac's general observations of human conduct clashed with his desire to write a passionate document in defence of his fellow-exiles. As he had said in the Preface, he is writing 'une histoire', not 'un roman', for the events he narrates have actually happened even if the characters are fictitious. Furthermore, the Revolution itself is the very stuff of the narrative:

> les hommes précipités du faîte de la grandeur et de la richesse, dispersés sur le globe entier, présentent l'image de gens waufragés qui se sauvent à la nage dans des îles désertes, là, chacun oubliant son ancien état est forcé de revenir à l'état de nature; il cherche en soi-même des ressources, et développe une industrie et une activité qui lui étaient souvent inconnues à lui-même. Les rencontres les plus extraordinaires, les plus étonnantes circonstances, les plus déplorables situations deviennent des événements communs, et surpassent ce que les auteurs de roman peuvent imaginer (p. 1549).

The value of *L'Émigré* as an historical account is not limited to the effects of the Revolution abroad. Much time is spent on describing the atmosphere of Paris from the eve of the Revolution to 1793, and as a former *Intendant* Sénac is well acquainted with the Ancien Régime and competent to discuss its defects. Through the Président de Longueil and the marquis de Saint-Alban he expresses personal views that are also to be found in other of his works, like the *Considérations sur l'esprit et les mœurs* (1787), *Considérations sur les richesses et le luxe* (1787) and the treatise *Des principes et des causes de la Révolution en France* (1790). The Revolution had not been inevitable; it was an accident for which the volatile and passionate temperament of the French nation was largely to blame. The monarchy had done nothing wrong except to tolerate the demagogic reactions too liberally, but the people, 'extrême dans ses idées et séduit par ses orateurs' (p. 1686), had come to seek the sovereign power itself and to regard the monarchy as an usurpation of its rights. The duc d'Orléans had sought power for himself and had engaged in every infamy (p. 1584), but above all the man most responsible for the general corruption of affairs was

Necker, whose recall to power (in August 1788) was the beginning of the end (pp. 1581–2). The influence of the Court meantime declined, at the same time as 'cinq ou six maisons' in Paris focused and directed the development of the nation's policy (p. 1580). Ministers were subordinate to Necker, whose ambitions and fears made him a servant of the *Assemblée Nationale* (p. 1746). Mob violence broke out, Foulon and Berthier (two high officials) were murdered (July 1789), but meantime the same taste for luxury, pleasure, gaming and theatre prevailed amongst the wealthy as before (pp. 1585–8). The aristocrats were as capricious as the rest; the Duchesse de Montjustin feels that her husband, had he lived, might just as easily have joined the revolutionaries as been one of their victims (p. 1638). And so law gave way to anarchy as the horrors mounted, until at last the King and Queen were executed. It becomes understandable in this light that the *émigrés* felt they no longer had a function to serve in France and that they could help the monarchy only from abroad (p. 1748). Yet the régime will not be restored by the *émigrés* alone and certainly not by foreign troops; only internal opinion in France can effect that. Doubtless here Sénac is invoking the hindsight of 1797, by which time it was manifest that the *émigrés* were militantly and politically impotent. Yet he never seems to consider the legitimate grievances that lay at the roots of the Revolution. Louis XVI is simply 'le meilleur des rois', Marie-Antoinette, somewhat more intriguingly, 'la plus intéressante des reines' (p. 1663). As befits a man who wrote moral essays, he sees the historical event not in terms of public policy and large causes but as the product of personal self-interest and inconstancy. This view is more significant as existential response to the tumultuous events than as explanation. Like the Marquis de Saint-Alban's father, Sénac's faltering confidence in human rationality had been destroyed by the Revolution; universal enlightenment of men leads only to barbarism, and total democracy is impossible of achievement (p. 1843). Men attain nobility, if at all, only in adverse circumstances.

Yet despite these pessimistic views, so far removed from the visionary hopes of a Condorcet, Sénac declines to accuse the *philosophes* of causing the Revolution. Their writings were, it is true, of value to the revolutionaries, who exploited them for their own ends, but merely as a secondary support (p. 1730). Considering the wave of anti-intellectualism that swept the Rhineland after

Louis XVI's execution,[13] this is a remarkably moderate conclusion. Furthermore, whatever its horrors, the Revolution had 'hâté la marche de l'esprit' (p. 1752). It will advance the time when France abolishes the death penalty, which Sénac, like Beccaria, believes to be ineffective as a deterrent, and a punishment which human beings have no right to invoke (p. 1752). Much has gone for good, and most of the Président's library (which has been confiscated) is no longer relevant: all the books on theology and jurisprudence, those that deal with feudal rights, as well as most histories, novels, and travel accounts (p. 1758). It is clear that the Revolution has formed a great cultural divide.

Despite this perception that the new society required new literature, Sénac does not seem to have realised its implications for his own work. The Président argues that, although the tragedies of Corneille, Racine and Voltaire seem destined to survive permanently, 'si un homme de génie donnait plus de mouvement à ses drames, s'il agrandissait la scène, mettait en action la plupart des choses qui ne sont qu'en récit, s'il cessait de s'assujettir à l'unité de lieu... ces hommes auraient un jour dans cet auteur un rival dangereux pour leur gloire'. Plays would be related to topical events and the new customs, the people would have a large part in them, unlike in pre-Revolutionary France where, subject to Court influence, 'la scène n'était remplie que par des comtes et des marquis' (pp. 1755–6). Sainte-Beuve read this as a prediction of Romantic trends in literature,[14] but Stavan's reaction seems more judicious when he argues[15] that Sénac has in mind the eighteenth-century discussions of theatre reform such as we have seen surrounding Sedaine's *Le Philosophe sans le savoir*. Nothing in *L'Emigré* seems to presage the new attitudes in literature, and this absence is all the more striking because the occasion for bringing them into existence has already occurred. Despite the Président's isolation in Düsseldorf, he does not convey any of that *Weltschmerz* of the wanderer which emerges so powerfully from Chateaubriand's novels. He begins to approach it in one phrase: 'Mon cœur est surchargé de son propre poids' (p. 1623), but goes no further. Instead of investigating the sentiment for its own sake he returns to the less fruitful line of blaming his troubles on the indifference of the natives around him. Nowhere does Rhineland society emerge as qualitatively different from French. At most Sénac evokes a traditional feudalism, incarnated particularly in the charmingly eccentric uncle of Victorine, the Commandeur de Loewenstein, who has a fanatical regard for the aristocratic caste (p. 1572). Stavan points out that *L'Émigré* is in this respect typical of *émigré* novels, sentimentality being more important than social setting.[16] Yet even in the matter of sensibility, although the Comtesse has, like her author, read *Werther*, the novel does not seem to benefit from it. Sénac is at his best in concrete detail of scenes well known to him, or in that dying *genre* of a more rational psychology, the *maxime*, where he is not unworthy of the honourable line extending from La Bruyère and La Rochefoucauld through Vauvenargues, Duclos and Chamfort; in these respects, however, he merely closes an age. *L'Émigré* gives a good description of the life of these exiles, but the novels which truly evoke the sense of displacement resulting from a clash of cultures lie beyond the field of our study: Chateaubriand's *Atala* (1801) and *René* (1802), Constant's *Adolphe* (1816).

The novel ends in the courtyard outside the Comtesse's room with 200 peasants mourning her death, a true apotheosis. Etiemble justly notes (in the *Préface* to his edition) that Sénac hereby signifies how 'tout est bien, somme toute, dans l'ordre féodal'. By contrast, the guillotine is so horrible in itself and for what it represents that Sénac spares both the Marquis and his father from dying by it (p. xxix). The latter point is more appealing to the reader than the first. Sénac safeguards the Commandeur's snobbishness from becoming unpleasant by never allowing it to conflict with genuine principles. In a similar way he views the Revolution in a void; it emerges as a series of accidents instigated by nefarious men. The Duchesse de Montjustin, throughout the novel a noble and attractive figure, consoles herself for her daughter's premature death by reflecting that had the latter lived she would quite possibly have wished to marry beneath her: 'Je n'ai jamais été, mon cher cousin, enivrée de l'éclat des titres et de la noblesse; mais je n'aurais pu voir ma fille se dégrader par une alliance honteuse' (p. 1639). One cannot help remembering the son of the Baron of Thunder-ten-tronckh in Voltaire's *Candide* who, after all the horrors through which he and his companions had passed in exile from their native Westphalia, could still forbid Candide to marry Cunégonde because she was socially a cut above him. Like the Duchesse, he has learned nothing and forgotten nothing; ultimately, one feels, so has Sénac. Although aristocrats in his view may have helped to cause the Revolution, he cannot envisage an order in which their place is insecure. He makes a brave concession in admitting that the Revolution has caused intellectual progress, but there is no comfort in it. Characteristically, in his last years he found some consolation in the company of another exiled aristocrat, the prince de Ligne. Otherwise it was a time increasingly out of joint. Sénac had wanted to be the Montesquieu of the Revolution, but it was not to be. *L'Émigré* is a fascinating attempt to come to terms with the new world, a kind of epitaph for a lost age and those who have briefly survived it. The hero of the title sums up the pathos of the situation. He fights not because he expects to win, and with great reluctance at leaving his beloved, but because he must. It is a moving affirmation of an aristocratic code in a world that no longer had a place for it.

NOTES

1. G. Lefebvre, *La Révolution française* (Paris: P.U.F., 1963), p. 274; D. Greer, *The Incidence of the Emigration During the French Revolution* (Harvard University Press, 1951), pp. 21–6; Sydenham, *The French Revolution*. M. Weiner, *The French Exiles 1789–1815* (Murray, 1960), gives a lively and effective account of the *émigrés'* life and problems.
2. J. H. Stewart, *A Documentary Survey of the French Revolution* (New York: Macmillan, 1951), p. 415.
3. Stewart, *A Documentary Survey of the French Revolution*, pp. 307–11.
4. See Chateaubriand's description:

> Une armée est ordinairement composée de soldats à peu près du même âge, de la même taille, de la même force. Bien différente était la nôtre, assemblage confus d'hommes faits, de vieillards, d'enfants descendus de leurs colombiers, jargonnant normand, breton, picard, auvergnat, gascon, provençal, languedocien.... J'ai vu de vieux gentilshommes, à mine sévère, à poil gris, habit déchiré, sac sur le dos, fusil en bandoulière, se traînant avec un bâton et soutenus sous le bras par un de leurs fils; j'ai vu M. de Boishue, le père de mon camarade ... marcher seul et triste, pieds nus dans la boue, portant ses souliers à la pointe de sa baïonette, de peur de les user.... Toute cette troupe pauvre, ne recevant pas un sou des Princes, faisait la guerre à ses dépens...
>
> From *Mémoires d'outre-tombe*, edited by M. Levaillant and G. Moulinier (Paris: Pléiade, 1951), 2 vols., Vol I, p. 319.

5. J. Vidalenc, *Les Emigrés français, 1789–1825* (Caen: Faculté des Lettres et Sciences Humaines de l'Université, 1963), pp. 52–4.
6. Vidalenc, *Les Émigrés français*, p. 136.
7. Greer, *The Incidence of the Emigration*, p. 20.
8. Greer, *The Incidence of the Emigration*, pp. 64–5, 68–70.
9. The only critical work of any substance devoted entirely to Sénac de Meilhan is H. A. Stavan, *Gabriel Sénac de Meilhan (1736–1803): moraliste, romancier, homme de lettres* (Paris: Minard, 1968). Chapter I (pp. 9–41) gives an account of his life.
10. Vol. XII (Paris: Garnier, 1857), pp. 378–93.
11. *Romanciers du XVIIIe siècle*, edited by Etiemble (Paris: Pléiade), Vol. II (1965), pp. 1545–912. All references will be to this edition.
12 H. Coulet, *Le Roman jusqu'à la Révolution* (Paris: Colin, 1967–8), 2 vols., Vol. I, pp. 443–4, gives a brief list of *rapprochements*.
13. F. Baldensperger, *Le Mouvement des idées dans l'émigration française (1789–1815)* (Paris: Plon, 1924), 2 vols., Vol II, pp. 35–6.
14. *Causeries du lundi*, vol. XII, p. 387.
15. *Gabriel Sénac de Meilhan*, p. 77.
16. *Gabriel Sénac de Meilhan*, p. 81.

13 Popular Reading Tastes

We have dealt at length with high literature, its context and its audience. What, however, was read by, let us say, the *archers* in *Manon Lescaut*? One does not know. We cannot guess with any accuracy how much they would have been influenced by the popular tastes that prevailed in the country or affected by the sophistication of city life. Given the high illiteracy figures, they probably did not read at all. Indeed, it may well be true if paradoxical that peasants had more contact with literature of a kind than the ordinary townsman, since their more settled existence allowed people to gather together in *veillées*, particularly of a winter evening, to be read to as they mended their tools or span around the hearth. At least we have some information about what was popular in the countryside, thanks above all to Robert Mandrou's pioneering study of the collection of popular literature still surviving at Troyes, and Geneviève Bollème's subsequent anthology. The cultural picture revealed in these works could hardly be farther removed from the world of the Enlightenment.[1]

The *Bibliothèque bleue de Troyes* is a fund of works (essentially digests and adaptations) comprising over a thousand titles, poorly printed on cheap paper, and dating from the seventeenth, eighteenth and nineteenth centuries. Scarcely an echo is heard of contemporary learning, whether Christian or freethinking in its outlook; Descartes, Bayle, Bossuet, the *philosophes* have no existence here. Orthodox literature contributes very little, and nothing from the eighteenth century has been found. 'Science and technology' mean in effect arithmetical calculations, quack medicine, travel guides for pilgrims and merchants, astrology and the occult. Religion holds the first place (though in decline by the eighteenth century) outwardly unaffected by the attacks of a Voltaire or the internecine strife of Jansenist and Jesuit. It is a world of political apathy and fatalism, one where change exists mainly as the seasonal round of seedtime and harvest: a world so harsh and drab that literature's principal function was to offer escape into a marvellous never-never land of magic and chivalry.

One of the most common items is the *almanach*, whose success was enormous, some being printed in 150,000 to 200,000 copies selling at three to six *sous* each.[2] For the first time in this study we glimpse something like the mass printings of our own age. The *almanach's* great advantage was that it marked off the months, days, and Church feasts in such a way that even the unlettered could use it.[3] As such it was of value to all those living on the land, like the shepherd and ploughman, who needed some simple timetable by which to live their lives. Though its success was declining by the eighteenth century as education became gradually more widespread, Madame Bollème has found no fewer than 200 varieties from this period still extant. She notes too that the function of the *almanach* was gradually changing, so that by this time it appealed less to the purely credulous and was offering more useful information, rather like a rudimentary encyclopaedia. But the change is only gradual; astrology and predictions remain an important element (indeed, as we know, they have not been outmoded in such *almanachs* to this day).

In *almanachs* and similar 'useful' literature the people discovered remedies for ill-health, bad hygiene, and sterility:

> Contre douleurs de dents, quelques-uns tiennent pour un secret que porter au col la dent d'un homme enfermé dans un noeud de taffetas, ou une fève trouée où il y a un pou enclos, ôte la plus grande douleur de dent qu'on pourrait endurer.
>
> Pour ôter la puanteur des pieds, mettez dans vos souliers écume de fer.
>
> Pour rendre féconde la femme qui ne peut concevoir, prenez une biche pleine de son faon, tuez-la, tirez hors du ventre la multre où gît le faon; jetez-en hors le faon et, sans la laver, faites-la sécher au four.[4]

As Goubert points out, this last prescription is based on the principle of magical transfer; but the others, in their less complicated way, partake equally of the miraculous. Even the informative works existed in a world of superstitious lore. Mandrou discovered very few technical books for practitioners of various trades (they included gardener, cook, blacksmith, and veterinary surgeon), which suggests that these skills were usually transmitted by word of mouth until the *Encyclopédie* proposed otherwise; and these too incorporate craft with witchcraft. All the more so, then, in books that dealt exclusively with the occult. There were magical recipes for making gold, avoiding wounds, speaking to the dead. Prayers are invoked on occasion in these, serving to remind us how closely superstition was linked to religious belief and practice. Nor was the magic always benevolent. One of the most commonly reported customs was to 'nouer l'aiguillette', which consisted of tying a lace during the wedding ceremony so as to invoke impotence upon the marriage.[5] The Devil, like God, was always close at hand; the existence of sorcery, suspected on every side, was enough in itself to demonstrate his existence.

Despite this evil element, however, the *Bibliothèque bleue* contains numerous fairy tales about limitless realms, castles, parks, jewels, a universe where magic spells upset the natural order of things but the good fairies always triumph in the end. Mandrou notes that there is scarcely ever any divine intervention. Did this make such a world more immediate and 'realistic' to popular imagination? At any rate it indicates the survival of a pagan element in this part of Christendom. Another variant was to situate great mythological heroes in the everyday world, characters like 'le bon géant Gargantua qui décroche imperturbablement les cloches de Notre-Dame',[6] Till Eulenspiegel and Scaramouche, nonconformist anarchists who rob the rich to feed the poor. One can include here too the historical figures of Cartouche and Mandrin who passed into legend as heroic brigands.[7] Some of this popular literature was devoted to historical myth based on the medieval *chansons de geste*, evoking the magnificent and generous France of bygone days when the great figures of the *Chanson de Roland* were alive, the world of Charlemagne and his enemies like *les quatre fils Aymon*.

But while the feudal aristocracy still survives in these legends, the common people virtually do not exist. The action centres round the nobility as it hunts or jousts or goes to war to defend Christianity against the Infidel in the Crusades. This aristocratic group has a positive function in society, fighting the unending epic struggle for God and the King (or Emperor), venerating loyalty but also upholding justice by defending the oppressed, even to the point of rebelling against the sovereign if necessary. It is an idealised picture of what nobility should be like, a wish-fulfilment on behalf of the eighteenth-century aristocrat who could no longer justify his privileges by claiming to be the protector of his vassals. But this literature does not serve mainly as an ideal mirror for the nobility; its significance lies in its being an image for the humble folk beneath them. There are no signs here, for instance, of the conflicts between *noblesse d'épée* and *noblesse de robe,* no contemporary scourges like the *gabelle* (salt-tax). Did such omissions indicate an implicit condemnation of the current social system? It would be dangerous to make such an assertion in the virtual absence of any overt criticism. At most one finds specific complaints by apprentices or journeymen about the tribulations of their various jobs, but scarcely any general expressions of unrest.[8]

This acceptance of the social *status quo* is reinforced by the dominant rôle religion plays: hymn-books, catechisms, Biblical commentaries, prayer-books, and above all lives of the saints. The Christian religion represented here is not that of theological controversy; it is a faith for the simple-hearted, focused on Jesus, his birth and Passion, emphasising homely details with which the readers could easily identify: the manger, the shepherds, the poverty, the women helping the Virgin. Saints' lives echoed this naïve approach. Such lives were pervaded by miraculous interventions; indeed, the exceptional presence of the divine at every moment in their lives was the proof that these were saints. Nothing has changed here since the hagiographical literature of the Middle Ages.

This then appears to be a literature which though destined for the common people virtually ignores them,[9] portraying as it does a world of well-born lords and ladies elegant and refined, or of saints impossibly virtuous. For the ordinary peasant no hope is held out of progress, moral, scientific or intellectual. Original Sin is part of man's nature, men are the product of their humours, passions and the influence of the stars. Divine intervention is necessary for human salvation. Yet we should not too readily establish a coherent philosophy from this mixed bag. Despite the fatalistic attitudes, imitation of Christ's life in all its purity and simplicity is still proposed as a practicable ideal. No similar basis, however, emerges for social and political attitudes. The common people must bear their lot, whatever its miseries. Rewards, if any, will come in the world hereafter.

How far this reading audience overlapped with that for slightly less popular literature is impossible, in the present state of our knowledge, to assess. As Goubert puts it: 'Il faudrait de longues enquêtes, et beaucoup de finesse, pour parvenir à retracer, au-dessus du seuil de l'écriture courante, les niveaux inégaux'.[10] Some light, however, has been thrown on what particularly appealed to the 'reading public' (as distinct from the illiterate, mainly 'listening public' we have been considering) in the last decade of the Ancien Régime.[11] The authors of the study surveyed the range of books for which permission to reprint was sought (almost entirely in the provinces), the inference being that all these works had already proved their popularity. The method has its limitations, since it refers to only fifteen per cent of all requests for permission to print during the period (1778–89), while the actual number of copies of each book run off is unknown. Furthermore, clandestine publications, and even those with a *permission tacite*, are completely ignored in this survey, so that the results will inevitably overstress the orthodox element. Even so, if not interpreted too nicely, the statistics provided by the authors give an idea of what constituted the main literary trends in the provinces at this time.

The favourites turn out to be, without question, religious works, making up about two-thirds of the total, and as in the mass literature we have previously been considering, it is not theology that bulks large but less intellectual forms – such as, in this case, popular liturgical works, manuals of mystical or ascetic character, books of hours. Even when one examines the secular works, the world of the Enlightenment still seems far distant. Arts and sciences are mainly constituted by works on morality and metaphysics (with other areas some way behind – and even then technology is overwhelmingly preferred to theoretical topics). Not a single work appears in this category by Voltaire, who is known to this audience only as a playwright or poet. 'Belles-lettres', a more popular category comprising nearly twenty per cent of the total, relies heavily on the novel, especially of the exotic variety owing much to *A Thousand and One Nights*. Only two *philosophe* works appear anywhere, one by Fontenelle, the other by Montesquieu; nor was the influence of the Church limited to the religious books – as the authors of the article are able to show, the correlation between literacy and the distribution of pious literature was high.[12] Their general conclusion seems proven: 'En dehors de l'école et de l'Eglise, de l'école tenue par l'Eglise et de l'Eglise qui est une école, le livre du monde des lumières n'a pas pénétré profondément la France provinciale: le roman seul y a inauguré, mais timidement, l'aventure culturelle de la modernité'.[13]

Whatever the degree of interpenetration between this literature and the *Bibliothèque bleue*, the same broad indications emerge. The *philosophes* were writing for a small *élite* culture. The mass of the country led lives of patience and resignation, which the sporadic revolts, flaring up over immediate issues like the shortage of food or the execution of a popular figure and dying down as quickly, in no way invalidate.[14] The sparks to fire the Revolution came from Paris and Versailles. As Chateaubriand put it in words that were to become famous: 'Les plus grands coups portés à l'antique constitution de l'État le furent par des gentilshommes. Les patriciens commencèrent la Révolution, les plébéiens l'achèverent.'[15]

NOTES

1. R. Mandrou, *De la culture populaire aux XVIIe et XVIIIe siècles: La Bibliothèque bleue de Troyes* (Paris: Stock, 1964); G. Bollème, *La Bible bleue: Anthologie d'une littérature 'populaire'* (Paris: Flammarion, 1975). See also G. Bollème, 'Littérature populaire et littérature de colportage au 18e siècle', *Livre et société dans la France du XVIIIe siècle*, Vol. I, pp. 61–92; P. Brochon, *Le Livre de colportage en France depuis le XVIe siècle* (Paris: Gründ, 1954).
2. G. Bollème, *Les Almanachs populaires aux XVIIe et XVIIIe siècles: Essai d'histoire sociale* (Paris/The Hague: Mouton, 1969).
3. 'L'almanach est d'abord un livre que l'on peut consulter sans savoir lire', Bollème, *Les Almanachs populaires*, p. 11.
4. C. Estienne and J. Liébault, *L'Agriculture et maison rustique* (1564), Vol. I, p. 12; cited in P. Goubert, *L'Ancien Régime*, Vol. I, p. 261. This work was re-edited many times right up to the eighteenth century, according to Goubert (p. 259). See also N. Belmont, *Mythes et croyances dans l'ancienne France* (Paris: Flammarion, 1973), pp. 49–113.
5. A. Poitrineau reports one such example in Auvergne in the eighteenth century (*La Vie rurale en Basse–Auvergne au XVIIIe siècle* (Paris: P.U.F., 1965), p. 617; cited in Goubert, Vol. I, p. 261). See Bayle, *Oeuvres diverses* (The Hague, 1737), Vol. III, p. 561; Voltaire, *Oeuvres complètes*, edited by Moland, Vol. IX, p.213, n. (note to *La Pucelle*); XIX, p. 448 (*Questions sur l'Encyclopédie*).
6. Goubert, *L'Ancien Régime*, Vol. I, p. 249.

7. Mandrin's importance is discussed in L. S. Gordon, 'Le thème de Mandrin, le "brigand noble" dans l'histoire des idées en France avant la Révolution', *Au siècle des lumières* (Paris/Moscow: S.E.V.P.E.N., 1970), pp. 189–207. The author argues that eighteenth-century popular literature is much more revolutionary in outlook than Mandrou and others had allowed, and he adduces one work in defence of his contention, Ange Goudar's *Testament politique de Louis Mandrin* (1755), which directs a fierce attack on the immorality of the *fermiers généraux*. This example, however, is not enough of iself to invalidate the general import of Mandrou's remarks.

8. It is always possible that if more works like Goudar's *Testament de Mandrin* are unearthed, this conclusion will have to be modified along the lines argued by L. S. Gordon in 'Le thème de Mandrin' (n.7): Until such time, we must assume that the *Bibliothèque bleue de Troyes* contains a representative collection and that therefore the conclusions of Mandrou and Bollème are sound.

9. See Bollème's speculations on whether these works could have been written for the ordinary people, *La Bible bleue*, p. 27.

10. *L'Ancien Régime*, Vol. I, p. 251.

11. J. Brancolini and M.-T. Bouyssy, 'La Vie provinciale du livre à la fin de l'Ancien Régime', *Livre et société dans la France du XVIII* siècle, Vol. II, pp. 3–37.

12. See above. p. 25.

13. 'La Vie provenciale du livre,' p. 32.

14. As late as the grain riots of 1775, which were extensive and serious, the notions of popular sovereignty and the Rights of Man had not yet begun to circulate among the urban and rural poor. The sole target was the man hoarding the corn or profiting by it; the riots were still purely about food. See G. Rudé, *The Crowd in History: A Study of Popular Disturbances in France and England, 1730–1848* (New York: Wiley, 1964), pp. 30–1.

15. *Mémoires d'outre-tombe*, edited by M. Leviallant and G. Moulinier, Vol. I, pp. 172–3.

14   The Way Forward: Madame de Staël (1766–1817)

De la littérature (1800)

Madame de Staël's long essay on the history of Western literature is a remarkable work on many counts. It presents a vast
sweep of development since the Greeks and Romans and finds
space in the modern period for the literatures of Italy, Spain,
England, Germany and France; and it attempts to prophesy
what the literature of the future, after the French Revolution, will
be like. Though the information is often limited, the comments
are personal, immediate, and interesting; often, as in her reaction
to Goethe's *Werther*, they are very shrewd and fruitful.[1] On one
level the book is a declaration of faith in liberalism and progress,
especially in Part II which devotes much time to the future and
bears comparison with Condorcet's *Esquisse d'un tableau historique*.
It is also, in effect if not intention, a plea to Napoleon not to suppress enlightenment in France.[2] When one remembers that the
work was published before the author's 34th birthday, the
achievement appears even more striking. Yet it is none of these
aspects which particularly claims our attention in this survey,
but the most central and probably the most original of all,
Madame de Staël's intention to consider literature in its relationships with society, as the full title of the work makes clear: *De la
littérature considérée dans ses rapports avec les institutions sociales*.

This idea was not entirely new when she began work (no later
than 1798).[3] The author was taking Montesquieu's system in *De
l'esprit des lois* as a model and extending its method to a new
domain. Where the latter had sought to establish the 'spirit of the
laws' and the influences determining it, Madame de Staël was
seeking to define the spirit of literatures at various times and

places and to trace its origins. Montesquieu had himself expressed some fragmentary thoughts on the latter subject;[4] specific aspects of the question had been considered in some detail; both Rousseau and Diderot were concerned, as we have seen, with evaluating the precise interaction of theatre and society. P. Dimoff points out that André Chénier had written a work on a similar theme to Madame de Staël's some fifteen years before; but Chénier's *Essai sur les causes et les effets de la perfection et de la décadence des lettres et des arts* was unpublished, probably unknown to her, and in any case weak on concrete examples.[5] In 1780 the Academy of Berlin had chosen for an essay competition the question: 'Quelle a été l'influence du gouvernement sur les lettres chez les nations où elles ont fleuri? Et quelle a été l'influence des lettres sur le gouvernement?' (The prize went to Herder.) Hume too had traced links between the nature of government and the vitality of culture.[6] It is clear that the general concept of literature as an expression of society was in the air.

Yet it was for Madame de Staël to take these scattered ideas and construct a unified approach to the subject. The aim of the work is announced with admirable directness in the opening sentences of the *Discours préliminaire*:

> Je me suis proposé d'examiner quelle est l'influence de la religion, des mœurs et des lois sur la littérature, et quelle est l'influence de la littérature sur la religion, les mœurs et les lois. Il existe, dans la langue française, sur l'art d'écrire et sur les principes du goût, des traités qui ne laissent rien à désirer; mais il me semble que l'on n'a pas suffisamment analysé les causes morales et politiques, qui modifient l'esprit de la littérature (p. 17).

For men and movements do not spring forth full-grown and autonomous. Homer, however great his genius, was not unique and divorced from other men of his time (p. 53); the Renaissance was not a qualitative break with the medieval past but the natural extension of it (pp. 146–7). In brief, 'il ne faut pas oublier le principe que j'ai posé dès le commencement de cet ouvrage; c'est que le génie le plus remarquable ne s'élève jamais au-dessus des lumières de son siècle, que d'un petit nombre de degrés' (p. 147). The individual writer necessarily partakes of the *Zeitgeist* and cannot be understood outside it.

What aspects, then, of religion, manners and laws does

Madame de Staël consider? On the religious side the dominant theme is the civilising effect of Christianity, which has promoted the abolition of slavery, made women the moral equals of men, strengthened conjugal love and established domestic happiness, encouraged the growth of sympathy, pity, philanthropy and respect for life (pp. 135–40, 154–5). Protestantism is the more enlightened form of Christianity, giving the Northern peoples a more philosophic attitude, grounded on faith in progress, emphasis upon virtue, and freedom from superstition (pp. 187–8). The Christian religion, indeed, represents the great divide between ancient and modern literature, constituting the main reason for the surprisingly low esteem which Madame de Staël shows for Greek literature in particular. For while the Greek gods aided the development of the imagination in literature, their presence restricted the evolution of abstract concepts (pp. 56–7).

From Christianity manners had developed; the status of women, the quality of family and personal relationships are all intimately bound up with the nature of one's faith and religious practices. But manners are also the function of the laws, which is to say of the whole political regime. As, for example, the Roman Empire became more corrupt, writers abandoned the unheroic mode of Augustus's reign and turned to a terser and more forceful style as a reaction against the tyranny and cruelty surrounding them (pp. 122–3). Madame de Staël is at her most suggestive in discussing the effects of forms of government upon literature. She relates the Athenian democracy to the excessive fondness for satire, the Roman aristocracy to the more dignified and philosophical tone of Latin literature. In the modern era Italian princes, through their patronage of intellectuals, made an important contribution to the Renaissance in arts and sciences but hindered the development of philosophy, which depends upon freedom of thought. The German federal system, on the other hand, was so decentralised that no cultural capital existed; German writers were thrown back much more upon themselves, a phenomenon which gave them freedom to develop their own ideas but excluded them from all the advantages of communication with one another.

As for French culture, its nature is determined by the situation of an absolute monarch surrounded by his aristocratic courtiers; in consequence, 'la cour influe sur le genre d'esprit de la nation, parce qu'on veut imiter généralement ce qui distingue la classe la plus élevée' (p. 265). Madame de Staël sees clearly how limited was the scope for reform under such a regime: 'on pouvait, comme Rousseau l'a fait dans le Contrat Social, vanter sans danger la démocratie pure; mais on n'aurait point osé approcher des idées plus vraisemblables' (p. 235). In France new ideas had to be acceptable to aristocratic tastes, since enlightenment 'descendait de la classe supérieure vers le peuple' (p. 236). This accounts for the greater refinement and wit in French philosophical works than in their English equivalents; Frenchmen like Montesquieu had a clear notion of their sophisticated audience in mind. In England, by contrast, where the writer is appealing to a much wider reading public, his situation is more that of 'un instituteur parlant à ses élèves' (p. 236). Hence (rather paradoxically) the reason for the prolixity of so much English philosophical literature. This last comparison between English and French culture is a good illustration of Madame de Staël's approach, with both its strengths and its weaknesses. The hypothesis about English verbosity is striking and not entirely invalid; but it is not wholly persuasive either. At the same time, the author lucidly notes the essentially aristocratic refinement of Ancien Régime literature and refuses to entertain the thesis which subsequently became fashionable, that the eighteenth century witnessed the triumph of the bourgeoisie. Voltaire, for example, 'le premier homme qui ait popularisé la philosophie en France' (p. 278), was successful in large part because he frequented the society of nobles and monarchs, possibly even shared their prejudices, and always insisted 'que les lumières fussent de bon ton' (p. 279). Madame de Staël is quick to see the problems of such a reformer for whom a civilised society and culture were paramount: 'il devait craindre même de renverser ce qu'il attaquait' (p. 279). She senses the ambiguous character of eighteenth-century French literature, often politically in opposition yet philosophically traditional still, not attacking fundamental concepts like natural law or reason.[7] At a time when the wave of philistine reaction against the *philosophes* was at its height amongst those who hated the Revolution, she could detest the developments of recent history yet still maintain a clear vision of the Ancien Régime and the situation of its intellectuals.

One needs hardly to stress that an *œuvre de synthèse* such as this, the first in the field, has many omissions of the kind that no sociologist of literature would ignore today. It is largely, one might say,

macro-sociology rather than micro-sociology. Detailed comments on particular authors are much less common than one
would like, especially when one sees that they can be, as with
Voltaire and *Werther*, so perceptive. Madame de Staël takes scant
account of the individual author's relationship to society as
mediated through family, educational background and class. In
particular the economic circumstances of the writer are ignored,
except possibly when she is referring to protection by persons in
authority, though then she seems mainly to have political aspects
in mind.[8] The present-day reader tires of her numerous generalities about national character, which testify to the survival, even
beyond the Revolution, of that penchant for abstract statements
stemming back to Descartes. True, she argues that national traits
are 'le résultat des institutions et des circonstances qui influent
sur le bonheur d'un peuple, sur ses intérêts et sur ses habitudes'
(p. 262); but she does not always remember to show the institutions and circumstances that created the nation, so that the
generalities often have a gratuitous air about them. Sometimes
she has to work hard to make the facts fit the Procrustean bed of
her creation. Since the Northern peoples must, for the sake of her
polarity between North and South, appear at all costs to be
melancholy, she has no interest in either Shakespeare's comedies
or those of the English Restoration. Where such works exist, they
must be seen as an aberration: 'Rien ne ressemble moins aux
Anglais que leurs comédies' (p. 214).

In brief, *De la littérature* suffers from two major weaknesses: it is
tendentious, and it spends too much time on general psychology
of a rather unfruitful kind. But let us not concentrate on the more
sterile side. The work, albeit not as systematically as one would
have liked, embraces an impressively wide range of considerations; within that range, Madame de Staël takes note of many an
important detail. She pays attention on several occasions to the
rôle of media: the importance of theatre and public performances
in Greece, not only for drama but for poetry and declamation too;
the fact that before printing was discovered censorship was more
lenient, since literature could not be easily broadcast; the differences between Demosthenes and Cicero as a function of their
audiences. Though more interested in ideas, she does not neglect
the relationship of form to social milieu, as we have seen, for
example, in her discussion of the gracefulness and good taste of
French literature. A whole chapter in Part II is devoted to style,

the author pointing out that any work of literature (by which she means, as she had said at the outset, 'son acception la plus étendue; c'est-à-dire, renfermant en elle les écrits philosophiques et les ouvrages d'imagination, tout ce qui concerne enfin l'exercice de la pensée dans les écrits, les sciences physiques exceptées' – p. 18) appeals not only to the reader's rational capacities but to his imagination and emotions as well. Hence the importance of structure, eloquence, imagery. Nor does she fall into the trap of seeing literature merely as a response to social causes, a weakness of which literary sociology is still not always free. For her, writers clearly have an autonomy within the wide framework of their times. She does not try to account for every last reaction; indeed, she recognises gradations of conformity to the *Zeitgeist*: the public orator must adjust his utterances to those he wishes to influence, but at the other extreme 'l'écrivain solitaire peut n'appartenir qu'à son talent' (p. 112).

The interrelating of literature and society has with Madame de Staël been inaugurated as a serious study, destined to a future that has not always been of the happiest. But it would seem that in recent years that corner has been turned and that the imaginativeness of genuine textual criticism is at last being properly combined with a study of the context in which the text was born. Madame de Staël is an honourable precursor of that view. In Roland Mortier's words, the year 1800 in which *De la littérature* appeared has itself a symbolic character. Madame de Staël's long and seminal essay is 'Synthèse du passé, phare tourné vers l'avenir'.[9]

NOTES

1. An interesting discussion of this particular contact occurs in R. de Luppé, 'Mme de Staël et *Werther*', *Madame de Staël et l'Europe: Colloque de Coppet (18–24 juillet 1966)* (Paris: Klincksieck, 1970), pp. 111–18.
2. Fargher, *Life and Letters in France*, p. 225.
3. P. Van Tieghem (editor) *De la littérature* (Geneva/Paris: Droz/Minard, 1959), 2 vols., Vol. I, p. xix. All textual references will be to this edition.
4. *Mes pensées*, Vol. III, xi: *Sur la littérature, Oeuvres complètes*, edited by R. Caillois, Vol. I, pp. 1054–5.

5. In *La Vie et l'œuvre d'André Chénier jusqu'à la Révolution française* (Paris, 1936, thesis); referred to in Van Tieghem (editor), pp. xviii–xix.
6. Gusdorf, *Les Principes de la pensée*, p. 486.
7. This point is well put by Gossman, *French Society and Culture*, pp. 121–4. It is essentially the same thesis as that argued, more dramatically, by Michel Foucault, who claims that classical thought of the seventeenth and eighteenth centuries is concerned with general categories only, a sort of colourless geometric representation, interesting only to the eye and excluding other sensory perceptions, ignoring the rich specificity of things (see especially *Les Mots et les choses* (Paris: Gallimard, 1966), pp. 145–69). This argument, impressively demonstrated, has the great merit of reminding us not to draw facile parallels between our world and that of 200 years ago. It reinforces in new ways the long-standing belief that eighteenth-century thought bears the heavy imprint of Cartesianism. As such, however, it excessively devalues the growing insistence upon the individual and upon the multitudinous quality of phenomena, to which we should like to think the preceding chapters bear considerable testimony.
8. Not exclusively, however; see, for example, 'Les hommes de lettres d'Italie ... ayant besoin *de la fortune* et de l'approbation des princes...' (p. 158, my italics). But such references are fleeting.
9. *Clartés et ombres du siècle des lumières*, p. 127.

Select Bibliography

Adam, A., *Le Mouvement philosophique dans la première moitié du XVIIIe siècle* (Paris: Société d'Éditions d'Enseignement Supérieur, 1967).

Alasseur, C., *La Comédie Française au 18e siècle: étude economique* (Paris/The Hague: Mouton, 1967).

Anchel, R., *Crimes et châtiments au XVIIIe siècle* (Paris: Perrin, 1933).

Atkinson, G. and A. C. Keller, *Prelude to the Enlightenment: French Literature, 1690–1740* (London: Allen and Unwin, 1971).

Baldensperger, F., *Le Mouvement des idées dans l'émigration française (1789–1815)* (Paris: Plon, 1924), 2 vols.

Baker, K. M., *Condorcet: From Natural Philosophy to Social Mathematics* (University of Chicago Press, 1975).

Barber, E. G., *The Bourgeoisie in 18th Century France* (Princeton: Princeton University Press, 1955).

Barber, W. H. *et al.* (editors), *The Age of the Enlightenment: Studies Presented to Theodore Besterman* (Edinburgh/London: Oliver and Boyd, 1967).

Barbier, E.-J.-F., *Journal d'un bourgeois sous le règne de Louis XV,* edited by P. Bernard (Paris: Union générale d'éditions 10/18, n.d.).

Barnard, H. C., *Education and the French Revolution* (London: Cambridge University Press, 1969).

Barthes, R. *et al.*, *L'Univers de l'Encyclopédie* (Paris: Les Libraires Associés, 1964).

Behrens, C. B. A., *The Ancien Régime* (London: Thames and Hudson, 1967).

Bénichou, P., *Le Sacre de l'écrivain, 1750–1830* (Paris: Corti, 1973).

Besterman, T., *Voltaire* (London: Longman, 1969).

Besterman, T. (editor), *Voltaire: Correspondence,* in *The Complete Works of Voltaire* (Geneva: Institut et Musée Voltaire, and Banbury and Oxford: Voltaire Foundation, 1968–77).

Buvat, J., *Journal de la Régence,* edited by E. Campardon (Paris: Plon, 1865), 2 vols.

Cahen, L., *Condorcet et la Révolution française* (Paris: Alcan, 1904).

Chartier, R. *et al.*, *L'Education en France du XVIe au XVIIIe siècle* (Paris: Société d'Éditions d'Enseignement Supérieur, 1976).

Cobban, A., *A History of Modern France* (Harmondsworth: Penguin, 1961), 2 vols.

Conlon, P.M., 'Voltaire's literary career from 1728 to 1750,' *Studies on Voltaire and the Eighteenth Century*, 14 (1961).

Darnton, R., 'The High Enlightenment and the Low-Life of Literature in Pre-Revolutionary France', *Past and Present*, 51 (1971), pp. 81–115.

——, 'Reading, Writing and Publishing in Eighteenth-Century France: A Case Study in the Sociology of Literature', *Daedalus*, 100 (1971), pp. 214–56.

Ehrard, J., *L'Idée de nature dans la première moitié du XVIII' siècle* (Paris: Service d'Édition et de Vente des Publications de l'Éducation Nationale, 1963), 2 vols.

Fargher, R., *Life and Letters in France: the Eighteenth Century* (London: Nelson, 1970).

Favre, R., *La Mort dans la littérature et la pensée françaises au siècle des lumières* (Lyon: Presses Universitaires, 1978).

Fontainerie, F. de la, *French Liberalism and Education in the Eighteenth Century* (New York: McGraw-Hill, 1932).

Ford, F. L., *Robe and Sword: The Regrouping of the French Aristocracy after Louis XIV* (Cambridge, Massachusetts: Havard University Press, 1953).

Francastel, P. (editor), *Utopie et institutions au XVIII' siècle* (Paris/The Hague: Mouton, 1963).

Gaiffe, F., *Le Drame en France au XVIII' siècle* (Paris: Colin, 1910).

Gay, P., *The Enlightenment*, Vol. II (London: Weidenfeld and Nicolson, 1970).

——, *The Party of Humanity* (Weidenfeld and Nicolson, 1964).

——, *Voltaire's Politics: The Poet as Realist* (New York: Vintage, 1965).

Gillispie, C. C. (editor), *A Diderot Pictorial Encyclopedia of Trades and Industry* (New York: Dover, 1959) 2 vols.

Glass, B. *et al.* (editors), *Forerunners of Darwin: 1745–1859* (Baltimore: Johns Hopkins Press, 1959).

Gossman, L., *French Society and Culture* (Englewood Cliffs, New Jersey: Prentice-Hall, 1972).

Goubert, P., *L'Ancien Régime*, Vol. I, *La Société* (Paris: Colin, 1969).

Green, F. C., *The Ancien Régime: A Manual of French Institutions and Social Classes* (Edinburgh: Edinburgh University Press, 1958).

Guéhenno, J., *Jean-Jacques* (Paris: Gallimard, 1962), 2 vols.

Gusdorf, G., *Les Principes de la pensée au siècle des lumières* (Paris; Payot, 1971).

Hampson, N., *A Social History of the French Revolution* (London: Routledge, 1966).

——, *The Enlightenment* (Harmondsworth: Penguin, 1968).

Johnson, N. R., 'Louis XIV and the Age of the Enlightenment: the Myth of the Sun King from 1715 to 1789', *Studies on Voltaire and the Eighteenth Century*, 182 (1978).

Jones, R. B., *The French Revolution* (London: University of London Press, 1967).

Kiernan, C., 'Science and the Enlightenment in Eighteenth-Century France', *Studies on Voltaire and the Eighteenth Century*, 59 (1968).

Labrousse, E. *et al.*, *Histoire économique et sociale de la France*, Vol. II, *1660–1789* (Paris: Presses Universitaires de France, 1970).

Lagrave, H., *Le Théâtre et le public à Paris de 1715 à 1750* (Paris: Klincksieck, 1972).

——, *Marivaux et sa fortune littéraire* (Saint-Médard-en-Jalles: Ducros, 1970).

Lanson, G., *Nivelle de La Chaussée et la comédie larmoyante* (Paris: Hachette, 1887).

Launay, M., *Jean-Jacques Rousseau: écrivain politique, 1712–1762* (Cannes/Grenoble: Coopérative d'Enseignement Laïc/A.C.E.R., 1971).

Leigh, R. A. (editor), *Correspondance complète de Jean-Jacques Rousseau* (Geneva: Institut et Musée Voltaire, and Banbury and Oxford: Voltaire Foundation, 1965–).

Léon, A., *Histoire de l'enseignement en France* (Paris: Presses Universitaires de France, 'Que sais-je?', 1967).

Livre et société dans la France du XVIIIe siècle, Vol. II (Paris/The Hague: Mouton, 1970).

Lough, J., *An Introduction to Eighteenth Century France* (London: Longman, 1960).

——, *The Encyclopédie* (London: Longman, 1971).

——, *Paris Theatre Audiences in the Seventeenth and Eighteenth Centuries* (London: Oxford University Press, 1957).

——, *Writer and Public in France from the Middle Ages to the Present Day* (Oxford: Clarendon Press, 1978).

Mandrou, R., *La France aux XVIIe et XVIIIe siècles* (Paris: Presses Universitaires de France, 1970).

Mason, H., *Voltaire: A Biography* (London: Granada, 1981).

Mauzi, R. and Menant, S., *Le XVIIIe Siècle: II, 1750–1778* (Paris: Arthaud, 1977).

Méthivier, H., *L'Ancien Régime* (Paris: Presses Universitaires de France, 'Que sais-je?', 1971).

——, *La Fin de l'ancien régime* (Paris: Presses Universitaires de France, 'Que sais-je?', 1970).

Moravia, S., *Il tramonto dell' illuminismo: Filosofia e politica nella società francese (1770–1810)* (Bari: Laterza, 1968).

Mornet, D., *Les Origines intellectuelles de la Révolution française (1715–1787)* (Paris: Colin, 1933).

——, *Le Sentiment de la nature en France de Jean-Jacques Rousseau à Bernardin de Saint-Pierre* (Paris: Hachette, 1907).

Mortier, R., *Clartés et ombres du siècle des lumières* (Geneva: Droz, 1969).

Mylne, V., *The Eighteenth-Century French novel: Techniques of Illusion* (Manchester University Press, 1965).

Niklaus, R., *A Literary History of France: The Eighteenth Century, 1715–1789* (London: Benn, 1970).

Ogg, D., *Europe of the Ancien Régime, 1715–1783* (London: Collins, 1965).

Pottinger, D.T., *The French Book Trade in the Ancien Régime, 1500–1791* (Cambridge, Massachusetts: Harvard University Press, 1958).

Proust, J., *Diderot et l'Encyclopédie* (Paris: Colin, 1962).

Richard, G., *Noblesse d'affaires au XVIIIe siècle* (Paris: Colin, 1974).

Roche, D., *Le Siècle des lumières en province: Académies et académiciens provinciaux* (Paris/The Hague: Mouton, 1978), 2 vols.

Roger, J., *Les Sciences de la vie dans la pensée française du XVIIIe siècle* (Paris: Colin, 1963).

Rudé, G., *Paris and London in the 18th Century: Studies in Popular Protest* (London: Collins, Fontana, 1970).

Sgard, J., *Prévost romancier* (Paris: Corti, 1968).

Shackleton, R., *Montesquieu* (London: Oxford University Press, 1961).

Shennan, J. H., *Philippe, Duke of Orleans: Regent of France 1715–1723* (London: Thames and Hudson, 1979).

Soboul, A. *et al.*, *Le Siècle des lumières*, Vol. I, *L'Essor* (1715–1750) (Paris: Presses Universitaires de France, 1977).

Starobinski, J., *L'Invention de la liberté, 1700–1789* (Geneva: Skira, 1964).

——, *Montesquieu par lui-même* (Paris: Seuil, 1953).

Stavan, H. A., *Gabriel Sénac de Meilhan (1736–1803): moraliste, romancier, homme de lettres* (Paris: Minard, 1968).

Sydenham, M. J., *The French Revolution* (London: Methuen, 1969).

Trousson, R., *Rousseau et sa fortune littéraire* (Saint-Médard-en-Jalles: Ducros, 1971).

Venturi, F., *Utopia and Reform in the Enlightenment* (Cambridge: Cambridge University Press, 1971).

Versini, L., *Laclos et la tradition: essai sur les sources et la technique des 'Liaisons dangereuses'* (Paris: Klincksieck, 1968).

Index